# The War Against the Atom

# THE WAR AGAINST THE ATOM

*Samuel McCracken*

Basic Books, Inc., Publisher   New York

Library of Congress Cataloging in Publication Data

McCracken, Samuel.
  The war against the atom.

  Bibliography: p. 190.
  Includes index.
  1. Atomic power.  I.  Title
TK9146.M37          333.79'24          81–66105
ISBN 0–465–09062–1                     AACR2

For

Emily S. McCracken

and

George E. McCracken

# Contents

# *Acknowledgments*

MY OBLIGATIONS are many. Hundreds of individuals at energy installations and research centers here and in Europe, and at many conferences, have provided grist for my mill. While I cannot acknowledge them individually, the debt, to colleagues and critics alike, is remembered.

Two friends have been especially and consistently helpful: Petr Beckmann, who first brought my attention to the state of the controversy over nuclear power, who made such good sense about it, and who continues to do so with infinite variety and detail; and Mark Mills, whom I met by the telephone the day of Three Mile Island, and who ever since has been sharing his encyclopedic knowledge and gift for illustration. Although this book would not have been written without them, they are guiltless of its imperfections.

Besides serving as a font of reason about energy matters, Lanny Tonning, formerly of the Public Service Commission of New Mexico, introduced me to a uranium mine and to those unique New Mexico institutions, the *New Mexico Independent* of Albuquerque and the Uranium Cafe, of Grants.

To Henrik and Stephan Rosenmeier of Copenhagen, I am grateful for services beyond the call of friendship in helping me to pursue inquiries in Denmark.

In the United Kingdom, Sir John Hill, then Chairman of the United Kingdom Atomic Energy Authority, was most generous in arranging a tour of U.K. facilities, and I am deeply in the debt of UKAEA people in Britain, including at the breeder reactor at Dounreay, the laboratories at Winfrith, and the safety and inspection center at Risley. Andrew Hills of the London office of the UKAEA was of great help in connection with Risley. Robert

Swift, of the South of Scotland Electricity Generating Board, made smooth the path to the power reactor complex at Hunterston, near Glasgow, and supplied more good talk on more topics than seems possible for a one-day visit. The staff at Hunterston were especially helpful.

To the American and British Ditchley Foundations, and to Sir Philip Adams, Director of Ditchley Park, I am greatly indebted for the chance to attend a 1978 conference on nuclear energy at that incomparable institution.

In France, M. Christian Clouet d'Orval, director of the French experimental reactor program, arranged a vastly informative day at the Center for Nuclear Research at Cadarache.

Boston University granted me a leave of absence to carry out my research, and my colleagues John Silber, Jon Westling, and Doyne Dawson have returned the ideas I have thrust at them very much improved.

Neal Kozodoy continues to be an editor of intelligence, taste, and ruthlessness.

My family has suffered my four years' monomania with great patience; additionally, Harry McCracken provided advice on computers and, as did Elizabeth McCracken, research assistance. Natalie McCracken had nothing whatever to do with typing the manuscript, but everything to do with the rest of it.

Genetic and environmental benefits of great importance are acknowledged in the dedication.

# Preface

THE UNITED STATES is poised to embrace an energy technology that will inflict untold damage on its natural environment, cost its citizens billions upon billions of dollars, and kill them by the hundreds of thousands. Yet friends of the environment, far from opposing this death-dealing technology with every stratagem at their command, have rather rejected the one workable source of energy free of such hazards and are willy-nilly working to insure an environmental and social disaster.

This is precisely what is involved in the present movement to restrain or abolish nuclear energy. For the only workable alternative to nuclear energy available to us is coal, and the grim picture I have just drawn is of the consequences not of an expanded use of coal but of our present use of it.

Practically everyone involved in today's energy debate agrees that we must use coal; and so we must. The truth is, however, that considered as a fuel, coal is not a panacea but a dreadful necessity. That it is considered a panacea is largely because of the present unmerited low estate of nuclear power and the widespread belief among decision makers that the nuclear option, for the time being at least, has been closed off. That this should be so is in turn largely due to a vigorously prosecuted war against nuclear energy, a war almost against the atom itself. In a real sense this war is a war against the future welfare of our society, because nuclear energy is the key to our present energy crisis.

The energy crisis itself presents us with a problem of fitting a complex range of energy sources to a complex range of energy uses. The basic argument of the antinuclear movement is that in all this complexity there is no place for nuclear energy. To show that there is such a place—as I shall do in this book—involves not only rebutting an immense amount of superstition about nuclear energy, but also demonstrating the faults of its competitors and the ways in which it surpasses them. Moreover, it involves showing how a small group of scientists and quasi-scientists, having gotten the public eye and ear, have badly misinformed educated Americans as to the simple facts.

The technical issues in the energy debate, although not simple, are perfectly accessible to any intelligent and unscientific layman willing to spend a little intellectual energy on them. Beyond these essentially technical issues lies a series of political and social ones that in the last ten years or so have all but dominated public discussion and overwhelmed the discussion of the technical merits of one form of energy as opposed to another. In the pages that follow I will be dealing with both sets of issues, in an attempt to clarify the terms of debate and to find where exactly the truth lies in this hopelessly controverted field.

Although, like much else in modern life, the energy debate has become ideologically charged in the extreme, the reader ought to understand that energy itself is not an ideological question. At present the opposition to nuclear power is lined up on the liberal to left end of the political spectrum, but there is no reason why this should be so. Affection or revulsion from technology is, politically speaking, a matter of fashion, and technology was once a left-wing shibboleth. Lenin's basic formula was "Soviet Power + Electrification = Communism," and the late Dr. Hewlett Johnson, the "Red Dean" of Canterbury, regularly published paeans to high technology (which he conceived to be an invention of Stalin) that would make most liberals today uncomfortable. His views of central electrical generation would make contemporary solar enthusiasts worse than uncomfortable.

That opposition to nuclear power has become an issue for those on the Left is adventitious. Nuclear power is often said to be in the interests of capitalists, yet it is being rapidly developed in the Soviet Union and its satellites and in the more developed portions of the Third World as well. Where the government is free from capitalist pressure, it has chosen as a major energy source not soft energy—as exemplified by solar panels—but hard energy— as exemplified by nuclear reactors. The same is true for Sweden, presumably the most leftward of the thoroughly industrialized states.

There is a marvelous paradox in this area. On the one hand, nuclear power is regularly claimed to be economically noncompetitive with other energy sources, including not only coal but also oil and solar energy. On the other hand, nuclear power is said to be the preferred energy source of monopoly capital, presumably because of the immense profits it provides. This, unhappily, is only one, and by no means the most striking, of the logical contradictions in the antinuclear position.

There are historical reasons why opposition to nuclear power has become bound together with other liberal and left-wing views, and I deal with these in chapter 5. Yet there is no irrepressible conflict between nuclear energy and liberal principles. For nuclear energy is part and parcel of the revolution that has helped raise the working classes from being beasts of burden to owners of hundreds of mechanical and morally unobjectionable servants. Unless we mean to reverse that revolution altogether, we would be well advised to take a just measure of nuclear technology, assessing candidly both its drawbacks (of which there are some) and its advantages (of which there are many, many more), and to guide our policy accordingly.

To do all that, however, it is necessary to clear away the accumulation of myth, distortion, error, and scare mongering that now surrounds this topic, which has become one of the great bugbears of our age. And that is the reason for this book.

# The War Against the Atom

# 1

## *Some Technical Background*

MOST DISCUSSIONS of nuclear power are conducted in a haze of misinformation. There are few areas of public controversy where there is so much to know and where everyone knows so little and so much of what everyone knows ain't necessarily so. Let us begin with some of the least controversial facts about the processes by which nuclear power is generated. These are neither many nor complicated, but it is essential that they be understood as a basis for discussing the more complicated and controversial issues that grow out of them.

The promises and problems of nuclear energy rest on the fact that the atoms of some forms of each element* are inherently unstable. Each element exists in a number of forms, known as isotopes. The various isotopes of an element are chemically identical because their nuclei are surrounded by identical arrangements of electrons. But the nuclei themselves are distinctive, and for this reason they behave physically in very different ways. The difference that most concerns us here is that which distinguishes stable and unstable elements.

Each atomic nucleus contains two sorts of particles: protons and neutrons.† (From the point of view of contemporary physics, this statement is a dreadful oversimplification, for physics recognizes two hundred or so particles in the nucleus; but the other members of the atomic zoo, as it is called, need not

* In nature, not all elements have unstable forms, but unstable forms of most of them have been produced in the laboratory.

† The exception is the common form of hydrogen, which has no neutrons.

concern us here.) Protons have a positive electrical charge and neutrons have no charge. In a stable form of an element the complement of protons and neutrons is such that they stay closely bound together in the nucleus. The atoms of such forms, unless tampered with by man in his laboratories, will remain as they are forever.* Even if individual atoms can be transmuted through bombardment, the remaining substance does not become radioactive.

In an unstable form, a certain proportion of the atoms in a given quantity are constantly undergoing disintegration or decay. In the disintegration, some elemental particles are expelled from the atom, sometimes along with a form of electromagnetic radiation known as the gamma ray, and the remaining particles now constitute an atom of a different element. Each of these two phenomena is of key importance in understanding nuclear power. The expelled particles and rays constitute the phenomenon of radiation, and in some of those elements that expel neutrons during decay the departing neutrons may hit something, with a variety of results. The result of interest here occurs when a neutron strikes a nucleus of the class called *fissionable* (nuclei of certain isotopes of uranium and plutonium are the best known). Then it may enter the nucleus and cause it to split.

There are three consequences of the split.

First, the nucleus breaks down into two lighter atoms, known as fission products. Each will be very roughly half the weight of the original atom. Unlike naturally radioactive isotopes, which are comparatively stable since they are the long-lived survivors of eons of radioactive decay, fission products are often highly unstable and decay at a furious rate. They are thus typically highly radioactive and short lived.

Second, neutrons escape from the disintegrated nucleus, and third, there is a massive release of energy. The other escaping neutrons may strike other nuclei, and these too may split; if enough fissionable material is present in a given volume of matter, there will be a self-sustaining chain reaction, releasing great amounts of energy. If the mass of fissionable material is great enough, such a chain reaction can, with considerable difficulty, be contained so as to produce an explosion.

A nuclear power plant of the type now being built or scheduled to be built in this country uses the chain reaction as a source of heat to make steam to operate turbines that spin generators. That is, except for the reactor itself, a nuclear power plant is much like a coal- or oil-fired one.

The naturally occurring supply of an element is a mixture of all the naturally occurring isotopes. (An immense catalogue of man-made isotopes also exists.)

* There are rare exceptions to man's monopoly on transmutation. See fn. p. 53.

4

# Some Technical Background

Natural uranium contains just such a mixture of isotopes, only two of which need concern us here: U-235 and U-238. (The numbers denote the total number of protons and neutrons in the nucleus.)

About 0.7 percent of all uranium is U-235, the fissionable fuel most in use as a fuel in power reactors. The rest, for all practical purposes, is U-238, an almost entirely nonfissionable isotope. In order to use natural uranium as a fuel, it is necessary to raise the proportion of U-235 in it by a process known as enrichment. Uranium for bombs must be enriched to nearly 90 percent U-235. In the power reactors used in this country, 3 percent U-235 will do. The enrichment process is extremely complicated and expensive, consuming vast amounts of capital for equipment and vast amounts of electricity to operate.* It also leaves over large amounts of U-238 for which at present there is no use except thermonuclear bombs and (because of its great weight) conventional artillery shells.

Another fissionable element of interest is plutonium, which occurs in nature only in traces but which is easily produced in reactors as a by-product. All uranium-burning reactors produce some plutonium incidentally, and breeder reactors produce it in large quantities deliberately.

Beyond these two fissionable isotopes—U-235 and plutonium-239 (Pu-239)—there are two that are said to be fertile. If a quantity of a fertile element is placed in proximity to a fission reaction, some of its atoms will capture neutrons from the reaction and be transmuted into fissionable elements. Some of these will fission as part of the chain reaction, and others can be recovered for fissioning later. This phenomenon is the basis of the so-called breeder reactor.

In the most common form of this, fertile U-238 is placed close to fissioning U-235. As a result of a series of changes, some of the uranium is transmuted to Pu-239, some of which is further transmuted to Pu-240. Pu-239 is the basis of most nuclear bombs and also makes an excellent reactor fuel. The other fertile isotope of interest is thorium-232 (Th-232), which when exposed to a chain reaction will be transmuted into U-233, an isotope with many of the same characteristics as U-235.

There are three types of nuclear reactor. A *burner reactor* uses a fuel composed entirely of fissionable material. Pure burners are not built in real life, but certain reactors, such as those that propel nuclear submarines, use highly enriched uranium and thus have comparatively little U-238 to transmute. A *converter reactor,* besides burning fissionable fuel, converts a certain amount of fertile material into new fuel. This amount will vary from some to a great deal, but it will always be less than the amount of fuel used to

---

* But not as vast as is sometimes suggested by nuclear critics; see p. 43.

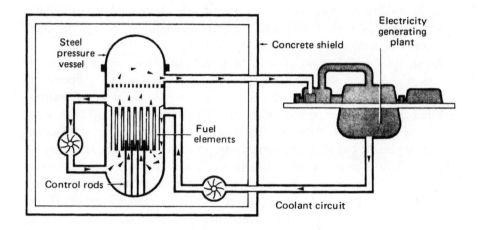

FIGURE 1–1

*Boiling-Water Reactor*

SOURCE: *World Energy Book* (Cambridge, Mass.: M.I.T., 1979), p. 30. Reproduced by the kind permission of the UKAEA.

provide the reaction. Finally, *breeder reactors,* besides fissioning material in their cores, also transmute fertile material placed around the core, so that over a period they produce more fuel than they burn.

Within and across these broad constraints, there is a considerable variety of possible reactor designs, and the choice among them has become a major issue of public policy.

Most of the nuclear reactors in the world today (and with one exception all those producing power in the United States) are light-water reactors. In these ordinary water is circulated around the reactor core and is heated by the nuclear reaction, thereby serving to cool the core. In one type of light-water reactor, the cooling water is allowed to boil into steam that is piped directly to the generating turbines. This is known as the boiling-water reactor (BWR). (See figure 1–1.)

In another type, the cooling water is kept under pressure, which keeps it from boiling, and is piped to a separate steam generator. This is known as the pressurized-water reactor (PWR). (See figure 1–2.) Water also serves the necessary purpose of slowing down the neutrons flowing through the reactor core so that they will be able to split nuclei. For this purpose, the water is called a *moderator,* and its presence is no less essential to a chain reaction than the fuel itself.

At present, light-water reactors are fueled with uranium enriched to contain

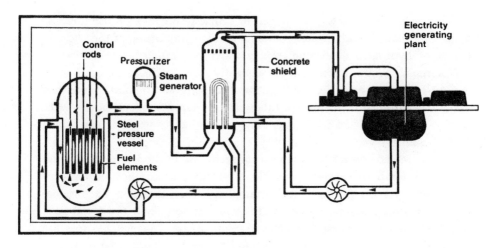

FIGURE 1–2

*Pressurized Water Reactor*

SOURCE: *World Energy Book*, p. 144. Reproduced by the kind permission of the UKAEA.

between 2 percent and 3 percent of U-235,* although they can also use plutonium or a mix of plutonium and uranium.

As with most engineering practice, the choice between the two types of light-water reactor is a matter of trade-off. The BWR is simpler than the PWR—and simplicity of design is a high virtue in engineering—but its design allows water made radioactive as it flows through the core to reach the generating turbines (in the form of steam).†

The considerable experience with the light-water reactor built up in the United States Navy was important in making it the basis of the U.S. commercial power industry. It is also now the most common form in use worldwide. But there are two other broad types in commercial use outside the United States.

* It should be remembered that the reactor core also contains over a hundred times as much U-238 as U-235. This is because it is not practical (or desirable) to produce pure U-235 for such a reactor. Some of the U-238 atoms in the fuel of a light-water reactor will be transmuted into plutonium.

† Some of the radioactivity is induced when neutron bombardment of the water molecules succeeds in transmuting normal hydrogen atoms into atoms of tritium, the heaviest of hydrogen's three isotopes and its only radioactive one, or when bombardment activates atoms of nitrogen dissolved in the water as part of the purification process. The rest is induced when the same bombardment transmutes atoms of minute impurities in the water—for example, microtraces of iron. Great care is taken to keep the levels of these impurities extraordinarily small, and once the high-level but very short-lived radiation has died away, the coolant is less radioactive than tap water and much less radioactive than Scotch whiskey or salad oil.

The heavy-water reactor, developed in Canada and in wide use there, is cooled and moderated by water containing a high proportion of the "heavy" isotope of hydrogen, deuterium. Heavy water is a much better moderator than normal, or light, water, and consequently the Canadian reactors, known as CANDUs, can be fueled with unenriched, natural uranium. Since they boil water in individual pressure tubes rather than in boilers, heavy-water reactors can be refueled while operating, unlike light-water reactors, which must be shut down.

The gas-cooled reactor has found widespread use in the United Kingdom. Such a reactor is moderated by blocks of graphite in and around the core and cooled by a gas (in the British examples, carbon dioxide). The original series of British reactors, known as Magnox reactors from the metal used to encase their fuel, burned natural uranium metal. Magnox reactors are among the most reliable in the world, and the earliest ones, having already lasted what was thought to be their useful lifetime, are now being readied for another run. A later series, the Advanced Gas-Cooled Reactors, use slightly enriched uranium.

Gas-cooled reactors have a much lower power density—the number of watts produced per liter of core volume—than water-cooled reactors. Accordingly, they are substantially less at risk from loss-of-coolant accidents. Moreover, their graphite moderators, which are physically prevented from meltdown by the fact that graphite has no liquid state, have immense capacities to store heat in an emergency. Their principal disadvantage is that they must be fabricated largely on-site, which means they are not well adapted to mass production.

The High-Temperature Gas-Cooled Reactor, of which there is now one medium-sized demonstration model operating in the United States (near Denver, Colorado), is cooled by helium and moderated by graphite. This design is substantially more efficient than any other thermal generator of electricity and has considerable promise as a supplier of industrial process heat.*

In the United States the breeder reactor is often talked of as something for the future, but the design goes back to the beginning of the atomic power program, and the first experimental reactor used in this country to generate power was a breeder. Breeder reactors surround the fuel, typically U-235 and Pu-239, with a "blanket" of fertile material, usually U-238, but possibly Th-232. They create, over time, more fuel than they use, but not in the sense that they literally make something out of nothing. What breeders can do is to produce more plutonium from U-238 than they burn up in the core.

These reactors do not have moderators, for the neutrons need to strike

* See pp. 180–182.

the fertile material at high speeds; hence breeders are sometimes called *fast reactors.* The breeder design now being developed worldwide is cooled by liquid sodium, a metal that has excellent heat-transfer qualities that allow it to be circulated at atmospheric pressure but that needs careful treatment to avoid contact with water, which can lead to an explosion.

The U.S. breeder program is in deep political trouble, but both the British and French have built and are operating successful medium-sized demonstration plants, and France is now building a large-sized plant. A similar medium-sized plant in the Soviet Union has had accidents in its steam generators and must be marked as the least successful of the three foreign programs, although it is certainly more successful than the U.S. program.*

Getting the fuel for any nuclear reactor is complicated, and getting it for the light-water reactor is the most complicated of all. Uranium ore must first be processed to produce uranium oxide, known as yellowcake. Yellowcake, as well as any chemical compound that might be derived from it, is useless as light-water reactor fuel, because—as mentioned earlier—only 0.7 percent of the uranium atoms in any given amount of any compound derived from natural uranium will be of the fissionable isotope, U-235. No chemical process will serve to change this proportion, for no chemical process can distinguish among the chemically identical isotopes of a given element. It is necessary to use a physical process. Physical processes for separating out the U-235—the process is called *enrichment* because it is thought of as enriching the U-235 content of the mix—exploit the fact that an atom of U-238, having three additional protons, is heavier than an atom of U-235.

Theoretically there are three enrichment methods possible, of which only one has been developed commercially. The least developed but potentially cheapest method involves the use of lasers to increase the proportion of U-235 in a given volume. Further developed, but much more expensive, is the centrifuge process, which uses, to the same end, the differing momentums attained by equally accelerated atoms of different weight. Finally there is the existing process, gaseous diffusion. In this method the yellowcake is converted to a gas, uranium hexafluoride, which is then passed through a membrane. The lighter U-235 atoms pass through the membrane a little faster than the heavier U-238 atoms, with the result that once past the membrane the concentration of U-235 atoms is slightly greater. This process must be repeated again and again to achieve even the modest enrichment—to 2 percent or 3 percent—needed for reactor fuel. The enriched uranium hexafluoride is then converted into uranium dioxide and fabricated into fuel rods.

This series of processes makes up the so-called front end of the cycle;

* For a fuller discussion of the breeder reactor and its place in a rational energy plan, see pp. 33–36 and p. 182.

that is, before the reactor. With present technology, each of these steps in the front end is mandatory for light-water reactors.

Once the fuel is loaded into the reactor and the chain reaction is started, the composition of the fuel rod constantly alters as fission products and transmuted elements build up. The proportion of fission products eventually reaches a point at which it seriously interferes with the chain reaction. At this point, the fuel rod has reached its optimum life and is removed.

From this point, the "back end" of the fuel cycle would end with the spent fuel reliably disposed of through one of two basic routes.* Both would begin with storage of the fuel rods in water-filled pools at the reactor site, for a period sufficient to allow the decay of the most ferocious and short-lived fission products, after which the rods are cooler and less radioactive. The two paths diverge in the next step: In a so-called "once-through" cycle, the spent fuel rods would, after suitable cooling, be discarded by burial in a stable geological formation.

In the more complex option, the fuel rods would be dissolved in an acid bath, from which the usable uranium and plutonium would be recovered. The remaining material containing the fission products, the waste proper, would then be buried in a stable geological formation. At present, nowhere in the world has the back end of the cycle reached the stage of geological disposal, but the British and the French have both closed the fuel cycle as far as the reprocessing stage and are storing reprocessed waste against the day when a suitable repository will have been completed.

The United States has not gotten that far. At present there is in storage a good deal of reprocessed liquid waste, most of it from bomb production (which has a fuel cycle analagous to that used in power reactors). None of this has been solidified for final disposal, and no fuel is being reprocessed. It was the position of the Carter administration that none would be, on the grounds that reprocessing makes nuclear proliferation more likely. The policy of the Reagan administration, although presumably pronuclear in general, has not yet been enunciated on this point.

Thus the back end of the cycle now consists simply of disposal, and this is currently being held at its first stage, maintaining the spent fuel in storage ponds at reactor sites. This will become increasingly troublesome as the ponds fill up, although there is no reason why they could not be expanded.

These, then, are the noncontroversial facts about nuclear energy. From here on in, all is dispute.

---

* I have tried in this technical introduction to limit myself to facts that are agreed upon by all sides in the controversy over nuclear power. I should point out here, however, that most if not all nuclear opponents deny the adequacy of any particular back-end cycle, and some may deny the adequacy of any imaginable solution.

# 2

## The Case Against the Atom: Charges and Rebuttals

### The Charges

THE OPPONENTS of nuclear power are more or less agreed as to what is wrong with it, and their charges are quickly summarized. These charges have been specified at great length in many sources, but as yet there has been no single influential exposition of the case against nuclear power. An annotated bibliography appears at the end of the book. The summary that follows is assembled from these and other sources. Most versions of the critique are interchangeable.

The routine operation of power reactors and their fuel cycles is said to be dangerous because such reactors release small amounts of radioactive material into the atmosphere, and it is said that there is unacceptable danger to humans from any amount of radiation, no matter how small.

It was once alleged that nuclear plants posed the additional danger of accidentally exploding like an atomic bomb, but this false charge is now rarely heard. The most common risk talked about with regard to light-water reactors is that of "meltdown," a process that may be initiated if the water cooling the reactor core stops flowing. In such an accident, the loss of water removes the moderator and stops the chain reaction itself, but the inherent heat of the radioactive fuel and fission products, if not cooled by water, will cause an inexorable rise in temperature that will eventually melt the fuel and everything beneath it, possibly leading to a serious release of radioactive materials into the atmosphere. In 1965 an Atomic Energy Commission report estimated that the worst possible meltdown accident—one in which all safety systems failed—would kill 27,000 people, injure 73,000, and cause $17 billion in property damage.[1] It is often said that in 1966, the Fermi I reactor near Detroit went into a "partial meltdown" and that in 1975 a fire at the Browns Ferry plant in Alabama brought a meltdown very near.

Plutonium breeder reactors, besides producing plutonium, a fuel alleged to be too dangerous to allow in society, are also said to impose a risk of nuclear explosion.

It is pointed out by critics of nuclear energy that homeowners' insurance policies exclude nuclear accidents; the risk of such accidents is said to be so great that no company will insure against them.

The problem of waste disposal sometimes appears to be not only insoluble but so dangerous as to be a sufficient cause for the abolition of nuclear power, sometimes even among those who believe nuclear power to be safe in every other respect. Besides being "uniquely dangerous," the fission products of a nuclear reactor are said to be "the longest-lived" substances known to man; plutonium, not technically a fission product, has been called "toxic beyond human experience." It is often pointed out that there have been leaks of wastes from the government storage facility at Hanford, Washington, and it is widely asserted that there exists no technology to deal with the wastes, which are said to remain dangerous for hundreds of thousands of years, and that none is foreseeable. One commonly hears of the need for a "nuclear priesthood" dedicated to safeguarding nuclear wastes into the infinite future.

A related charge is that retired nuclear plants present a serious radiation hazard, one that can be obviated, if at all, only at great cost, since the so-called "decommissioning" of a nuclear plant may cost upward of a third of its original price.

It is very widely alleged by critics that nuclear power is uneconomical, partially because its routine costs are said to be much higher than the costs of other forms of power generation and partially because nuclear plants are said to be much less reliable than other types.

Critics say that nuclear plants are guilty of "thermal pollution," that is, they can raise the temperature of the cooling water they discharge into lakes, rivers, and oceans by many degrees, with catastrophic consequences for aquatic life.

Further, it is alleged that nuclear power plants are overly complicated for the tasks they perform and operate at excessively high temperatures for the purpose at hand.

The mining of uranium is said to impose unacceptable risks on the workers involved, and the same goes for operating the rest of the nuclear fuel cycle, including the reactors themselves.

Plutonium is claimed to be a potential boon to terrorists in two ways. First, it is said that simply as a poison, a few kilos of plutonium, properly dispersed, could kill everyone in the world. Further, it is often said that a dedicated band of terrorists could acquire enough plutonium to construct its own atomic bomb, with predictably horrific results. To thwart both these dangers, it is alleged that it will be necessary to construct security systems that will create garrison states.

Finally, it is said that a nuclear power industry is inextricably tied up with nuclear weapons proliferation because nations that do not currently have a nuclear weapons capability will be able to attain one by using plutonium reactor fuel to make plutonium bombs. The best-known advocate of this view was President Carter.

These charges against nuclear power would be terrifying if true. Indeed, were no more than half of them true—or even plausible—nuclear power would almost certainly be too dangerous to offer a solution to the energy crisis and to be allowed to continue at the present level. If these charges were true, there might even be some sense in the slogan "Split wood, not atoms." But they are not true.

Unfortunately, they can be stated more succinctly than they can be refuted. The refutation is, in effect, the first part of the case for the atom.


# Rebuttal: Radiation

The belief that a functioning nuclear reactor and its fuel cycle pose a radiation threat illustrates a common habit among the antinuclear lobby: holding nuclear reactors to a standard of safety that if generalized would forbid not only all other forms of power generation but also most of the things man makes or finds in nature. It is a standard of safety so demanding that only a nuclear reactor can hope to meet it.

In order to see why this should be so, first of all we need to understand radiation, a phenomenon that cuts through the antinuclear case. It cuts across almost all boundaries and lurks always as the most potent argument against the atom. For this reason, before answering the antinuclear case point by point, I shall discuss, as background for almost everything that follows, radiation and how it works.

That radiation should be at the heart of the nuclear controversy is not conducive to public understanding. Among scientists it is a phenomenon, on the whole very well understood by scientists and not subject to immense controversy,* but—perhaps owing to the impossibility of its being perceived without scientific instruments—it is much misunderstood by the general public. Indeed, it is precisely because radiation is not perceptible to the unaided human senses, because it is invisible, odorless, and tasteless, that it has been possible to present one of the most easily measurable forces in nature as a mysterious and infinitely threatening phenomenon.

There are many types of radiation besides those at issue in the nuclear controversy. Most of them are considered to be thoroughly harmless even when this is patently not so. Sunlight is a case in point. The energy contained in it is quite sufficient to kill an exposed human being in a few days as long as he gets no water.† That light and FM radio transmissions are forms of radiation in which we all bathe constantly should suggest that the phenomenon in general is neither unnatural nor malevolent.

Although we all pass through life bathed in a sea of radiations, including, but not limited to, candlelight, Walter Cronkite, Radio Moscow, heat generated by angry dispute, the sound of our own voices, and the warmth received by kittens snuggled up to their mother, only four types of radiation are at issue in the nuclear debate. These I shall henceforth call simply "radiation," trusting the reader to remember Walter Cronkite and those kittens.

Alpha radiation consists of particles identical to the nucleus of a helium atom: two neutrons and two protons. Beta radiation consists of free electrons, and gamma radiation is better known under the name X ray. Finally, neutrons, particles normally contained within the nucleus, become radiation when they are expelled outward.

We should be well aware that radiation, like good claret, water, or jogging, can kill human beings, and like all of these needs to be thoroughly understood and approached with some care.

The production of nuclear power does not involve radiation in its most violent forms—as with bombs—if only because in nuclear energy installations great care is taken to contain radiation, whereas in nuclear bombs the whole point is to get it out. That, however, does not matter much to the nuclear critics, whose essential aphorism is that "there is no safe level of exposure to radiation." If one qualifies this remark carefully enough, it is probably

---

* There are some severe *little* controversies swirling around it, but they are not of the order of, say, the controversy among cardiac surgeons over bypass surgery or among nutritionists over the role of cholesterol in heart disease.

† C. S. Forester's unforgettable mad dictator, El Supremo, understood this well. Scorning the elaborate methods of both his Inca and Spanish ancestors, he executed his prisoners simply by tying them to stakes in the sun. "He will die when the noonday sun shines on him. They always do," explains one of El Supremo's lieutenants to an appalled Captain Hornblower.[2]

true, but not in any sense useful. It is true that if one alpha particle hits one cell squarely enough, a single collision could cause one cancer. The question is, How often does one alpha particle hit a cell squarely enough to result in cancer? Since, as antinuclearists are fond of telling us, cancers do not carry tags saying how they were caused, there is no way to answer such a question with any assurance. But it is possible to make some highly educated guesses derived from negative evidence.

Even without nuclear power plants, every human being is exposed to a great deal of radiation. (With such plants, every human being is exposed to radiation greater by an infinitesimal amount.) This comes from two sources: external radiation from the environment and internal radiation from the human body, radiation that would be there even if there were no external radiation whatsoever. Humans, like other living beings, are inescapably and naturally radioactive.

Before looking at the implications of this fact, let us consider some of the elements of the process by which radiation can be dangerous to life. It should be understood, first of all, that an atom of a radioactive substance poses no radiological threat so long as it remains in existence. The problem comes during its death throes, when it disintegrates and casts out dangerous debris in the form of radiation. Now let us imagine a group of 1 billion radioactive atoms that have a half-life of 1 billion years. That means that after 1 billion years, half of these atoms, or 500 million of them, will have disintegrated. That sounds like a lot of disintegrations, but it works out to only one every other year.

Let us next look at an actual radioactive element: Pu-239, the form of plutonium used to make bombs and reactor fuel. Pu-239 has a half-life of approximately 24,000 years. This means that of 1 billion atoms of Pu-239, half, or 500 million, will have disintegrated in 24,000 years. That is approximately twenty-one disintegrations a year. Let us suppose that a human being receives at the age of twenty an internal burden of 1 billion atoms of Pu-239 and lives to be eighty. During his life about 1,200 of those atoms will disintegrate. These are the only atoms of plutonium that can pose any threat, radiologically speaking, to the person in which the plutonium resides.

Our understanding of the relation between radiation and cancer has not progressed to the point at which we could guess what proportion of those 1,200 disintegrations has even the potential to cause cancer. But we do know that the human body contains a radioactive form of potassium, K-40, and that this isotope alone supplies every human being with a lifetime internal irradiation composed primarily of alpha particles. During seventy years, the average human being undergoes a bombardment of radiation from this cause. Yet the average human being never gets cancer.

This is evidence of the most persuasive kind that if no level of exposure to radiation can be called absolutely safe, most human beings can experience substantial exposure to radiation without developing cancer. For we must remember that it is not clear how many members of the population who get cancer get it from radiation. Radiation is not by any means the only carcinogen in contemporary society; in fact most people who develop cancer get it from some other cause.

The evidence for the proposition that radiation is a minor cause of cancer lies in the fact that the national cancer rate seems to be largely independent of background radiation. Denver, for example, with one of the highest background radiation rates, has one of the lowest cancer rates in the nation. Consulting a map indicating cancer rates cannot teach one much about background radiation in the United States, but it will teach one a great deal about industrial concentrations containing, inter alia, many facilities burning coal.

In any event, the average exposure to radiation across the country is 170 millirem* (mrem) a year. Nuclear critics say that this is quite enough and that we do not need to add any more radiation to what we already have. This argument may be superficially persuasive on the ground that any amount of a bad thing is too much. But are the effects of the nuclear industry so severe as this suggests, compared to various other components of the background?

One inescapable radiation from nuclear power is that emitted by a reactor in routine operation. The Nuclear Regulatory Commission (NRC) allows a person living at the boundary line of a nuclear plant—that is, a member of the general public who does not court voluntary exposure by visiting or working at the plant—a yearly exposure of 5 mrem. In point of fact, no plant actually operates at so high a level of emission. Should any plant actually emit as much as a *fourth* of its legal limit during any three-month period, it is required to report the matter to the NRC and conduct an investigation to see what is causing the emission. But the law does allow such an emission, which can be put into perspective by noting that the average American receives a yearly exposure of 5 mrem from color television. If an American has a

---

* It will be possible for the reader to follow my argument without having the slightest grasp of what a millirem is as long as he remembers that 1 mrem is a great deal less than 170 mrem. The millirem is a measure of the biological effect of radiation on human beings. The millirem is one thousandth of a rem, a term that stands for roentgen-equivalent-man (the roentgen is the basic unit of radiation). The rem takes into account the effect of radiation on a particular species: Because various kinds of radiation have differing effects on humans, a rad—a dosage of absorbed radiation that is equal to 100 ergs per gram of irradiated material—of one type of radiation will give a different rem-equivalent than that of another type. Roughly, one rad of X rays is equal to one rem. Doses of this magnitude are comparatively rare among the general public, so most of the figures I shall be citing will be in one thousandths of a rem, or millirem.

color television set and lives a few blocks from a nuclear power plant, he receives more irradiation from the television set.

We could go through a large number of similar examples. One gets about 5 mrem of exposure from a single coast-to-coast jet airliner trip (one spends several hours without the protection of much of the atmosphere and is thereby more exposed to cosmic radiation). Were one to move from Boston to Denver, one would increase one's average yearly exposure not by 5 mrem but by 50 mrem. Because granite is rather radioactive, one gets more than 5 mrem a year from working in or at the boundary of a granite building. News vendors working on the sidewalks at Grand Central Station in New York and anxious to reduce their radiation exposure would be well advised to move to the Indian Point nuclear station upstream on the Hudson.

(Connoisseurs of irony in energy will appreciate that the granite for Grand Central was quarried near New London, Connecticut, at Millstone Point, now the site of two operating reactors with a third in construction. The removal of the granite from the Millstone Point area probably reduced the exposure there by a greater amount than the reactors have increased it.)

All these comparisons are to a reactor's permitted boundary dose of 5 mrem, but the actual exposure to the average American from the entire nuclear industry is very much smaller. And other sources—jet travel, color television, granite buildings—inflict much greater exposure than nuclear power does. Put another way, whatever risk is posed to the general public by radiation, the radiation exposure from nuclear power plants is one of the most trivial of all sources.

And there is excellent evidence that this trivial exposure has trivial health effects. The statistics here are quite unambiguous. For the purposes of tabulating the causes of cancer, the International Commission on Radiological Protection (ICRP) adheres to the linear hypothesis, which assumes in the face of increasing evidence to the contrary that even very small amounts of radiation cause small amounts of cancer. This assumption may well exaggerate the number of cancer deaths due to radiation, but on the basis of it, and assuming 148 mrem total exposure a year, there will be, out of 181.9 cancer deaths per 100,000 population, 1.85 due to radiation.

This is a tiny enough figure, made tinier if we remember that nuclear power plants account for only a minute fraction of the total of 148 mrem. The number of cancer deaths attributable to nuclear power is, according to this calculation, two thousandths of one death a year per 100,000 deaths from all causes.

If this abstraction is hard to grasp, we can replace it with an estimate of the actual number of cancer deaths due to nuclear plants a year. There were about 400,000 cancer deaths in 1980, of which about 40 were due to radiation. Of these, about four hundredths of one death was due to nuclear power plants. At this rate nuclear power plants will kill a whole person every twenty-five years. Expansion of the nuclear industry will, to be sure, increase this figure—perhaps, one day, to the extent that in one year the effects of the entire nuclear industry might approach those of a single coal-fired power plant.

This is a very low estimate. What of the higher ones? In 1979 a report of the Biological Effects of Ionizing Radiation (BEIR) committee of the National Academy of Sciences estimated that between the years 1975 and 2000 some 2,000 people will develop cancer as a result of exposure to radiation from nuclear energy.[3] New and higher estimates of the effect of radiation appeared to underlie this figure; it was reported that the academy committee that produced the estimates was deeply split over them. A year later the BEIR committee issued a new report lowering the estimates once again.[4]

But let us suppose that the original estimates were sound. Can we tolerate such a death toll from nuclear power, amounting to 80 a year? The *New York Times*[5] account of the 1979 report mentioned in passing that the cancer deaths from nuclear power should be compared to those caused by the alternative of coal, but specifically cited only the death toll among miners, which is a small part of the total. Moreover, the *Times* report had a curious label for the question of "public health trade-offs of nuclear versus coal-fired plants": It called it an "esoteric" issue, but the question is not esoteric at all, involving as it does the routine death by cancer and respiratory diseases of thousands of Americans each year. Eighty deaths a year at present is a little over one person per operating reactor. At a very conservative estimate, a 1,000-megawatt (MW) coal-fired plant kills 30 people a year;[6] over the twenty-five-year span covered in the National Academy of Sciences study, only three such plants would kill as many people as the study estimates for the entire nuclear industry, current and future. A moderate estimate is that a 1,000-MW coal plant kills 110 people a year; on that estimate, a single coal-fired plant would kill more people over twenty-five years than the entire nuclear power industry!

Nuclear critics claim that since cancer caused by radiation takes years to develop, we do not know the true number of victims from accidents at plants like Three Mile Island for a generation. As it happens, we have good reason to believe that there will be none even in twenty years.

By any objective measure, the accident at a plutonium-production reactor at Windscale in northwest England in 1957 was very much worse than Three Mile Island in terms of radiation release. In the most contaminated areas, milk was confiscated for as long as forty-four days.[7] Twenty-three years later, *no* pattern of increased cancer has been attributed to this accident.[8]

## The Case Against the Atom: Charges and Rebuttals

In the late summer of 1980, a study appeared that provided additional confirmation from actual health records of the negligible effect of low-level radiation—though the levels involved were very much higher than those at Three Mile Island. The study dealt with two areas, in one of which the background radiation was about three times as high as in the other. About 70,000 people lived in each area, and about 20,000 in each area were interviewed. It was established that the families of about 90 percent of the people responding had lived in the area for at least six generations. Persons who had significant *occupational* exposure to radiation were excluded from the sample, and the figures were also adjusted for medical irradiation. Some 400 people in each area wore radiation monitors for two months, and the readings from these confirmed that the actual doses received were about three times as high in the high-radiation area. The study was run for four years—1972 to 1975—and the health records of the two populations were compared for cancer, genetic disease, and chromosome damage.

The excess radiation received in the high-radiation area was over 100 millirems a year, or about fifty times the average dose received by people living within fifty miles of Three Mile Island. The study showed no significant increase in cancer, genetic disease, or chromosome damage in the persons living in the high-radiation area. (Indeed, in some categories there were fewer health defects than in the low-radiation area, but these differences were also too small to be significant.) Incidentally, the area being studied was in Guangdong province, China, and the sponsoring agency was the Ministry of Public Health in Beijing.[9] Working out the practical implications of such facts, Professor Bernard Cohen of the University of Pittsburgh's Department of Physics has provided a neat illustration of the real risk from the emissions of a nuclear reactor. If one lives at its property line and wishes to move away in order to escape the risks of the 5 millirems a year maximum emission permitted—in practice, remember, no reactor comes near the permitted maximum—one must take care not to move to a house more than 500 feet farther away from work. If one does, the increased risk from an auto accident will overbalance the decreased risk from radiation.

Although the opponents of nuclear power talk as if it were generally accepted that minute amounts of radiation result in genetic damage to human beings, it is not generally realized that this assumption rests on laboratory results with animals that are contradicted by actual experience with humans. In Hiroshima and Nagasaki, thousands of humans were exposed to levels of radiation that not even the harshest critic of nuclear power believes can come from a reactor. Thirty years later no increase in genetic abnormality has been detected in this population. In September 1981, *Science*[10] published a new study suggesting strongly that previous estimates of the genetic effect of radiation on humans, based on animal studies, have been exaggerated as much as four times.

There are undoubtedly risks of cancer from exposure to radiation. That they are tiny is evident from the fact that any number of highly radioactive (but nonindustrialized) sections of the country combine high background radiation with low cancer rates. The important point is that nuclear reactors, routinely operated, are among the most negligible emitters of radiation and thus among the most negligible causes of cancer from radiation.

# Reactor Accidents

The most serious accident that could befall a nuclear reactor, a meltdown,* would begin with a failure in the water supply to the core, either from a break in one of the pipes carrying heated water or steam from the reactor core to a heat exchanger or a turbine, or from a pump failure. All reactors have redundant systems to supply emergency cooling water, but if all these were to fail, even though the lack of a moderator would shut down the chain reaction, the heat growing out of the fission products contained in the core would no longer be carried away and the fuel would begin to overheat. If cooling water were withheld for more than a few minutes,† the fuel would begin to melt.

The stainless-steel pressure vessel covering the reactor proper is designed to contain the effects of this, but if it should fail, the domed containment structure is designed to hold in the various radioactive products dispersed within it. Only if this containment structure should fail—and it is designed to withstand an impact from a crashing jetliner—would there be a serious release of radioactive material into the atmosphere.

What would happen next would depend on the location of the reactor and the weather. The consequences would range from none to very serious indeed. There would be none if a minimum of radioactivity were released and it were very widely dispersed over sparsely populated areas. And there

---

* The following discussion of nuclear reactor accidents follows fairly closely an account originally written in the summer of 1977, a year and a half before the accident at Three Mile Island. Although I have substantially expanded the argument and rewritten parts for greater lucidity, the accident as it actually occurred required only one substantive revision of what I—or any other reasonably well-informed person—thought about meltdowns in 1977. The single revision was to the benefit of nuclear power.

† This, as we will see (see pp. 27–28), is the major revision in this passage required by the accident at Three Mile Island.

would be very serious results if a great deal of radioactivity was emitted and dispersed in a concentrated fashion over densely populated areas.

Light-water reactors are designed to prevent such an outcome through what is known as defense in depth. In order to prevent the initation of a loss-of-coolant accident in the first place, they are provided with not one but several systems to supply emergency cooling water to a reactor whose operating coolant systems have sprung a leak. In everyday terms, this can be compared to a car that was provided with two or three standby radiators, each with its own supply of water or antifreeze and each prepared to supply coolant to the engine were the regular radiator or its hoses to fail. In a reactor, these alternate sources of coolant are known as the Emergency Core Cooling System (ECCS).

For many years nuclear critics have complained that there has never been a full-scale test of the ECCS used in all modern light-water reactors. A similar complaint might have been made prior to 1923 against Frank Lloyd Wright's Imperial Hotel in Tokyo; designed to survive a major earthquake, its integrity could be definitively tested only by such an earthquake (a test that it eventually passed with flying colors). In the case of an ECCS, which is designed to prevent a meltdown after a cooling loss in a full-sized reactor operating at full power, the only definitive test would be such an accident.*

Failing this, the Atomic Energy Commission (AEC) and its successors devised the Loss-of-Fluid-Test (LOFT) program. In the LOFT program, a very large scale model of a nuclear power plant (one-fifth the size of a large commercial reactor, and operating at much less total power but at equivalent power density) is subjected to procedures simulating a major loss-of-coolant accident, and the results are analyzed.

The first series of six tests was conducted at an AEC test facility in Idaho without operating nuclear fuel in the core. None of these tests was designed to simulate a real accident; the intention, rather, was to gather data about the safety of the system for the next series, using an operating core. The first test in the second series was carried out on December 10, 1978. This test simulated the worst-case loss-of-coolant accident, a so-called double-guillotine cut, in which a considerable segment of a main coolant pipe is destroyed, allowing full flow of water at both ends of the cut. Computer simulations had predicted that the ECCS would restore cooling in ninety seconds and that the fuel temperature would rise to 1,350 degrees F. As it turned out, cooling was restored in forty-four seconds and fuel temperature did not rise above 1,000 degrees F.[11] Subsequent tests have continued this success.

---

* Rather lost in the hullabaloo over Three Mile Island is the plain fact that such a test occurred there and that, even with evidence of substantial error, the ECCS did what it was designed to do.

But let us assume that all the systems that make up the ECCS in an operating reactor have failed. The next barrier is the reactor vessel, a stainless-steel structure primarily designed to contain the pressurized coolant.* An uncontrolled meltdown would probably get through the bottom of this pressure vessel and come to rest on a thick concrete slab. Above the fuel, as mentioned earlier, is the containment building, a reinforced concrete structure whose walls are designed to withstand a crashing jetliner. The next barrier under the melted fuel would be the earth itself, the largest heat sink we have. The earth would rapidly carry away the heat of the melted fuel until it congealed again, where it would reach stability. Although nuclear critics often suggest that melted fuel would strike groundwater, causing a steam explosion and opening an avenue for radioactive contamination, reactor sites are checked for the absence of groundwater to depths of greater than a hundred feet.

Given these facts, it is easy to see why the Kemeny Commission—convened by President Carter to investigate the accident—concluded that if there had been a meltdown at Three Mile Island, it would have been contained.[12]

Now, although there is some disagreement as to the precise magnitude of casualties in the worst possible meltdown disaster—that is, one that would be, however improbably, uncontained—all parties agree that the worst possible meltdown disaster would be a major one. The real disagreement comes on probabilities.

Probabilities are essential to understanding the real risk of anything. In general, the worse the accident the lower the probability. For the entire earth, the worst possible accident is probably a collision with a large asteroid. No asteroid is now known to be on a collision course with earth, and given the great volumes of space, such a course is exceedingly unlikely. No one would want to discount the possibility—purely from the theoretical viewpoint—of an as-yet undiscovered asteroid with an exceedingly elliptical orbit that might bring it into collision with earth. But the likelihood is so remote as to make it unworthy of serious attention.

The worst possible airline accident is something like a fully loaded 747 crashing into the Rose Bowl on New Year's Day, an event that might kill more than 30,000 people. The worst possible electric power generation accident is not a nuclear meltdown but the failure of a hydroelectric dam at the head of a heavily populated valley. This might kill as many as a quarter of a million people and destroy many billions of dollars worth of property. If such an accident were very much less probable than a meltdown, we might discount the fact that it threatens a much higher death toll. As it

---

* The term *pressurized-water reactor* is slightly misleading if taken to mean that in boiling-water reactors the coolant is not under pressure; it is, but at a substantially lower level.

happens, the dam accident is substantially more likely than a major meltdown accident.

In 1975 the Atomic Energy Commission published a massive attempt to calculate the probability of reactor accidents, the *Reactor Safety Study* (*RSS*),[13] familiarly known as the Rasmussen Report after the director of the study, Norman Rasmussen of M.I.T. The *RSS* concluded that the maximum possible light-water reactor accident would result in 3,300 deaths immediately, with 45,000 deaths from cancer over a period of thirty years, and $17 billion in property damage. It also concluded that the chance of such an accident was vanishingly remote, perhaps 10,000 times smaller than similar death tolls from such disasters as dam failures and tropical storms. With 100 reactors operating, the probability that 1,000 people would be killed in a single accident is the same as the probability of 1,000 people being killed by a single meteorite—once every billion years.

Before Three Mile Island, the *RSS* was subjected to very severe criticism from both the American Physical Society and the Union of Concerned Scientists. The most telling claims made included that the system of analysis it used was developed to predict relative, but not absolute, safety and that it paid inadequate regard to the possibility that failure in one component might lead to failure in another, as, for example, when water spilling from a broken pipe disables a safety device.

If the probabilities were not themselves so remote, the work of the critics would have been more disturbing. Absent the desideratum of a reworked *RSS,* there was much sense in the conclusion reached by a Ford Foundation report that although the risks of a meltdown may be greater than indicated in the *RSS,* they are still very remote.[14] Moreover, they are not greater in likelihood and intensity than risks that society already accepts and has learned to live with. In this century, the Ford Foundation report noted, the United States has already seen two hurricanes that have taken over a thousand lives each and resulted in billions of dollars of property damage.

Early in 1979 the NRC reacted to a study report it had commissioned of the Rasmussen Report. The NRC withdrew its endorsement of the so-called executive summary, an abstract designed to make the report's conclusions more accessible. This event was widely misreported as the NRC's repudiation of the Rasmussen Report itself. What went unreported were statements by the chairman of the study commission that he continued to be strongly supportive of nuclear energy and that his commission had found that uncertainties in the Rasmussen methodology were as likely to overestimate danger as to underestimate it.

Shortly thereafter, events at Three Mile Island were to provide extensive new empirical data on the subject. As it happens, this accident was on the whole badly reported, and if we are to understand how what happened at Three Mile Island has a bearing on nuclear power, we need to look more closely at the events of late March and early April 1979.

What follows is adapted from the chronology issued by the Nuclear Regulatory Commission. In order to understand it, it is necessary to keep in mind a few facts about the construction of the reactor at Three Mile Island.

It is of the pressurized-water type, in which cooling water is handled in two separate circuits (see figure 1–2, p. 7). The primary circuit, which is kept at pressure sufficient to prevent boiling even at 650 degrees F, takes water to the reactor core, where it is heated, and then to a sort of boiler called a steam generator where it makes thermal—but not physical—contact with the secondary circuit, giving up its heat to it. It is then pumped back to the reactor core.

Water in the primary circuit becomes slightly radioactive as neutrons in the core alter occasional atoms of hydrogen and nitrogen and various trace impurities. The secondary circuit water, which is not pressurized and hence can boil, goes—in the form of steam—from the steam generator to the turbine and then to the condenser, where it is cooled back to water. It is then pumped back to the steam generator to be reheated again.

As can be seen, taken together the two circuits have a dual function. They are at once cooling devices and heating devices, and the turbine is a part of the cooling system for the core as well as a source of energy to turn the generator. Any interruption in any part of either circuit raises an immediate problem with regard to both of these functions.

On March 28, about 4:00 A.M., an incident occurred in the secondary (or nonnuclear) circuit of Three Mile Island unit 121. A main feedwater pump, which has the job of pumping water from the condenser back into the steam generator, tripped. Immediately the turbine and its associated generator were automatically stopped. Pressure began to rise in the primary system, and, as designed, a valve automatically opened to relieve pressure. However, pressure rose enough that another automatic system instantly shut down the reactor by inserting its control rods. Thus far, approximately thirty seconds into the accident, everything happened as planned. From this point on, the chain reaction was shut down, and all the heat left in the core derived from the decay of highly radioactive fission products within the fuel rods.

This decay heat, amounting to less than 1 percent of the total output of the reactor, is constantly produced even in a shut-down reactor. It must be removed from the core in order to avoid damage to the fuel. To do this, the primary circuit continues to carry the heat to the steam generator, where it must be transferred to the secondary circuit and carried away to the condenser even if the turbine has been turned off. In order to accomplish this, reactors are equipped with auxiliary feedwater systems that are designed to supply water to the steam generator after a turbine trip. Thirty seconds after the original failure, the three auxiliary feedwater pumps were started up. However, they failed to supply water to the steam generator because their discharge valves were closed.

A minute into the accident, the steam generators were running short of water. Moreover, the pressure-relief valve in the primary circuit, automatically opened when the pressure exceeded 2,255 pounds per square inch, failed to close again when the pressure fell within operating bounds. The pressure continued to drop, and two minutes into the accident the ECCS automatically injected water into the primary system. Shortly thereafter, the water level in the pressurizer—the part of the primary circuit that regulates pressure— began to register very high levels, actually going off the scale. The operator then turned off the ECCS, as he was supposed to have done with such an indication.

Eight minutes into the accident, the operator opened the discharge valves of the auxiliary feedwater pumps, and water began to be supplied once again to the steam generators. Three minutes later, he restarted the ECCS and the pressurizer level came back on scale. At this point the accident was eleven minutes into its course.

Four minutes later, the failure of the relief valve to close led to a leak in the tank to which it drained, and radioactive water flooded into the containment building. This water was eventually pumped automatically into an auxiliary building, leading to some release of radiation outside the plant.

During the second hour of the accident, the operator turned off the pumps circulating the primary coolant. Following this action, the temperature in the core began to rise, and during the next several hours cooling in the core was inadequate to prevent fuel damage, which is now estimated to have occurred, in greater or lesser degree, to about half the fuel. It is clear that the top of the core was uncovered; estimates of how long this state lasted range from four to fifteen hours. Once cooling water had been restored, the problem was to find ways to bring the reactor to the state known as cold shutdown, in which the coolant temperature falls below the boiling point and convection currents in the unpressurized coolant are sufficient to carry off the decay heat from the core. A detailed chronology shows a steady alternation of ups and downs toward this end. One of the ups received wide publicity. The overheating of the core generated hydrogen, which accumulated in the reactor pressure vessel, hampering further cooling. The hydrogen bubble first appears in the NRC chronology on March 30; by April 2, it was significantly reduced in size and by April 5 seemed to have become negligible.

Also highly publicized during the early days of the accident were various releases of radioactive material into the atmosphere. Some of these were inadvertent and some were deliberate. Their existence, and the possibility of more of them, led to the recommended evacuation of pregnant women and small children from the immediate vicinity of the reactor.

These are, in essence, the salient noncontroversial elements of what happened at Three Mile Island. If one reads them in the form of the NRC's "Immediate Preliminary Notice" documents, comparatively undigested summaries of events and data prepared in the first instance for the commissioners themselves and senior NRC staff, and then for the media, one is struck by the fact that the whole affair seems a good deal drier and less panic-stricken than the press reports made out.

One exception to the general tenor of press coverage was the normally sensational *National Enquirer,* which ran an antisensational story holding that as the whole problem had been handled quickly and calmly by the professionals, the very idea of a crisis was a hoax. The tone of this account, although it made the event seem more routine than it was, was more accurate than most treatments. The *Enquirer,* arguing that the event involved a wildly improbable concatenation of human and mechanical malfunction, also suggested strongly that the accident was the result of sabotage.

The press in general was quite restrained in reporting a bit of overseas nuclear news: Three Mile Island apparently induced the Soviets to confide more about their own nuclear program. A congressional delegation was told in late April 1979 that yes, there had been some accidents in Soviet reactors, but none that harmed the public. An earlier American group had been told that the absence of an antinuclear movement in the Soviet Union was attributable to the superior safety of the People's reactors. Similar claims were made about the safety of Soviet reactors on this occasion, all dutifully reported in the American press.

What was not generally reported was that most Soviet reactors have *no* containments. Had a Three Mile Island–type accident happened at one of these uncontained reactors, there would almost certainly have been very serious releases of radioactivity.

The weeks following the accident at Three Mile Island were crowded with man-made and natural disasters. On two occasions accidents involving industrial chemicals forced widespread evacuations in the United States. There were very serious floods in this country, a major earthquake in Yugoslavia, and a major volcanic eruption in the Caribbean. In all these events many thousands of people were threatened with death, and many more thousands were evacuated from their homes. These events were routinely reported in the press. Had anyone pointed out that they posed greater threats than Three Mile Island, the antinuclear lobby would doubtless have replied that even if they did, one good disaster does not deserve another. True; but on the other hand, there is no upside, as the cost-benefit analysts put it, to an earthquake or a flood.

A little over a year after Three Mile Island, Mount Saint Helens was to provide an instructive contrast. Although the news media carried a certain proportion of super-alarmist stories about the possible long-term destruction of agriculture in northeast Washington, by and large such coverage was again restrained. Late in the summer of 1980, there appeared a fascinating report: Mount Saint Helens was radioactive. The mountain had spewed out substantial amounts of the radioactive elements radon, polonium, and thorium, and radioactive isotopes of lead and potassium. The total far exceeded the release at Three Mile Island.

This is significant not because the release of radiation from a volcano proves that the release of radiation from a reactor is good—although one should note that the volcano eruption was an entirely "natural" phenomenon—but because of the source of all that radioactivity. Mount Saint Helens did not find its radioactive material in a waste dump or manufacture it in a reactor. It simply fired a chunk out of the earth itself, which is more radioactive than a reactor in the midst of an accident.

The single most important question about Three Mile Island concerns the seriousness of the accident. Did we, as it is said with great regularity, come very near to a meltdown?

Here one must distinguish between the melting of fuel cladding and of some fuel and the phenomenon of "meltdown," that is, an uncontrollable syndrome in which all the fuel in a reactor core melts and as a semiliquid mass generates enough heat to melt through the bottom of the reactor vessel and the containment building. This process, once it starts, is irreversible. There is no such thing as a partial meltdown, although one is often said to have happened at an accident near Detroit in 1966 and the same thing is likely to be said of Three Mile Island.

For a full meltdown in this sense to occur it is necessary for some of the fuel itself to melt. This requires a temperature of approximately 5,000 degrees F. How near did we come to this temperature in the fuel at Three Mile Island? There the temperature never reached more than about 3,000 degrees F. This fact is a better gauge than all the vague press reports of "possibilities," and certainly better than the bogus report that circulated widely on March 31 to the effect that the reactor bubble was expanding rapidly and that an explosion or a meltdown was likely within forty-eight hours.

It appears that, if anything, Three Mile Island makes meltdowns seem less likely than we had thought. Before March 28, 1979, it was widely agreed on all sides that if the core of a recently shut down reactor were to be uncovered for more than a few minutes, a meltdown would follow. This was the way the "experts" put it in the film *The China Syndrome,* and in the real world few experts could have been found to disagree.

As it turned out, the core was uncovered not for minutes but for hours, and there was no meltdown. The core survived the erroneous and deliberate disabling of its emergency cooling system. Those nuclear critics who deal with the matter at all treat it as something quite mysterious. One—Dr. Helen Caldicott—even attributed it to the hand of God.* But the nuclear engineers are less puzzled. The steam in the reactor vessel, although a less adequate cooling medium than cold water, did in fact cool the core and prevent a meltdown. (The cooling ability of steam also appears to explain the fact that in the 1978–1979 tests the LOFT reactor cooled down faster than expected when a loss-of-coolant accident was initiated.) The inference to be drawn is quite clear: For this particular design of light-water reactor, the probability of a meltdown is much less than expected. Some engineers have speculated that meltdowns may be next to impossible as long as some water can be supplied to the reactor vessel.

Wire service reports of the April 27 attainment of shutdown at Three Mile Island continued to speak of an uncovered core not as an actual event but as a horrible threat posed by the hydrogen bubble, from which we were mysteriously saved. Thus another reasonable question is, How near did we come at Three Mile Island to a hydrogen explosion? With regard to hydrogen explosions in the atmosphere of the containment building, it seems clear that we had such an explosion: The NRC explains a sharp rise in containment pressure the afternoon of March 28 that is otherwise unexplainable as the result of a small hydrogen explosion. It should be noted that the explosion was neither heard nor felt and could only be inferred on the basis of readings from sensitive recording instruments.

As to the possibility of an explosion of the hydrogen bubble within the reactor dome, it is clear that there was never enough oxygen available, whatever the hydrogen supply, to allow for a hydrogen fire, let alone an explosion; and while the possibility of such an explosion was splendidly *frisson*-making, we never even headed in the direction of such an explosion, let alone got near it.

"Well, then," one can imagine a nuclear opponent saying, "suppose we concede that we didn't get very close to a worse accident. What we had is quite bad enough, because there were many releases of radiation, and there is no safe level of radiation. The death toll at Three Mile Island, in the

---

* To the *literal* hand of God, that is, seen as holding the top of the reactor vessel down and preventing the release of radioactivity.

form of an increased cancer rate in the area, won't show up for twenty years."

There are a number of ways to evaluate the magnitude of the radiation releases. One is to consider the maximum exposure the most exposed member of the public might have gotten. This, according to NRC figures, amounted to 80 millirems. That is the equivalent of two chest X rays. It is also a little less than the difference between the annual natural, or "background," exposure in New Orleans and Denver. That needs to be appreciated: A resident of New Orleans offered a choice between a year in Denver or five days, starting March 28, 1979, on the banks of the Susquehanna, staring at Three Mile Island, would, on radiological grounds at least, be well advised to spend the time in Pennsylvania. The average exposure to persons living within fifty miles of the reactor was slightly less than 1 mrem. This is, by a neat coincidence, the same exposure each of them gets each year from color television.*

There is another accurate measure of radiation exposure: The NRC set up a whole-body radiation scanner in Middletown, and offered to test anyone who wished to be tested for increased body radiation. Of some 750 individuals, none showed radiation levels above normal.

Still another measure is the contamination of milk by radioiodine. The highest iodine-131 reading in milk in the area around Three Mile Island was some 40 picocuries per liter. This is one-tenth of the reading permitted by the reactor license for routine operation, and a third of 1 percent of the level at which the Food and Drug Administration recommends placing cattle on stored feed.

A wide variety of other samplings—of vegetables, soil, air, and water—showed no radiation above normal. Finally, even with the discharge of some mildly radioactive water into the Susquehanna, the plant was well within its quarterly limits for discharge into the river.†

There were also tales chronicled by such journals as the *Village Voice* of monstrous births, fallow cows, and the like. Such stories are common in rural areas. Similar ones circulate about weather-modification research under-

---

* To a certain extent, nuclear energy has become a victim of its own exceptional concern with safety. The NRC sets highly conservative limits for radiation release, which in practice reactors never come near. When, in an accident, a reactor emits radiation that exceeds these conservative limits even slightly and temporarily, it is said that safety standards have been violated and there must be danger. This would be an accurate conclusion only if the safety standards were set as laxly as possible, rather than as tightly as possible, as is the case in fact. It is as if a bank promised to calculate interest on savings accounts to the fifteenth decimal place before rounding off and a depositor interpreted a minor error in the twelfth place as evidence that he was being robbed blind.

† For a further discussion of the possible exposure at Three Mile Island, see pp. 142–144.

taken at nearby Pennsylvania State University years ago, notwithstanding the fact that it had been confined to the speculation of the laboratory.

Predictably, the critics had a field day with the venting of krypton gas from the containment building, a necessary first step to entering it and beginning the process of restoration. Yet here too the risk to the average resident of the immediate area was approximately that of watching a minute or so of color television and much less than that of driving to Atlantic City to avoid the threat. When the venting was finally carried out, Joseph M. Hendrie, member and former chairman of the NRC, took his family camping in the immediate area during one of the sessions. This act—which should not be called brave but was certainly imaginative—put the venting in its proper perspective.

Altogether, according to nuclear critics, the "lesson" to be learned from Three Mile Island goes something like this: "They told us this sort of accident couldn't happen; now it has happened; they have lied to us." It is hard to imagine a statement more false.

To begin with, no one, certainly not the authors of the Rasmussen Report, ever maintained the impossibility of a loss-of-coolant accident. No one ever maintained even that such an accident was so unlikely as to be unworthy of serious consideration. To the contrary, the nuclear industry has always maintained that loss-of-coolant accidents were not merely possible but probable enough to require complex mechanisms to deal with them. That is why reactors are equipped with Emergency Core Cooling Systems. The Rasmussen Report maintained merely that the probability of a loss-of-coolant accident not controlled by the ECCS was extremely low. This prediction is not disproved by Three Mile Island, for the ECCS worked as designed, and even though it was disabled through human error, it prevented overheating: There was no meltdown. (There may have been some melting of fuel cladding, but that is a different matter; a meltdown is the irreversible destruction of the core.)

Because there was no meltdown, there was no decisive evidence concerning another Rasmussen prediction, that it is extremely unlikely, even after a meltdown, that a serious release of radioactivity will occur. Still, after analysis of the performance of the containment at Three Mile Island, the experts of the Kemeny Commission concluded that had there been a meltdown, it would have been contained.

Although, as I have shown, one lesson to be learned from Three Mile Island is that light-water reactors are rather safer than we thought they were, the "lesson" generally learned by the public and the media goes in the opposite direction: Nuclear reactors are much more dangerous than we thought they were. This widespread mistake is possible largely because of a general misapprehension of the laws of probability and how they applied to the accident.

Probably few concepts are bandied about so much and understood so little as probability. If someone estimates that the chance of something happening is 1 in 10 billion, he may be right or he may be wrong. But the odds are that he will be understood as saying that it is impossible. He is not saying that; to call something highly improbable is inescapably to call it possible. If an event predicted to be highly unlikely actually happens, the prediction is not thereby discredited. It can only be discredited by repeated occurrences at frequencies too close to be accommodated by the prediction. That is, if someone predicts that a given event is likely to occur once in 10 billion years, its occurrence next Thursday does not disprove the prediction. Indeed, since part of the prediction is that the event will happen eventually, the occurrence next Thursday serves to confirm the prediction. If the event happens again next Friday, the prediction is still not demolished, but it would be quite natural to suspect that it may have been seriously off the mark. At a repetition on Saturday, the likelihood arises that the predictor was completely misguided, and each repetition thereafter—short of an interval measured in tens of billions of years—makes that diagnosis more persuasive.

These principles can be better illustrated in the more familiar arena of coin tossing. There is no more widely tested and believed estimate of probability than that which says that if you flip a coin long enough, it will fall heads and tails an equal number of times. And there is probably no more widely understood commentary on a special case of probability than the statement that you may have to flip the coin awhile to get even rough parity.

The calculation of even chances is a statement of the average, and to strike an average you need a number of tries. If one tosses a coin once a second, the probability for heads is once in two seconds. That probability is not disproved by a ten-second run of tails. Such runs, and longer ones, are not uncommon in real-life coin tossing, where variations in the "flip" need time to be averaged out. Similar runs even occur in computer simulations, in which the "flip" is an identically replicated random-number generation.

The matter is more complex when one comes to estimates of the probability of reactor accidents. By their very nature, such estimates cannot be "proven" empirically within a reasonable time. This is true most of all of those reactor accidents that the experts treat as literally impossible. For example, the possibility of a bomblike explosion in a light-water reactor is zero. The same laws that explain how it works as a reactor show that it cannot work as a bomb, for it lacks uranium sufficiently enriched in U-235 to support an explosion. The only empirical and absolute proof of this proposition would be an infinity of reactor years in which no explosion occurred. But the theoretical proof here has gradually won over even the most obstinate critics.

Taken as a whole, the accident at Three Mile Island generally confirms what we have been told about nuclear power. Where it does change our understanding, it not only suggests ways we can improve nuclear safety, but also that we have in some respects underestimated the degree of the safety we have already attained.

There was failure of equipment, there was operation of the plant contrary to its legally mandated technical specifications, and there was serious operator error. But even so, the system and its operators averted any injuries to the public or damage to its property. That, after all, is what the system and its operators are supposed to do.

Even if there had been a substantially more serious accident, it would have been necessary to consider it in perspective. As it is, the generation of replacement electricity in the three-state power pool (Pennsylvania, Maryland, and New Jersey) will shift sources from 46 percent coal-fired to 50 percent coal-fired. That change will have inevitable health effects as sulfur dioxide and other pollutants increase in the three-state area; there will indeed be victims of Three Mile Island, but they will be victims of a temporarily lessened dependence on nuclear power.

The closing of the two reactors at Three Mile Island—TMI-1, not involved in the accident, was shut down for refueling when it happened and has not been allowed to restart—is in effect a local moratorium on nuclear power. One study of a similar moratorium, that enforced by the Browns Ferry fire in 1975, estimates that as many as fifteen miners and between sixty and two hundred members of the general public will have been killed as a result of the increased coal burning it made necessary. It will not be possible to make similar calculations about Three Mile Island until we know how long it will be out of action, but the cost will not be small in any case. Petr Beckmann has calculated that replacement power generated from fossil fuels, primarily coal, to replace the damaged TMI-2 is killing four people a month. That death toll, regrettably, is unavoidable. It is not a cost of nuclear power but of the loss of it; if TMI-2 had been built as a coal-fired plant, it would have exacted a monthly toll of seventy-five deaths over its forty-plus year life.[15]

Another four deaths a month *are* avoidable. These are the Americans being killed by the fossil fuels burned to replace the output of TMI-1, not damaged in the accident, but shut down ever since.

Both the NRC and the nuclear industry responded promptly to the imperative of Three Mile Island. The industry promptly set up and funded an

Institute for Nuclear Reactor Operations, designed to conduct constant research into ways to lessen the chances of a repetition of Three Mile Island. The NRC set up a so-called Lessons Learned Task Force, which within three months of the accident had issued an interim report and made a number of short-term recommendations, including one to develop positive signaling to the control board on the open/closed status of all relief valves; to supply pressurized-water reactors with indicators to indicate the water level in the reactor; to install or have available hydrogen recombiners at all reactor sites; to improve the leak-proofness of areas outside the containment; to reclassify auxiliary feedwater systems as safety devices and to signal their availability to the control board; to improve radiation monitoring; to redefine responsibilities at the plant and to establish several new high-level technical positions; to establish new rules for reduced operation when safety systems are not available; and a host of other and more technical recommendations.

It will be noticed that the NRC did not take the simple and irresponsible path of recommending the shutting down of all nuclear power plants. Such fantasies are three a penny with those who are not accountable to the public, but they are not available to those who are actually accountable for their actions and must always ask themselves "Compared to what?"

# Breeder Reactors and Plutonium

Breeder reactors are widely condemned because they both burn and produce plutonium. Plutonium, the best-known man-made element, is also the most sensationalized. It is said to have been named for "Pluto, the god of hell," a statement that is erroneous as to fact (it was named by astronomical analogy as the element beyond Neptunium) and ignorant of the Greco-Roman notion of Hades. It is regularly said to be the most toxic substance known to man, and sometimes even to be toxic beyond human experience. It is hard to disagree with Petr Beckmann's characterization of such statements as "melodramatic piffle."

It should be first observed that plutonium is a waste substance only if it is not used as a fuel. If it is a waste substance requiring long-term storage, it is only because we make it so. Plutonium is of course a very toxic substance, but it is not uniquely so. Bernard Cohen has estimated that if the entire electric power industry of the United States operated with fast breeder reactors, the annual production of plutonium would, if dispersed with maximum efficiency and then inhaled, be sufficient to cause 1 trillion deaths. This indeed sounds terrifying. But two things must be remembered: The annual production of plutonium could not possibly be dispersed with such efficiency, and we routinely handle far more dangerous substances. Our present annual production of hydrogen cyanide, if similarly dispersed and inhaled, would cause 6 trillion deaths; our annual production of ammonia, 8 trillion; our annual production of phosgene, 18 trillion; and our annual production of chlorine, no fewer than 400 trillion deaths.

Cohen also points out that there is more danger to us from the radium deposited in the earth's crust than from prospective plutonium production. Specifically, if all the present generating capacity were fired by fast breeder reactors producing as much plutonium as they consumed, the total amount of plutonium in existence would be no more radioactive than the radium that already exists in a little over half a foot of the earth's crust.

Even this comparison overstates the danger from plutonium. When ingested, naturally occurring radium is forty times as toxic as plutonium, and it is a source of the dangerous radioactive gas radon. If we correct for this, we will see that all the plutonium produced by an all-breeder power system would, if dispersed throughout the earth's crust, be no more dangerous than the radium occurring naturally in *4 millimeters* of that crust. It should hardly need to be pointed out that this plutonium would not be dispersed throughout the environment but would be in reactors and processing plants.

Nor need one confine oneself to naturally occurring radioactive substances when looking for things that are more poisonous than plutonium. When ingested, arsenic trioxide is fifty times more toxic than plutonium. Yet we import this insecticide in quantities that would exceed the wastes from an all-nuclear economy, and we spray it about very nearly at random, often on food, and have no plans whatever for disposing of it in any manner.

Plutonium is, additionally, often characterized by such terms as "searingly radioactive," a phrase applied to it by *Time* magazine. This is exceptionally ignorant and misleading. Plutonium radiation consists of alpha particles, and these can be stopped by a sheet of paper or a few inches of air. Indeed, they are stopped by the epidermis and pose a threat to humans only when ingested or inhaled. Their principal threat is as a carcinogen, and there is general agreement that in this regard plutonium is extremely potent. The extent of the danger is a matter for debate, but no one regards the problem as something to be ignored. But for a society that tolerates cigarettes, to use this hazard as an excuse for rejecting the extraordinary benefits of plutonium is irrational or cynical.

A great deal is made of plutonium's half-life of 24,000 years. (This is the half-life of its most common isotope, Pu-239. Its other isotopes have half-lives ranging from less than a second to 80 million years.) It is, on this basis, frequently called "one of the longest-lived substances known to man." This characterization is particularly idiotic as it obscures the fact that the longer-lived a radioactive substance is, the less dangerous its radiation is—for it emits radiation at a lower rate. But the characterization obscures something even more important: Radioactive poisons are the only poisons that have half-lives as *short* as 24,000, or even 80 million, years. Stable isotopes are eternal and have infinite half-lives. A gram of plutonium will eventually end up as slightly less than a gram of lead. A gram of arsenic will always be a gram of arsenic.

Moreover, as a power plant the breeder is alleged to present even more serious safety problems than the light-water reactor. The principal allegation about the operation of the reactor itself is that should it suffer a meltdown, it is possible for the melted plutonium fuel to reassemble itself in such a way as to achieve critical mass and undergo a nuclear explosion. The technical community is divided on this issue, and it would be foolish in the face of such division for a layman to maintain that it could not happen. But it is important to understand what it would involve and how highly unlikely it is.

As yet there is no body of data on operating breeders that would allow any hard assessment of risks of a meltdown comparable to those made on light-water reactors. But the design of such reactors makes it very unlikely. In the best contemporary breeder designs, the reactor core is enclosed in a so-called "swimming pool" of sodium. The liquid sodium coolant is circulated at atmospheric pressure, which makes the probability of pipe rupture less likely in prospect and less serious in actuality. So a loss-of-coolant accident is very unlikely, as is the prospect that all emergency systems would fail.

There is persuasive evidence that breeder reactors can survive the failure of emergency systems far more successfully than light-water reactors. The United Kingdom Atomic Energy Authority maintains a fast breeder reactor at Dounreay, in Scotland. In a recent series of tests, the reactor was shut down precipitately and the sodium pumps—contrary to design—shut off. There was no fuel overheating: Convection currents within the sodium were sufficient to cool the core. Moreover, although the matter has not been tested empirically, calculations indicate that the pumps could be turned off with the reactor in operation, and again the convection currents would serve to cool. The pumps appear to be redundant, and this particular breeder reactor design, which is already supplying electricity to the United Kingdom grid, may well be the safest power reactor in the world. Any close student of the nuclear debate runs across many examples in which the public perception of reality is topsy-turvy. None is as striking as the alleged dangerousness of the breeder reactor.

Even if a breeder were to suffer a meltdown, it does not follow that the fuel would reassemble so as to form a critical mass, and any explosion that did occur would be of a different order than a bomb explosion. Reactor-grade plutonium is heavily contaminated with Pu-240, which makes it a less than ideal weapons material. (Nuclear critics consistently mislabel reactor plutonium as "weapons-grade.") Further, since much of the art in making an atomic bomb is in elaborate mechanisms to contain the explosion long enough for it to build up, an accidental critical mass would lead to a fizzle rather than a real explosion. It is probable that such an "explosion"—equaling the force of a few hundred pounds of TNT—would be held within the containment structure, which is constructed for the purpose. The risk of such an explosion occurring and releasing radiation must be akin to that of being hit by a meteorite.

An overheating incident in 1966 at the Fermi I breeder plant near Detroit has been the subject of John G. Fuller's extremely ignorant and sensational book, *We Almost Lost Detroit*.[16] I deal with this book at greater length in chapter 6. For the moment it is perhaps enough that say that the next specialty Mr. Fuller developed after nuclear energy was spiritualism.

Briefly, the Fermi reactor suffered a serious accident during which its safety systems prevented injury to any member of its staff or the public. Accounts of the accident normally note that the reactor is now shut down, but they never point out that it was successfully restarted in 1970 before being shut down for economic rather than technical reasons in 1972.

# Insurance

The principle of the half-truth is nowhere better illustrated than in the antinuclear movement's discussion of insurance. It is true that homeowners' insurance policies exclude damage due to nuclear accidents. But this is because nuclear accidents are covered separately under insurance set up in 1957 by the Price-Anderson Act. Under the act, a coverage is established of $560 million per accident. A portion of this—currently $500 million—is covered by insurance purchased from private insurance companies and assessments on utilities. The balance is covered by insurance purchased from the federal government. As new plants are built the limit will be raised. And should an accident occur, all operating plants will be assessed a retrospective charge of $5 million.

The critics' perennial question—"If a major accident that would cost $17 billion is so extraordinarily remote, why won't the insurance companies sell insurance for it?"—is easily answered. Although the extreme case is highly unlikely over any span of years, it could—however unlikely this may be— occur tomorrow. Although no premium would have been paid that nearly covered the cost, the cost would have to be paid. And because should a major nuclear accident occur, the resultant outcry would make the death of the industry a high probability, there would be little chance of recovering the cost out of future premiums.

A similar principle occurs in insuring fireworks displays. The premium drops proportionately to the length of experience and future stability of the firm lighting the fuse. A bunch of college students with no experience and little future as customers for pyrotechnic insurance pay a heavy premium. Or to draw an example from a more common type of insurance, if the death of one policyholder of a life insurance company were likely to lead to cancellations by all the rest, no company would write much life insurance.

Should a nuclear accident occur beyond the insured limits, it seems very likely that the government would provide retrospective compensation. This is precisely what happened after the eruption at Mount Saint Helens: The government promptly provided hundreds of millions of dollars to aid the affected areas.

Price-Anderson insurance is superior to other forms of disaster insurance in that it is no-fault insurance and is not paid for by the beneficiary. Actuarially it is similar to federal flood insurance—in major floods, all the customers of the insurance companies suffer serious loss. This makes the writing of flood insurance—in the absence of prohibitively expensive antiflood construction—economically impossible. The federal program makes flood insurance available at a reasonable rate. Price-Anderson insurance, being written against a very unlikely event, is so cheap that the government can afford to give it away.

Nor do antinuclear advocates often mention the fact that the utilities are able to buy—and afford—insurance to values of hundreds of millions of dollars on their own property. The alleged noninsurability of nuclear power is one more bogus problem.

# Waste Disposal

It is evident that the single most frightening charge made against nuclear energy is that it produces extraordinarily dangerous wastes that must be guarded for millions of years. We are called on to remember our obligations to our descendants and regularly told that we have as yet devised no means to deal with the waste problem. No part of the antinuclear dogma is more suffused with ignorance and sensationalism than this charge.

Let us begin by considering how the fission products are created. As the nuclear reaction proceeds in the core of the reactor, besides energy being liberated, some of the atoms in the fuel rods are transmuted into a wide variety of radioactive isotopes. With the exception of plutonium, these are largely useless. (Plutonium is not waste at all but an immensely valuable—indeed, the most valuable—fuel.)

After some months of operation, the waste products begin to affect the efficiency of the fuel rod, and it is removed from the reactor and replaced with a fresh one. Besides the waste products and plutonium, the spent rod contains unfissioned uranium. It is intensely radioactive and physically hot as well.

The spent rod is immersed in a tank of water near the reactor, where it gradually becomes less hot in both senses. It should be understood that length of half-life and intensity of radiation are inversely proportional. If a radioactive isotope has a half-life of one second, one-half of the atoms in any quantity of it will disintegrate each second, creating intense radioactivity. On the other hand, any given quantity will be essentially annihilated in about ten seconds. If a radioactive substance has a half-life of a million years, it will take one million years for one-half of the atoms in a given quantity to disintegrate. This is a very slow rate of disintegration and produces a much lower level of radiation. In fuel rods the various radioactive isotopes decay at a rate proportional to their radioactivity, the hottest ones most rapidly, and the level of total radioactivity in the fuel drops sharply.

The last paragraph, regrettably, describes the entire operational U.S. nuclear waste management program as currently conducted. The steps that should follow it have been suspended by order of the federal government. In theory there is no reason why we cannot continue storing spent fuel rods in this way indefinitely, given the building of additional storage capacity, but there are two very good reasons why we should not. First, the plutonium and uranium in the rods represent an immense fuel resource; and second, as the rods cool the plutonium becomes increasingly accessible to thieves.

The next step should be reprocessing—the dissolving of the fuel rods and the extraction of the plutonium and uranium for use as fuel. A great deal of separated waste of this sort, left over from reprocessing before the suspension, is now being stored in tanks about the country, most of it from bomb waste but some from earlier power-reactor waste. The actual danger posed by these wastes is grossly exaggerated.

The wastes are of two general types. Fission products, elements lighter than uranium and highly radioactive, are the debris of the split nuclei and have comparatively short half-lives. These are also called *high-level wastes*. Transuranics, elements heavier than uranium and caused by its irradiation, have long half-lives. These are also called *low-level wastes*.

A principal claim of nuclear critics is that there has been a series of leaks of high-level wastes from storage tanks at the government's Hanford, Washington, facility. These leaks, deplorable enough in themselves, are regularly cited as representing risks in current techniques. One is never told that the tanks in question are of early postwar design and have long since been superseded. It is as if the safety record of the railroads in 1845, when accidents were very common, had been invoked in 1925 to justify closing them down.

The most common assertion one hears in this area is the flat statement that we do not now know how to dispose of high-level wastes, which must be isolated from contact with the biosphere for many thousands of years. However, in reality this challenge has already been met.

The technology for this disposal, which has been demonstrated in a pilot project at Hanford and actually used in Europe, involves first "calcining" the waste to a sandlike substance of greatly reduced bulk and then using this "sand" as a component to make glass ("vitrification"). The resulting glass is radioactive but chemically inert. It can then be buried deep in geologically stable formations, where no water has flowed for millions of years. It will require no surveillance, let alone a "nuclear priesthood."

Our present suspension of reprocessing makes impossible the implementation of so rational a waste-management strategy. Until recently it was proposed to bury spent fuel rods, still containing large amounts of uranium and plutonium, at a site in New Mexico. This dubious plan has been withdrawn, but nothing has been adopted in its place, although the NRC has begun to work out plans for developing criteria of choice. This development, little as it is, is at least an improvement over past inaction, and by 1980 Congress was on the way to establishing serious timetables.

As indicated, after reprocessing should come calcination/vitrification, and the vitrified waste should be entombed in geologically stable formations. After about a thousand years, the level of radioactivity in the glass falls away to a point lower than that of the uranium ore from which the waste was originally derived. That is, over thousand-year spans the effect of a light-water reactor is to *reduce* the level of radiation in the world. A breeder reactor, which annihilates uranium atoms at a faster rate, reduces radiation even faster.

This chain of events from spent fuel rods to glassified waste is not simply a proposal or even a pilot project. All the steps except entombment are

39

now in use on a commercial scale in France,[17] and that final step simply awaits the cooling down of the vitrified waste to a temperature satisfactory for further handling. Most nuclear critics simply ignore this process or lump it together with a number of purely speculative suggestions, such as launching wastes by rocket into the sun. Ralph Nader, for example, ignores it except to quote an outdated government press release noting that it will not work for the Energy Research and Development Administration's (ERDA) inventory of *weapons* waste. The problem has now been corrected by a new process developed at Hanford. Nader also claims that technology cannot guarantee geologically stable areas in which to deposit wastes. This is true but irrelevant. Nature provides such areas and technology can locate them.

It is perhaps not surprising that antinuclear advocates should wish to perpetuate the false assertion that waste disposal is an unsolved and unsolvable problem. But the nation does not have the luxury of agreeing with the antinuclear movement. Existing reactors have produced and will produce wastes, and these must be dealt with, as indeed they can be.

Most of the liquefied waste now stored in this country is from our weapons program, so that the necessity for successful waste management would remain even if every power reactor in the country were to be shut down tomorrow and, indeed, if we never made another bomb, for we have the wastes from those we have already made. The problem would be especially acute under nuclear disarmament, for we would need to find a means to dispose of the existing stockpile of nuclear weapons. The important point is that we have large amounts of liquid waste on hand because of our failure to adopt a strategy for permanent storage; thirty-year storage of liquid high-level waste is not essential to waste management in a world that knows of the vitrification process or alternatives now under development, such as the conversion of liquid waste to a ceramic form.

The antinuclear movement confuses two very different requirements. One is the technological necessity of developing sound programs for managing radioactive wastes and the other is the political necessity to choose such a means from among those that technology develops. The former has been accomplished, but in this country the latter remains to be done. It is as if people went about saying "We have no idea how to make an airliner that will fly faster than the speed of sound," ignoring the existence of the Concorde. (Lest I be misunderstood here, I should say that the mere existence of the Concorde does not in itself disprove the statement "We have no idea how to make a *commercially successful* airliner that will fly faster than the speed of sound.")

Finally, the residual risks to future generations from nuclear waste disposal are tiny compared to those inherent in our consumption of petrochemical feedstocks for fuel. Any energy policy based on fossil fuels is a policy that will, in the long run, deprive future generations of the chemical basis of modern society in the bargain. If the policy also foreswears the nuclear option, it will sharply limit future access to energy more concentrated than that produced in wood-burning stoves and the bodies of mammals. There is a scandal indeed.

# Decommissioning

It is claimed that after forty years or so a retired plant will pose a major radiation hazard and that protecting us against the hazard, if possible, will cost immense amounts of money. There are thus two components in the charge, a technical problem that is analogous to the waste problem and one that is essentially economic.

To begin with the technical issue: It is important to understand the true scope of the problem presented by a retired nuclear plant. First, as the chain reaction has been forever stopped, there is no production of new radioactivity, and the remaining level will drop steadily. Second, as the core has been removed for reprocessing and waste disposal, the overwhelming majority of radiation hazard—the fission products—will be gone. The residual radiation will issue from so-called activation products. These are produced when nuclei of nonradioactive elements, mostly in the structure of the reactor itself—for example, the iron in the reactor vessel—and also in comparatively trivial amounts of impurities from coolant water lodged in the piping—so-called "crud"—capture neutrons from the chain reaction. They are then transmuted into unstable, hence radioactive, elements. These vary as to half-life, with, as usual, the longest-lived ones being the least dangerous.

It should be understood that these radioactive elements are not lying around on the floor as dust or blowing out the windows of the former plant as gas. They are entombed, as it were, in the structure of the reactor steam supply system, and they are of no use to anyone, no matter how evilly intentioned. The most depraved and capable terrorist group imaginable would have no use for an only moderately radioactive pressure vessel weighing many tons. No mad dictator could fabricate a bomb from activated steel piping smuggled out of a retired plant. Therefore, it is a little hard to understand why anyone thinks it necessary to dismantle former plants and bury them as waste. Entombing them in concrete seems extraordinarily cautious, and the fact is that probably a chain-link fence bearing the radiation symbol ought to be enough to prevent their causing any harm for the full length of their existence. We can afford to envision actually dismantling such plants and carting them away because the cost even of that complex operation, amortized in advance over a generation, is trivial.

The source of the notion that the cost of decommissioning runs at 35 percent of original cost is derived from an estimate made by Jersey Central Power and Light for its Oyster Creek plant ($35 million in 1969 dollars).[18] This figure was derived for the purpose of establishing a rate base charge for decommissioning. In order to provide this sum by the time it is needed, the amount added to the cost of electricity is about a third of a mill—that is, a thirtieth of a cent—a kilowatt-hour. (Over thirty years, a 650 megawatt reactor like Oyster Creek, operating at 65 percent of capacity, will generate some 100 billion kilowatt-hours of electricity.)

The smallness of this charge illustrates the important truth that it is possible to build up very large sums indeed if one can collect a little bit of money from a lot of people over a long period of time and invest the bits in a sinking fund. But even so, Oyster Creek is atypical: It is a comparatively large plant built just before the great nuclear plant price rise, and therefore it is certain to yield an abnormally high ratio of decommissioning to construction cost. Decommissioning one large reactor is much like decommissioning another, and the $100 million it would cost in 1997 to decommission the $110 million Oyster Creek plant would, at 7 percent annual inflation, rise to about $200 million in 2009, which would be sufficient to decommission a $1 billion plant that had gone into operation in the early 1980s. This would be not 35 percent of capital cost but 20 percent. And that would have been generated in the cheapest way possible, by comparatively small additions to a sinking fund over a generation. Jersey Central's figures are compatible with Department of Energy estimates of the cost of decommissioning as between .32 and .69 mills/kilowatt-hour.[19]

We should, in this context, remember that there is yet little reliable information on the useful life of a mature nuclear power plant. Most figures are only assumptions made for depreciation purposes. The estimates for Oyster Creek, for example, assumed a useful life for the plant of thirty years, which is historically reasonable, based on the performance of fossil-fuel plants. But it may turn out to be useful for fifty years; we will be lucky indeed if we develop an energy source that makes fission power obsolete before then. There is some evidence that such estimates may be overconservative. The United Kingdom's first Magnox reactors, originally scheduled to last fifteen years, have recently been given the go-ahead for a second lifespan of the same length.[20]

The "problem" of decommissioning, then, is simply another bogeyman.

# The Economics of Nuclear Energy

The economic argument against nuclear power is made in multifarious ways. Sometimes it appears to grow out of simple ignorance, as when the utilities are alleged to prefer expensive nuclear plants because higher rates can be charged with great capital investment, quite as if that capital did not have to be recovered out of income. Sometimes it is based on the implied assumption that the government ought never to subsidize the development of a new technology, as when it is claimed and then objected to that the government does not make a profit on its fuel enrichment operation. Those who so object are of course often eager to have the government subsidize their own pet projects, such as solar energy.

Additionally, it is very common to exaggerate the actual amount of subsidy, typically by charging the cost of all nuclear-related research to the present generating program. This would be the equivalent of debiting Amtrak with the cost of ongoing research on advanced passenger trains, just because Amtrak or its successors may some day make use of it. Estimates of the amount actually spent by the government on developing the present light-water reactor program range from $3 to $10 billion.[21] Amortized over thirty years, this is at the most 5 percent of the total price of electricity sold, a remarkable bargain considering the millions of barrels of OPEC oil that we are not now importing because of our present nuclear capacity.

Sometimes the charge is based on manipulation of the facts, as when figures for western low-sulfur coal burned near the mine in comparatively cheap power plants are misapplied to plants burning high-sulfur coal in very expensive scrubber-equipped plants. And sometimes it is based on the bizarre charge that the total energy needed to build and operate a nuclear plant is greater than what it produces—the idea being that the nuclear industry has made no net addition to the nation's energy supply. This preposterous notion is arrived at partly by exaggerating the amount of electricity consumed by the nation's fuel-enrichment plants by multiples of five or more. Some of it can also be explained on the assumption that antinuclear accountants charge the cost of electricity used to enrich weapons uranium and nuclear ship fuel to nuclear power plant fuel. But even this error will not account for the charge, for in fact building and operating a light-water plant, including the enrichment of its fuel, uses 6 percent of its lifetime output. This is actually slightly better than the competition, for a coal-fired plant uses between 6.7 and 7.8 percent, depending on whether it burns surface or deep-mined coal.[22]

Detailed forms of the argument that nuclear power is expensive are scarcer than vague charges based on the fact that nuclear plants have a higher capital cost than fossil plants. (The gap is narrowing as environmental regulation lies heavier on coal-fired plants.) This is a naive view of economics, and a two-edged sword in the bargain, since on the same standard solar power is, and always will be, more expensive than any other source. Sometimes a parallel argument is made that the price of uranium has been increasing, quite as if other fuels had not been increasing by a much higher ratio.

One of the best-known exponents of this method of economic reasoning is Charles Komanoff. In a piece published in the *New York Review of Books*[23] a month after Three Mile Island, which he called a "near disaster," Komanoff asserted that nuclear electricity is more expensive than electricity from coal. He quoted and denigrated a utility industry estimate that costs per kilowatt/ hour are 1.5 cents for nuclear, 2 cents for coal, and 3.9 for oil. But he did not propose any figures for these three items that would be in his opinion more correct. Rather, he fell back on the false argument that the capital costs of nuclear power have been increasing, refusing to integrate capital costs and operating costs to get actual estimates of costs of production.*

Had he done so, he would have been forced to see that the cost comparisons favor nuclear. This is true not only of cost comparisons undertaken by the electrical industry, but also by the Department of Energy, which reported the costs for three forms in 1979 as 20.7 mills for nuclear and 22.35 mills for coal.[24] Oil, not included in the survey, would have cost much more. Moreover, 1979 was a year in which the capital costs of an unusual number of inoperative reactors—the two at Three Mile Island, the five shut down for earthquake studies—had to be counted against revenues.

Perhaps a more persuasive set of figures comes from the United Kingdom's Central Electricity Generating Board (CEGB). It is worth reviewing this institution's credentials. The single electric generating utility in England, it is larger and more experienced by far than any single U.S. utility. It operates a very wide range of generating facilities. It is owned by the British government. It has no stockholders to please. Indeed, in the United Kingdom, the energy industry generally is publicly held, the various components of the nuclear industry being owned by the Crown outright or by consortia in which private companies have a minority interest. It is, in short, unlikely that the CEGB is incompetent to calculate costs and beyond all reason that it should lie about them. For years, under Labour as well as Conservative governments, CEGB has reported that its nuclear power stations operate substantially more cheaply than its fossil-fuel plants.

---

* Frequently the piece is not only logically, but also technically, defective. Komanoff says that nuclear power can produce only electricity, whereas the Very High Temperature Reactor currently well along in development in Japan and well-known to anyone *au courant* with nuclear development will produce process heat suitable for, among other things, steelmaking.

Perhaps most striking, the CEGB announced that in 1979, one of its latest nuclear stations, Hinkley Point B, outperformed an equivalent-size coal-fired plant 1.52 pence to 1.35 pence,* despite the fact that Hinkley Point B, still in its shakedown stage, was available only 43 percent of the time as against 79 percent for the coal-fired plant.[25]

A common claim of critics is that nuclear plants are less reliable than other types. In part this charge is based on a half-truth, namely, that stringent safety standards require nuclear plants to be shut down for comparatively trivial reasons and that the discovery of a problem in one plant may lead to a temporary shutdown in all plants of the same general type. Such incidents are sometimes badly misreported: thus, when a hairline crack, releasing no water or radioactivity, was discovered in a standby cooling pipe at the Commonwealth Edison Dresden plant near Chicago, twenty-three plants with similar standby systems were ordered to close down for inspection. No cracks were found in any of these, but the incident was reported as one in which twenty-three plants had been shut down because of cracks in their cooling systems. Less widely reported is the fact that Commonwealth Edison's nuclear plants have proved just as reliable as its coal plants.[26]

Still more dubious is the practice of stating reliability factors for nuclear plants in isolation, without comparing them to other types or to much smaller conventional plants. The fact is that, over the nation, nuclear reactors are about as reliable as fossil-fuel plants of equivalent size.

There are two basic measures of reliability: the availability factor, which measures the proportion of the time a generator is actually ready to generate electricity, and the capacity factor, which measures the proportion of capacity actually used. In 1980 in the United States, nuclear plants still attained a higher capacity than either coal or oil plants, used for the same purpose,[27] to generate baseloads, the electricity that the utility must generate twenty-four hours a day. Nuclear plants are used only to generate baseloads, but other types are used also for both *load-following*—generating electricity at times of the day when the demand is higher for a substantial period—and for *peaking,* generating electricity during brief spurts when demand is highest. While in the same years the nuclear plants attained availability factors a few percentage points lower than coal and oil, it is the capacity factor that is significant for the economics of power generation. And if fossil-fuel plants were held to safety standards as rigorous as nuclear plants, they would post a still lower availability factor. Indeed, as still unreliable scrubbers become more common on coal-fired plants, this is just what will happen.

---

* These figures are not directly comparable to the American figures cited previously, which are bus-bar costs that ignore the costs of distribution.

Ralph Nader maintains that

a definitive statement on nuclear economics is the number of plants that have been cancelled or deferred. By November 1975, 130,000 Megawatts-electric had been cancelled or deferred, representing over two-thirds of all cancellations or deferrals of power plants within the industry.[28]

Such figures are quite meaningless except in context. First of all, when a utility defers a nuclear plant, it does so because it plans to delay adding new capacity that had already been planned for. Recently such deferrals have occurred because the rate of growth in demand has finally slowed and we are clearly not going to need capacity that before the energy crisis it seemed reasonable to plan for. But a deferral is not a vote of no confidence in nuclear power; to the contrary, it is a statement that when there is adequate demand to employ a new plant, it will be nuclear rather than otherwise.

Although utilities cancel power plants for a variety of reasons, most do so because of reduced demand projections. Had the electric industry, in the days when it was placing orders for future demand, regarded nuclear power as the only form worth ordering, it would have placed even more orders for nuclear plants and would now be cancelling even more nuclear capacity. Thus the fact that, in Nader's words, "100% of all capacity deferred or cancelled has been nuclear" would derive from the industry's confidence in nuclear power as opposed to other forms. The statistics that would be really indicative are the megawattage of nuclear capacity cancelled and replaced by some other form of generation. Nader would not be eager to publish this figure; in early 1981, it still stood at zero.[29]

Nor should we expect Nader to publish an accounting of the net cost to householders of "environmentalist" delaying tactics. Each stage in the approval and construction of a nuclear plant is now routinely opposed by organizations of nuclear critics. The heavy legal fees thus incurred by the utilities end up on the electric bill. Still worse is the inflationary cost exacted by delay. Almost as sure as death and taxes is the continuing rise in construction costs.

The antinuclear lobby delights to quote cost overruns, but it rarely notes the influence on these of the delays that it works to cause. These costs too are borne by consumers and are cruelly regressive upon the poor.

One of the most vexed issues in reactor economics is construction work in progress (CWIP). It is sufficiently explosive as an issue to have played a major part in the 1978 gubernatorial race in New Hampshire and possibly to have elected a governor. The concept of CWIP is simple enough, and derives from the fact that utility rates are regulated. In determining the rate that a utility is allowed to charge, state regulatory commissions typically come up with a figure representing the net investment of the company and allow profit as a certain percentage of it. In calculating investment, the rate-setters have historically counted only plants that are actually generating power. Those that are not generating power have, in the past, generally been obsolete plants that have long ago been depreciated, so excluding them from the so-called rate base has presented no problem.

But there is a problem when an excluded generator is an unfinished, expensive, and unpaid-for nuclear plant. Largely because of regulation, nuclear power plants now take over a decade to complete. Under conventional rate-setting practice, the plant cannot be added to the rate base, that is to say, cannot start earning money, until it is actually in use. But such plants begin costing their owners long before they bring in any income, for they must be paid for as they are constructed. If a $10 million reactor vessel is delivered in year 6 of a twelve-year construction period, the utility will pay for it in year 6 and wait until year 12 to start recouping the expense.

This would present no particular problem if utilities were immensely rich charitable foundations. But they are not. They are backed only by the people who buy stock in them as an investment. Such a utility must borrow the $10 million in year 6 and pay interest on it until year 12. At a 10 percent interest rate, this will increase the actual cost of the reactor vessel to nearly $18 million. Someone will have to pay that extra $8 million when the plant finally goes into operation. It will not be the utility executives or the stockholders. The $8 million will be paid by the customers of the utility.

This should not be surprising: Every penny of the costs of a utility is eventually paid by the customers, plus whatever rate of profit the state will allow. This is because of a simple economic fact: Investors do not invest for their health. They expect to get back every penny they advance to the firms in which they invest, plus an annual return. If they fail in this simple desire, it will be because the enterprise has proved unprofitable. While occasional fits of unprofitability may be cured by firing the management and getting a new one, prolonged unprofitability leads to an emigration of investors into more profitable areas.

A corporation—or an industry—that fails to win the affection of investors is dead. It has a kind of bogus hope of resurrection through nationalization, but that would be CWIP on the grand scale. Indeed, the essential hypocrisy of the Naderite position can be understood when one realizes that the same people who object to paying farthings for energy through CWIP would often be delighted to pay pounds for it through nationalization.

It must be understood that a nonregulated company—say, General Motors or Sam the Shoe Repairman—will bill its customers for construction work in progress any time it can do so within its price structure, borrowing capital from banks and investors only when cash flow is insufficient. It is only regulated industries in which the issue of CWIP can arise.

The choice implicit in the question of CWIP is simple: Given the fact that the rate payers are going to pay for a plant eventually in any event, should they incur heavy interest charges in order to avoid paying for the plant before it is in use? At 10 percent interest, the price of the earliest stages of a nuclear plant can be nearly doubled if CWIP is not allowed. It is, at the least, arguable that the customers are better off paying CWIP now and avoiding eventually paying not only for the completed plant but also for debt service. The matter can be best put in perspective by remembering that the effect of CWIP on the average electric bill is never more than a dollar or so a month.[30]

Needless to say, the opponents of CWIP rarely cite the figure in this way. As is the case with rate increases, the numbers are always given in the form of the totals paid each year by millions of customers. Opponents of CWIP ought to be asked two questions: (1) In a given case, how much would CWIP add to the average monthly bill? and (2) How much would not having CWIP add to the average monthly bill? Until the day comes when the banks lend money as a public service, interest-free, (2) will always be greater than (1).

# Thermal Pollution

The "thermal pollution" charge laid at the door of nuclear power plants is a mixture of half-truth, exaggeration, and sentimentality. First of all, the root phenomenon is not peculiar to nuclear plants. All thermal power plants waste a great deal of heat and all of them must dispose of it, into bodies of water or through cooling towers into the atmosphere or through a combination of both methods. Light-water reactors, having a slightly lower thermal efficiency than fossil-fuel plants, discharge more heat, but breeder reactors are at least as efficient as fossil-fuel plants, and high-temperature gas-cooled reactors are much more so. If thermal pollution is really an argument for rejecting nuclear energy, it is also an argument for rejecting most of our electricity.

The most commonly attacked thermal pollution involves the discharge of waste heat into bodies of water. Critics cite the temperature rise at the discharge exit, which may be as high as 70 degrees F. They usually do not cite the temperature rise over a few acres, which will be only a few degrees. But even this slight change will have an effect on the aquatic life near a reactor, as it makes the water an unsuitable environment for some species—while also making it more suitable for other species, as the fishermen at the seafront park at the Pilgrim reactor in Massachusetts will attest.

More striking than these casual fishers is the extent to which "thermal pollution" encourages fish farming. Lobsters, for example, thrive in the slightly warmed water near a reactor. In the summer of 1980, *Newsweek*[31] had a story on how fish of various sorts were being raised in the outflows of various power plants, several of which were said to be coal-fired. None were said to have been nuclear-fired, although at the Hunsterston nuclear reactor in Scotland an organization that only the English could have invented—The Whitefish Authority!—raises soles commanding top prices in the demanding French market. The oddity of the *Newsweek* story is that nowhere in it can one find any indication that it is in fact about thermal pollution.

Thermal pollution has its other side, to be sure. For example, when a reactor shuts down, as for refueling, a species that has moved into warm water may have difficulty surviving a temporary cooling of the water. Much has been made of the fact that menhaden, fish important in fertilizer and pet food, are enticed into the slightly warmed waters near reactors located on the Atlantic and then killed off when the water cools during a shutdown. Less has been made of the not dissimilar phenomenon when the elderly of the human species die of cold during a natural gas shortage. If we had no need of energy, it would perhaps be possible to let our hearts bleed for the menhaden, who no doubt would prefer ending up as fertilizer or cat food to dying by thermal pollution.

The fact is, however, that our need for safe energy is crucial, and only those who have never known what it is like to be without energy can seriously contemplate a policy of sacrificing human interests to those of animals. In a related piece of folly, the opponents of the Seabrook plant in New Hampshire have opposed its cooling system on the grounds that it would inhale and destroy a certain diet of aquatic life each day. The amount involved is about what three or four whales consume, but one does not hear the same people urging a moratorium on whales.

# Cutting Butter with a Chainsaw

A good deal of the conventional wisdom in antinuclear circles is based on a very imperfect grasp of technology, physics, and medicine.

An excellent example is the oft-repeated claim that nuclear power plants are an overcomplicated way to boil water. (This is often maintained by observers who have never seen the inside of a "conventional" power plant and have little or no sense of how complicated it is.) In the extreme form of this claim, propagated by Amory Lovins,[32] the nuclear reaction is said to operate at trillions of degrees of heat, obviously extravagant if all one needs is water at 212 degrees F.

To begin with, this figure is wildly inaccurate. The hottest temperature in a reactor is at the center of the fuel pellets, and approaches 4000 degrees F. The reactor itself typically operates at about 500 degrees.

Among others, this error is repeated by Barry Commoner and Helen Caldicott, who often claims that using nuclear energy to produce steam is like cutting butter with a chainsaw. On the same reasoning, wood-burning locomotives ought to be more efficient than coal-fired ones, and diesel-powered submarines more efficient than nuclear ones, although of course not as efficient as those powered by wood or paper. Most of those who make this argument are in the grip of a misunderstanding of the laws of thermodynamics sufficient to keep them from understanding anything useful about the way steam and other heat engines work. They appear to assume that water vapor has some inherent power that operates steam engines, and that in order to make them work, all it is necessary to do is to boil water and get steam.

As it happens, and as every high school graduate ought to know, the water in a steam engine is simply a heat-transfer medium; and, given a complex set of natural and engineering constraints, the hotter the steam the better. Loosely put, the more heat one can cram into steam the more energy can be extracted by the piston or turbine it drives. The history of progress in the steam locomotive was almost entirely the history of ways to increase the temperature of the steam. Gas turbines, as used in jet aircraft, trains, and experimental cars, are more powerful than piston engines largely because they operate at much higher temperatures.

Indeed, flame temperatures in fossil-fuel power plants sometimes exceed the melting temperature of nuclear plant fuel. That is, temperatures in a coal-fired plant can exceed the highest temperature reached in a nuclear reactor. One of the reasons why fossil-fuel plants are a little more efficient than nuclear plants—and this is a matter of the most elementary physics— is that they run somewhat hotter. Considerable research is being expended on various ways to make nuclear reactors run hot enough to produce the level of process heat that have been commonplace with fossil fuels for decades.

# Occupational Risk

Coal mining is the most dangerous large-scale industry in the United States, and coal miners have an unhappy familiarity with the dangers of their craft. About coal mining two things are obviously true: It is too dangerous an occupation to compel one to enter, and, even if one did not believe in the right of the citizen on his own account to seek employment of his choice, it is too essential an occupation to prevent anyone from entering. The same is true, *mutatis mutandis,* for a variety of other occupations—steelmaking, construction work on tall buildings, nursing during epidemics, fire-fighting, and many more.

A sound policy toward occupational safety has three components. First, every worker must have a precise and accurate understanding of the risks that face him, and the burden of assuring this must lie with the employer. Second, those risks ought to be no larger than necessary to accomplish the work in question. Third, beyond these basic requirements, safety in the workplace is a legitimate subject for collective bargaining between employees and their employers. Beyond this, it is doubtful that in a free society those not directly involved have a right to demand anything more.

Any consideration of occupational safety in nuclear energy must begin with the uranium mines. It would be tempting to dismiss the subject simply by comparing the number of uranium miners killed in mining accidents to make a million megawatts of nuclear-fired electricity with the number of coal miners killed in such accidents to make an identical amount of coal-fired electricity. The ratio is about 1 to 100, and on this score if we ought not to dig uranium, we ought not to dig coal a hundredfold.

Estimates for the lung cancer rates among uranium miners range widely, but all are high. This indicates clearly that a lifetime of breathing radon gas is a highly carcinogenic lifetime. "But the question is confounded by the interaction of tobacco and radon. It is generally agreed even by such antinuclear scientists as Dr. John Gofman that the risk of lung cancer from radioactive sources is greater for smokers than for nonsmokers; such was his testimony at the Karen Silkwood trial in 1979 in Oklahoma City. Detailed studies now under way, which compare nonsmoking to smoking uranium miners, will probably provide a definitive answer to this question; early results confirm the idea that smoking seriously increases the risk from radon, but the studies are not yet complete." The inference to be made is that smoking and radon have a synergistic relationship in which the carcinogenic force of each is increased by the presence of the other. Or perhaps smoking renders the lungs unduly sensitive to radiation. (This leads to speculation as to the still-unknown mechanism that underlies the statistical correlation between smoking and lung cancer in the population at large. Can it be possible that smoking renders one unduly sensitive to the background radiation?)

The cold fact appears to be that nonsmoking uranium miners are less susceptible to lung cancer than smoking fudge makers. When discussing the occupational hazards of uranium mining, nuclear critics often dwell on the fact that many of the miners are American Indians. Since uranium is often found in areas where there are large numbers of Indians, it would seem that their absence in the mines could justifiably lead to charges of job discrimination. In discussing the plight of such Indians, many antinuclearists seem unaware that these men are hard-working, skillful, and well-paid workers who give every evidence of liking the work they do and enjoying the salaries they get for it. These sometimes approach $40,000 a year, and as one who has been down a uranium mine, I can testify that they earn every penny of it.

# Terrorism

The campaign to ban plutonium, a substance that contains more energy for its volume than any other, rests on the spurious grounds that it will inevitably be stolen and used by terrorists or acquired by nonnuclear national states as a means toward nuclear weapons proliferation. It is important to separate the terrorists and the national states, for they represent very different cases.

Let us deal with the terrorists first. An essential distinction to bear in mind is that terrorists will in all cases be working against the law and elaborate safeguards. Terrorists are alleged to be able to make use of plutonium in two ways: as a poison and as a bomb material. The difficulties in acquiring a stock of the substance are the same in either case.

They are immense. The only time plutonium is vulnerable is after it has been separated in a reprocessing plant and before it is loaded into a reactor— that is, when it is in the form of reactor fuel. At any other time, it is so poisoned by fission products as to be both dangerous and useless. And stealing it in fuel form would be extraordinarily difficult. It would be practically impossible to smuggle plutonium out of a facility in little bits: It is radioactive, and on the person is detectable in amounts as small as a gram. In order to extract the ten kilograms needed for a bomb, a smuggler would need to execute at least 10,000 separate thefts, or one each working day for forty years. By "theft" I mean not only the successful diversion each day of one gram of plutonium from the processing line, but also its successful (and daily) smuggling past the radiation detectors. If, as has been argued by Amory Lovins, the amount of plutonium needed for a bomb is only about half this amount, then it would take a smuggler only twenty years of successful daily smuggling to get enough plutonium past the sensors.

Raids on plutonium depositories do not look much more promising: A demonstration in which an army assault team using mortars and high explosives required fourteen hours to get into such a vault suggests the unlikelihood of covert theft from stationary deposits. This means that the plutonium would have to be hijacked from a convoy. The difficulties here are extraordinary. Hijacking a shipment of plutonium on the way to a reactor would have to be an oxymoronically covert semimilitary operation. Plutonium has been shipped in this country as part of weapons production since its start, and formidable precautions have been developed. These include radio tracking of the trucks, devices that disable the trucks if hijacked, and escort vehicles carrying armed guards. A group of terrorists improbably equipped to overwhelm such a convoy would be better advised to steal a tactical nuclear warhead ready-made.

A more fundamental question is whether plutonium is useful for terrorists. In its role as a radiological poison, it would not seem to be so. No terrorist movement has in the past made use of a threat that would, at worst, give some people cancer who might not have gotten it anyway many years later. Worse, some of these might well be supporters of the terrorists or the terrorists themselves.

It must be realized that plutonium's limited potential as a mass poison can be realized only by distributing it indiscriminately into the atmosphere. One absurd scenario has envisioned the terrorists advancing through the city spraying plutonium from aerosol cans. As silly as this scheme is, it is not much sillier than the average. Dumped in a water reservoir, for example, plutonium is harmless, much less toxic chemically than such common compounds as hydrogen cyanide.

It is, furthermore, a matter of considerable controversy as to how useful reactor plutonium is as a bomb material. To understand this controversy requires a brief digression into the isotopic composition of plutonium. Like all elements, any given amount of plutonium is a mixture of various isotopes that are chemically identical but physically distinct owing to differing nuclear composition. Plutonium as a man-made* element produced either in nuclear reactors or nuclear explosions has no "natural" isotope in the sense that

---

* There is actually a little "natural" plutonium. In Oklo, Gabon, there are the remains of a large natural reactor that operated for perhaps half a million years roughly 2 billion years ago. The plutonium and the fission products have remained in place ever since.

the ninety-two natural elements do, but Pu-239 is the most common isotope, as well as the one of greatest interest to reactor and bomb designers.

The isotopic composition of a natural element is a constant around the world, although in any element having naturally radioactive isotopes, the composition is always slowly altering as the relative proportion of shorter-lived isotopes becomes smaller. As a case in point, uranium once had a substantially heavier concentration of U-235 than it has now and will eventually have a substantially lower one. (Given enough time, it will be zero. All natural atoms of one element, technetium, have already decayed on earth. It has recently been "re-created" in the laboratories and reactors. Technetium might almost have been given to help us understand the pointlessness of the natural-artificial distinction.)

And so, although the process is slow, our stock of fissionable uranium is slowly decreasing whether we use any of it or not, which makes it (along with thorium) unique among fuels. We cannot, over the long haul, just leave it in the earth until we need it, as is the case with the fossil fuels. It will not be there tomorrow, at least on the very long time scales that the environmentalists have taught us to consider.

The composition of any lot of plutonium produced in a reactor is a function of how long and how hard the reactor has been run. Remove a fuel rod after a few days of operation, and the plutonium within it will be nearly pure Pu-239. Leave it in for three or four years, and it will be perhaps 30 percent other isotopes, of which Pu-240 and Pu-242 are the most prominent.

There is widespread agreement on two facts about Pu-240. Its presence in reactor plutonium makes it less satisfactory as a bomb material, but it does not make its use in a bomb impossible. Within those bounds, there is a massive disagreement as to how much of a problem reactor plutonium presents a bomb designer. In the summer of 1980, Amory Lovins published an article in *Foreign Affairs*[33] arguing that reactor plutonium, whether irradiated for a few days and thus nearly pure Pu-239 or irradiated for four years and thus heavily Pu-240 and other isotopes, is useful for bomb manufacture by professionals and amateurs alike.

Lovins tells us that he must conceal part of his argument in order not to aid terrorists. That is a plausible position, but it is difficult to evaluate his scantily supported assertions that clever amateurs can use spent fuel heavily contaminated with Pu-240 to make powerful and reliable bombs.

A related fright is that safeguarding plutonium from terrorists requires a police state that will inevitably destroy our civil liberties. This view ignores the fact that we are already shipping plutonium around the country in substantial quantities for military purposes, that it is not hijacked, and that we have had to establish no repressive mechanism to achieve this result. It is possible that establishing a mechanism to track down terrorists who make sensational but false claims involving plutonium as a poison or a bomb might require such a mechanism, but that problem will exist whether they acquire any plutonium or not. In any event it is largely the creature of the antinuclear movement, whose scenarios can only have the effect of lending credibility to terrorist claims.

The chances of terrorists constructing bombs need to be evaluated in the light of the considerable difficulty that faces nation-states, only a handful of which have as yet managed to build a plutonium bomb. The single explosion by the most recent nuclear power, India, involved what is widely considered to have been not a bomb but a "device"—that is, it was not compact enough for military use. If, as we are told, building a plutonium bomb is something that can be accomplished by clever amateurs, and if, as we are told, a good deal of plutonium is missing, it is remarkable that nations seem to have such trouble in getting the bomb and that in every case when a nation has gotten the bomb, it has not been through power reactors or stolen plutonium but through dedicated plutonium production reactors. Is it really likely that a band of terrorists can accomplish what India—scientifically the most advanced nation of the Third World—achieved only with difficulty?

# Proliferation

The use of power reactors by nation-states to develop nuclear weapons is a different question. On the one hand, none of the known nuclear-weapons states developed their capacity from a power program. In all cases except India, the power program was not developed until after the nuclear weapon capability. One thermonuclear power—China—still has no nuclear generating plants.

Diverting plutonium from a power reactor is not the ideal way of making plutonium suitable for weapons. It is more efficient to use a research reactor for the purpose, and as a matter of fact that is precisely how the Indians appear to have made the plutonium for their bomb: in a research—not power—reactor supplied them by Canada. (This fact is obscured by constant misstatements to the contrary by people who should know better, including *The New Republic*'s TRB.)[34] And the United States, having no monopoly on research reactors, is just as powerless to prevent nuclear proliferation by putting an embargo on them.

But a nation-state's diversion of plutonium from its power plants would have its attractions: The act itself would be at worst only formally illegal. The diverters would presumably be highly trained physicists and engineers, operating with the covert sanction of the state. Given a nation with full control of a set of power reactors and a reprocessing plant, there is considerable credibility in scenarios that involve clandestine diversion of plutonium for bomb production. But few countries fit this description now, and none need join the list. The countries signatory to the Nuclear Non-Proliferation Treaty (NPT) have agreed to international inspection of their nuclear facilities. The only countries that have not signed and have nuclear power plants are Argentina, Brazil, Pakistan, India, South Africa, France, and Spain. All of these nations would be quite capable of making bombs through research reactors, as indeed India has. And other nonsignatories have research facilities adequate for the purpose: Egypt, Israel, Colombia, Chile, and China. Of these China exemplifies the problem, for it has hydrogen bombs but no power reactor.

The most striking case is that of Iraq, a signatory to the NPT that proposed to operate a large research reactor that required high-enriched uranium fuel and for which it had no plausible civilian use. This fuel, if diverted before loading into the reactor, would have been directly usable in uranium bombs of simple design. The destruction of this reactor by Israel on June 7, 1981, is entirely plausible as an act of self-defense when seen as an attempt to destroy not the reactor but the French rationale for supplying it with fuel. Loaded with high-enriched uranium, the reactor could have been a slow but inevitable producer of bomb-grade plutonium.

Although from the point of nuclear power, it would be possible to dismiss the destruction of the Iraqi reactor on the ground that it was not a power reactor,* it is more important to remember that Iraq, when it apparently wanted to develop a nuclear weapon, turned not to a nuclear power plant but to a much cheaper and simpler research reactor. Lovins maintains that present safeguards on nuclear power are inadequate. His conclusion, expressed in the *Foreign Affairs* article and elsewhere, is that the United States can and should be the energy policeman of the world, forswearing the nuclear option and bullying and jollying others to follow in our path. It is exceedingly unlikely that we could succeed in this if we tried, for it is unlikely that either the Soviet Union or France will sit on their nuclear export programs just because we tell them to.

But if we were to succeed in imposing Lovinsian energy policies on the rest of the world, we should become the most hated of nations, and for

---

* It was widely so misrepresented in the U.S. press; see chapter 7.

good reason. We would be perceived as urging others to cut down on bread while we continued eating our cake.

Rather than pursue this arrogant and imperialist policy, we should move to get international approval of strengthened safeguards. We should bear in mind that the Soviet Union, ringed on the west by its potentially hostile satellites, regularly supplies them with civilian power plants. Surely if the Soviet Union supplies Poland or Finland with nuclear power plants, such plants do not equal nuclear bombs. Not even Lovins would argue that the Soviet Union would supply such states with a cheap and easy *force de frappe*.

The Soviet system is simple: The U.S.S.R. maintains a monopoly on reprocessing. Such a system could be internationalized. There is no reason why reprocessing facilities need to be diffused more widely than the existing nuclear-weapons states, where the horse has already bolted from the stable.*

The United States, Great Britain, France, the Soviet Union, and China (possibly joined by Germany and Japan) ought to provide an adequate base for reprocessing plants operating under the supervision of their own national authorities and, as well, the International Atomic Energy Authority. Such plants could provide reprocessed fuel for nuclear power stations in nonweapons states. Such supply could be made, subject to acceptance of stringent controls, a matter of right for nonweapons states.

Lovins argues that even if plutonium containing large quantities of Pu-240 and Pu-242 is inadequate for weapons use, a determined state possessing a civilian power program could remove fuel rods prematurely so as to extract plutonium that would be nearly pure Pu-239. But under an arrangement such as the one I am sketching here, it would be possible to restrict the reserve supply of fuel in any one country to the statistically reasonable, and to require the return of all spent fuel pins before supplying fresh ones. And, lest a country briefly irradiate enough fuel to make a bomb and hope to build the bomb before it needed new fuel in the normal course of events, it would be simple to require that the covers of reactor pressure vessels—which must be removed before any fueling operations—be taken off only in the presence of three international inspectors chosen at random just before the removal. Suitable monitoring devices could make it impossible to remove the cover without the presence of inspectors. Under such conditions, diversion of fuel rods for clandestine reprocessing would be impossible in a light-water reactor.

There are two types of reactor—the CANDU heavy-water reactor developed in Canada and the Magnox reactors that formed the backbone of the highly successful first stage of the British nuclear power program—that can

---

* Germany and Japan, two highly advanced nuclear powers that lack nuclear weapons only through forebearance, present special problems.

be refueled while operating. Theoretically, production of weapons-grade pluto-nium in such reactors is easier than in reactors that must be shut down. As it happens, all reactors of this type are currently in the hands either of countries that have nuclear weapons (for example, Britain or France) or nations unlikely to want to acquire them (for example, Canada or Italy). The solitary exception is India, where a heavy-water research reactor was used to produce a weapons capability. Prudence suggests that such reactors, when exported, should not go to Uganda or Paraguay unless there are stringent international controls on reprocessing.

It must be remembered even so that a pile of irradiated fuel rods containing 10 kilograms of Pu-239 is not 10 kilograms of bomb material. Making that conversion still requires a massive, complex, and very expensive reprocessing plant. These are currently the monopoly of the existing nuclear-weapons powers. But even without such controls, Magnox and CANDU reactors, both of which have superb capacity factors in excess of those obtained by coal-fired plants, could be supplied to the Denmarks of the world, who can be trusted with them.

If Lovins and his ilk were genuinely concerned with the production of energy, they would pursue such schemes for perfecting safeguards rather than using the proliferation issue as a club with which to beat nuclear power. Nuclear proliferation is, of course, an excellent thing to be against, but it is very doubtful that U.S. energy policy can have any effect whatsoever on its course. The most obvious reason for this is that those countries that lack a backstop of coal and oil—France first among them—will develop breeder technology for their own needs whether we do or not, and will finance that development by exporting breeder technology.

There is simply no possibility that the United States can prohibit the world-wide production of plutonium by sitting on the breeder reactor. It cannot sit on it because it does not yet have it, and even if it did, the French, with their Superphenix, are rushing to commercialize it.

In his argument that nuclear reactors equal nuclear bombs, Lovins agrees that one form of reactor fuel is really ill-adapted to weapons design. It is, ironically, the mixed-oxide (plutonium and uranium) fuel used in fast breeder reactors. That is to say, in forgoing the breeder reactor for nonproliferation reasons, the United States may be forgoing the one fuel cycle admitted even by Amory Lovins to produce only a seriously unwieldy bomb.

The prevention of nuclear proliferation is a grave problem, but it must be solved on its own terms if it is to be solved at all. It cannot be solved by false nostrums that require the adoption of a suicidal energy policy.

# 3

# The Case for the Atom: Considering the Alternatives— Fossil Fuels

THUS FAR the case for nuclear energy has been almost entirely negative: the refutation of a wide variety of false allegations made by its critics. The affirmative case for nuclear energy can be outlined in a single sentence: Nuclear energy is environmentally the most benign of major energy sources except natural gas, the most benign in terms of public health, the safest in terms of major accidents, and the only major source able, over a long period of time, to give us large amounts of flexible energy.

To demonstrate the truth of these assertions, we must again proceed in a comparative fashion, testing nuclear energy against the alternatives. Even to begin such a procedure is to reveal some astonishing facts. For example: If one were to list the three energy sources providing the *most* radioactivity to consumers, nuclear energy might not make the list. Natural gas would, for natural gas comes into one's house direct from deposits that may contain radon. Energy conservation would make the list, for energy-efficient houses are poorly ventilated by design and trap radon gas, thus doubling the total exposure to radiation of those living within them.[1] Nuclear energy would be at most tied for third place with coal.

We will consider these alternate-source exposures to radiation in detail. The important point is that none of them is controversial, in the sense that no one, not even the fiercest critics of the atom, disputes their existence. Yet one could read a thousand pages of antinuclear writing without coming across any of them.

I have deliberately picked exotic (and fairly trivial) examples to introduce the topic. But it is when one gets to comparing energy sources in terms of major health hazards that nuclear energy begins to shine. The notion that it is not our safest major form of energy depends on the widespread habit of forgetting the actual deaths caused by existing technologies and comparing the void thereby created with hypothetical (and exaggerated) deaths possibly to be caused by nuclear energy. These hypothetical deaths are still no more than that. But the actual deaths caused by other technologies are countable and many.

We can begin with coal. Coal-fired electricity* now costs a great many lives each year, a figure, even on the most conservative estimate, well into the thousands nationally. A minority of these deaths are occupational: As we have seen, the mining of coal kills people, and by almost two orders of magnitude more per unit of electricity generated than the mining of uranium. But it may be possible to pass over this if we argue that the number is not after all so high, and the miners work by choice.

It is otherwise with the public health effects of coal, the burning of which is a very nasty business even with the best contemporary technology. The combustion products of coal are many and diversely carcinogenic and mutagenic. Some of them reside in the solid wastes produced by power plants, the rest in the gaseous and particulate effluent that goes up the smokestack. "Scrubbers" designed to remove sulfur dioxide from the smoke reduce these hazards, but they far from eliminate them. First of all, they do not begin to trap all the dangerous components in the effluent, and those that they do trap are not annihilated—as, by contrast, plutonium is annihilated in the core of a reactor—but converted into immense amounts of sludge that must be put somewhere. And no one proposes to treat that sludge—containing, among other much more dangerous substances, uranium, thorium, radium, and polonium, all of which are radioactive—with anything approaching the care accorded nuclear wastes.[2]

The Office of Technology Assessment estimates that improvements in pollution control will, over the rest of the century, about keep pace with our increased use of coal. We will continue to kill, on its view, about 50,000 Americans a year by burning coal.[3]

And so the electricity generated by a 1,000-megawatt (MW) coal-fired generator carries two price tags, one in dollars and one in lives. D. J. Rose

* The production of electricity is, of course, hardly the only industrial use we make of coal. It is crucial to the steelmaking process and figures wherever industrial heat is needed.

and colleagues at M.I.T. have calculated this second price tag. If we add up the number of coal miners killed in accidents, coal miners killed by black lung disease, and workers killed in transporting coal from the mine to the power plant, we see that each such plant kills at least eleven people a year.[4] (One can imagine how quickly the nuclear industry would be shut down if a single plant killed eleven people a year.)

Furthermore, if we add members of the public killed by pollution from the plant, the exact number of which is a matter of controversy, we see that the price tag will list between 20 and 100 more human lives.[5] This, it must be remembered, is the cost per year of one large coal-fired plant: between 31 and 111 lives a year. These deaths, it also must be remembered, are of actual people who die every year in order that coal-fired plants may be operated.

In contrast, when a similar calculation of all the deaths caused by a 1,000-MW light-water reactor—including all those killed by the fuel cycle, by the operation of the reactor, and by waste disposal—we arrive at a total of a one-half death a year. This half death, by the way, is still largely hypothetical, since it includes amortized figures for a number of accidents that have not yet happened. While a few uranium miners are killed each year, no one has ever been killed by a commercial power reactor. (In this country there have been three deaths resulting from an accident at a small military experimental reactor.)

The death ratio between the two systems of power generation is thus seen to be between 60 and 225 to 1, in favor of nuclear. Incredibly, coal is the fuel we are now being urged to adopt in preference to "dangerous" uranium.

It is one of life's little ironies that coal contains small amounts of radioactive elements, mostly radium and thorium, and that the typical coal-fired plant has a level of radioactive emission greater than that allowed for a nuclear plant. If the Nuclear Regulatory Commission had responsibility for regulating our coal-fired plants, they would have to be shut down.

The antinuclear lobby implies that waste disposal is a problem unique to nuclear power. The fact is that coal-fired plants also have a disposal problem, and it is a very serious one. A large coal-fired plant burns about a million tons of coal a year. Because burning is a chemical reaction, it neither creates nor destroys matter. Hence we know that when the million tons of coal are burned, there will be at least a million tons of waste. There will in fact be more, for burning is a process whereby the carbon in the coal is joined with oxygen from the atmosphere, and the total annual waste product of a large coal-fired plant is about 1.5 million tons. This waste is, among other things, radioactive, for it contains about a ton of uranium.

Coal-fired plants solve part of this problem by disposing of their wastes into the air and thence into our lungs, and the rest by dumping. The amount disposed into the atmosphere comes to some thirty pounds a year for each American. The solid wastes carted away to the dump from coal-fired plants total tens of millions of tons a year: some 36,500 truckloads a year for a 1,000-megawatt plant.[6] These contain not only such nonradioactive poisons as mercury, selenium, vanadium, and benzopyrene, but radioactive materials such as uranium and thorium in amounts that would be impermissible for emission from a nuclear plant. This is hardly a "solved" waste-disposal problem.

A massive commitment to coal would raise yet another problem, the possibility that a substantial increase in atmospheric carbon dioxide would lead to a long-term warming of the earth—the so-called "greenhouse effect." The greenhouse effect would be to people what "thermal pollution" is to fish. That is, it would be a change in climate. Now, I have argued that thermal pollution is a trivial issue because, weighed against human needs for energy, the forced migration of some fish (not all fish in the area of a reactor, because some will prefer the slightly warmer temperature) is a trivial event. The greenhouse effect, which might raise the average temperature of the entire earth by as much as 7 degrees F—as compared with a typical reactor, which raises the temperature of six acres of ocean surface by only 4 degrees F— is environmentally a much more serious threat. It would pose the possibility of massive shifts of growing zones, problems from increased melting of the polar ice caps, and substantial problems of human adjustment to changed climate.[7]

The precise degree to which the burning of fossil fuel contributes to the buildup of carbon dioxide remains a matter of controversy, and so it is not absolutely clear how serious a threat fossil-fuel plants pose in this regard. But can anyone doubt what would be said in protest if it were credibly argued that nuclear power plants might raise the average temperature by 7 degrees?

The costs of these and other assaults on the environment from coal have been addressed by several writers. Petr Beckmann has made an estimate of the health costs of the 1975 fire at the Tennessee Valley Authority's Browns Ferry plant (widely merchandised as proof of the dangers of nuclear energy). These costs do not derive from the nuclear plant, where no one was injured, but from the use of coal to generate power while the nuclear plant shut down. He estimates that fifteen miners will lose their lives to generate the coal to replace Browns Ferry and that pollution from this coal-fired generation will kill between 60 and 200 members of the public. This is the true cost of the Browns Ferry fire.[8]

Browns Ferry is an example of a brief and localized nuclear moratorium.

## The Case for the Atom: Fossil Fuels

Professor Walter Meyer of the University of Missouri has made estimates of the economic and health costs of a five-year nationwide moratorium on new nuclear construction. Assuming that the lost nuclear capacity were replaced with coal-fired generators, by 1988 between 10,000 and 20,000 people would die annually from the environmental hazards posed by such plants. Assuming these coal plants were used for a thirty-year life, the total deaths would be between 300,000 and 600,000.[9]

These deaths could be reduced by replacing nuclear power instead with oil-fired power, but only at great economic cost. By 1988, to have replaced a five-year nuclear moratorium with oil-fired generation would cost as much as $40 billion a year. Even if the lost capacity were replaced with coal-fired generation, the annual cost would be as much as $10 billion a year.

It is not surprising that nuclear critics rarely dwell on the dangers of coal. When they deal with the matter at all, it is to obfuscate matters by suggesting that the Mine Safety Act of 1970 (which has about halved the number of mining deaths) will somehow close the gap between the two fuels. It is also misleadingly suggested that coal has been made benign by scrubbers. Scrubbers, as I have said, deal with one type of dangerous emission and convert the problem from one of gaseous emission to one of solid waste disposal. (If all new power plants were coal-fired and used scrubbers, the annual production of this sludge would be between 120 and 300 million tons a year.)

Critics of nuclear power generally lay great store by conservation as a means of reducing demand and thereby the need for new nuclear capacity. The first problem with this position is that it is not enough merely to reduce the need for new capacity. For even were it possible to generate all our electricity with fossil fuels, it would not be desirable. That is, over the long run, nuclear power is needed not only to add to the present capacity but to replace it. At a minimum, as obsolete fossil-fuel baseload* plants are retired, they ought to be replaced by nuclear plants.

The second problem with the advocacy of conservation is that all too often, among the critics of the atom, "conservation" becomes a euphemism for "dedevelopment."

There is no way to argue against genuine conservation. Waste—that is, the avoidable expenditure of anything when avoidance would be cost effective—is never defensible. Our present use of oil and coal as fuel when they

---

* That is, the plants that meet the minimum daily demand, the ones that would if possible be run twenty-four hours a day, 365 days a year. At the other end of the scale, the top of the peaking load, demand is met with highly inefficient devices such as converted aircraft turbines. This is a service unsuited to large plants such as nuclear ones, and it is unlikely that any of this demand can be met from the atom. For the intermediate range, so-called load-following, nuclear plants may prove more adaptable.

could be replaced by other means—partially solar, largely nuclear—is an outstanding example of waste, one we are now committed to increase. There clearly are a number of ways in which the United States could engage in genuine conservation, that is, the elimination of true waste. More careful insulation is one. Another one is co-generation, common in Europe but rare here. In co-generation, a thermal power plant is run on the waste heat from some industrial process. Even though the size of such plants must usually be small, the fact that the fuel cost is, effectively, close to zero makes them very efficient. A related means of conservation involves using the waste heat from a power plant for home heating, a use West Germany is investigating on a massive scale. And a third uses the waste heat from a plant to warm soil in order to grow exotic crops. Peanuts and cotton are already being grown in the Ruhr Valley by this means.[10]

But much of the waste alleged by the antinuclear lobby is in fact simply expenditure on ends they do not approve. Air-conditioning, that *bête noire* of the pseudo-conservationists, is an example of this. It is perfectly true that humanity has lived for most of its existence without air-conditioning, and by that crude measure it must be thought a luxury. As a matter of fact, humanity has lived most of its existence with no means of combating smallpox or appendicitis, but one does not hear improvements in that regard condemned as wasteful merely because newfangled.

It should also be obvious that to the extent to which such "conservation"— not genuine improvements in efficiency but reductions in economic activity— succeeds, it must be an enemy of economic growth. Many solve this problem by stating that growth is nasty anyway, but no one has come up with persuasive evidence that we can live comfortably without it.

One frequently asserted claim is that the Swiss and the Swedes maintain our standard of living and use half as much energy as we do—ergo, half our consumption must be waste. The short answer to this is that in common with the rest of the industrialized world, the United States has a low energy consumption for its gross national product, and our use in fact lies on the curve of lowest consumption.[11] A somewhat longer answer has been added by Beckmann, who points out that we could get by with less energy if we had no energy-intensive industry and instead made watches and wrote insurance, imported most of our food, and arranged to have a new geography typified by mountains and plentiful hydropower sites.[12]

This comparison is a part of the false myth that Americans are energy hogs. This myth is supported by statistics showing that the United States has about 5 percent of the world's population and uses about 30 percent of its energy. Yet it is not often pointed out that the United States produces about 30 percent of the world's energy, and that as the world's major exporting nation we export much of the energy we use rather than spend it on ourselves. For example, one thing we do with our energy is to grow food for the rest of the world. Our agriculture uses about 25 percent of all our diesel fuel and a third of our agricultural product is sent out of the country. The energy used to produce that food should, in any totting up of energy extravagance, be debited to the consuming country.

By importing food, comparatively backward countries like the Soviet Union are enabled also to import both the energy contained in the food and all the other energy used to produce it along the way. If it takes $x$ amount of petroleum to produce a bushel of wheat exported from the U.S. to the U.S.S.R., then the Soviet Union uses that petroleum just as surely as the owner of a 15-mile-per-gallon American car uses the gasoline to drive to the grocery store. The difference is that the U.S. consumption is debited to the U.S., whereas the Soviet consumption is debited—to the U.S.!

The clear facts are not only that Americans do not use more energy than anyone else, but also that they produce more than anyone else. These facts are essential to any understanding of our energy consumption.

Another crucial factor is geography. Sweden and Switzerland are both endowed by nature with massive hydropower potentials, which they have had the good sense to exploit. And hydropower, in which the human-controlled energy input is limited to the energy cost of building a dam, is the most efficient of all sources of electricity. When one combines hydroelectric generation with electric railways, as is the case in both Sweden and Switzerland, one gets an almost preternaturally efficient means of transport. The U.S. is proportionately much poorer in hydroelectric sites, and the railways were able to make only a stab at electrification before the roof fell in on them.*

But the crucial geographic factor is size. We are the only country that combines massive production, much of it for export, with massive and rather sparsely populated area. This factor affects our energy use per capita in several ways. First, we travel more. In a given year, the U.S. automobile fleet typically logs twice as many miles per capita as the European fleets. Moreover, for reasons that relate to the difficulty, in a sparsely populated country like the United States, of operating railroads competitively with automobiles, we

---

* Cheap coal and cheap oil made electric railways comparatively unattractive except in mountainous territory, where trains running downhill help to power trains running uphill. West Virginia and the Pacific Northwest thus have most of the U.S. electrified mileage. The great exception, the electrification of the Pennsylvania/New Haven main line between Washington and New Haven, the backbone of Amtrak's Northeast Corridor, was an early twentieth-century development in which the environmental desideratum of reducing air pollution in what was then industrial heartland went hand in hand with the superior acceleration possible with electrification, no less a desideratum for a heavily traversed commuter route with manifold stops and starts.

use the comparatively energy-efficient railroads for very little passenger travel. Typically, European trains travel as much as ten or twenty times as many miles per capita as those in the United States.

It is argued that comparatively low use of passenger trains is part of a conspiracy to force cars on us instead. The conspiracy is rather one of geography. If one starts out by train from New York City before dinner, by lunchtime the next day one has still not gotten to Chicago. If one leaves Cologne by train a little before lunch, by dinnertime one is in Copenhagen. Part of this advantage is because of faster European railways, but not all. (Even the crack Rhine–Copenhagen express must cross the Baltic by ferry for about an hour at 15 knots or so.) Most of it is because Europe is so much more compact.

It is about as far from New York to Detroit as from Berlin to Paris, and the distance from Chicago to San Francisco is 300 miles more than from Paris to Moscow. New York to San Francisco is 700 miles farther than Paris to Baghdad! At such distances and low population densities, trains cannot compete with airplanes. (The phenomenon is not limited to this country. Russians traveling between Moscow and Vladivostok do not take the Trans-Siberian Express, arguably the best passenger train in the world. They fly. The express is for tourists making the whole run and Soviets making partial ones. Similar considerations led to the demise of the Orient Express.)

Once we understand that the United States is not an unparalleled energy wastrel and that therefore we cannot expect to save immense amounts of energy painlessly, we can make an assessment of what genuine economies there are to be made. We should realize first of all that the importance of waste is relative to the abundance, both short and long term, of what is being wasted.

For the short term, for example, we ought not to waste OPEC oil because it is extremely expensive, not only financially but politically. But for the long term we ought not to waste any oil at all, because it is a finite resource in the Persian Gulf quite as much as in the United States. This imperative drives us to put a high priority on making automobiles more efficient.

In the short term we can afford to waste coal, because we have so much of it that it is hard to imagine using it all up within the lifetime of our immediate descendants.* But on the long term, we ought not to waste any

---

* I suspect that for most people, posterity is appreciable most strikingly in the form of their great-grandchildren (real or imagined) or perhaps the children of their great-grandchildren. It is not reasonable to expect personal contact with descendants any more remote than that, and after that posterity must be no more than a mass of utter strangers, to some of whom one stands in the relation of ancestor and to others of whom one stands in the relation of cousin, uncle, or aunt. This is a hardly more intimate relation than that which obtains between any two persons now alive chosen at random. There is no logical reason to value such stranger-

coal at all because our remoter descendants are going to need it all for petro-chemicals.

We need also to realize that it is possible to waste an asset through disuse quite as much as through use. For example, during the historic period when the price of gold was stable the French peasants who keep their little all in Napoleons in a box under the bed saw the value of the asset reduced each year by the amount of inflation and saw a further loss from the opportunity cost of not earning interest on it in some safe investment that would have been the Gallic equivalent of a federally insured savings account.

The steady upward pressure on the price of oil makes it entirely plausible for those nations with a surplus to leave some of it in the ground, where it has been lately appreciating faster than any other investment of comparable security.

In the short term the nuclear fuels—uranium and thorium—are appreciating in the ground. But in the long term they are depreciating. They are quite unlike oil, which when undisturbed really is certain to be there forever. A deposit of uranium is most assuredly not forever. On the very long term, a deposit of uranium—or thorium—is a deposit of lead, a substance with very inferior prospects as an energy source. Indeed, wait long enough and *every* atom of every radioactive substance will be transmuted, through natural causes, into lead.

It is, assuredly, a very long term: It will take 700 million years for half of the U-235 now in existence to disappear, and even longer for the U-238 and Th-232. But if we are to consider such matters in terms of our remotest imaginable posterity, we ought to consider seriously fissioning such atoms while they still exist. For nuclear fuels are the only fuels that can be wasted through inaction.

From the point of view of the present, however, it is useful to consider the total efficiencies of several energy systems for producing electricity. Strip-mined coal, for example, if burned in a power plant, produces delivered electricity with an energy value 24.9 percent of that contained in the coal as it lay in the earth. The 75.1 percent loss is attributable to the energy expended in mining the coal, transporting it, converting it to electricity, and distributing it to the customer. Natural gas, at 23.5 percent efficiency, is close behind, with pit-mined coal third at 17.8 percent and uranium fissioned in light-water reactors a close fourth at 16.3 percent. (Uranium fissioned in

---

posterity born in 2101 any more highly than those born in 21001. Once one starts worrying about one's obligation to generations yet unborn, at least unborn in the next century or so, one must worry about that obligation to them all. The thermal death of the universe, currently predicted to occur in some billions of years or so, is the only thing that will dissolve the obligation.

breeder reactors would do much better.) Offshore oil is 12.9 percent, onshore, 9.8 percent.[13]

From such figures we can draw one easy conclusion, namely, that on considerations of energy efficiency alone, oil should have a very low priority as a fuel for generating electricity. But we can generalize this conclusion and rank the other fuels in order of desirability according to their system efficiency. The problem with such calculations is that they take a naive view of efficiency, depending purely on the comparatively abstract realm of physics. This allows for substantial simplification.

But the real calculus of energy sources is complex, for the energy problem is rooted in the real world. For example, which is more efficient, a steam engine that burns very high-cost coal at 32 percent efficiency or one that burns very low-cost coal at 28 percent?

For the purpose of this example, we must assume that the price differential of the two coals is not directly proportionate to their energy content. In that case, and that case alone, the economic efficiency of the two engines is identical. Otherwise—if, for example, the higher-priced coal is higher priced because it produces less pollution but contains no more energy—the physically less efficient engine may well be economically the more efficient one, as well as environmentally (and politically) the less efficient.

Even more striking is a comparison between heating a house with electricity generated from nuclear sources and heating it directly with oil burned in a furnace. No one would deny that heating with nuclear-generated electricity wastes between one-half and two-thirds of the energy in the fissioned atoms simply from the conversion loss inherent in any thermal power plant. But by substituting domestic uranium for OPEC oil, we can gain substantial political and economic advantages that counterbalance the loss of physical efficiency. Still more important, the oil, besides being dangerous to us fiscally and politically, is also good for other things besides heating houses—not only in such presently irreplaceable uses as airplane fuel but in the vast, essential, and irreplaceable nonfuel use of petrochemicals. On the other hand, unfissioned uranium and thorium are essentially trash. Which then is the more efficient, a heating system that runs at 75 percent efficiency on liquid gold or one that runs at 23 percent efficiency on solid trash?

Amory Lovins would reject such an argument on the ground that the question we should be addressing is not how to generate electricity in central power stations but whether we should do it at all. He decries the use of electricity for any purpose for which it is not indispensable, for example, electric light and electronic devices. Since he believes we already use too much electricity, he has little patience with any scheme to generate more. In effect this position says that it is better to heat our houses with oil—an immensely useful substance of which we do not have nearly enough—than to heat them, via electricity, with uranium or thorium, otherwise essentially useless substances of which we have a great deal.

Our nuclear fuel supply is constrained only if we deliberately limit it to the 0.7 percent of natural uranium that is U-235. If we adopt the fast reactor technology that would allow the use of U-238 and Th-232, our nuclear fuel supply would be, for all practical purposes, renewable.*

I have already suggested the superiority of nuclear power to the existing alternative, comprising coal, oil, and natural-gas generation of electricity. Nuclear opponents, however, almost never compare nuclear energy to such existing forms of energy but rather to as-yet undeveloped forms. The fashion for such forms is just now in the ascendant, and not merely among those who advocate them as substitutes for nuclear energy. For the most popular of the "alternatives"—those belonging to the so-called "soft path" popularized by Amory Lovins—are invariably said to be easier and cheaper than anything else, and inexhaustible in the bargain.

It is necessary to put quotation marks around "alternatives," because even though the term suggests a practical choice with which to replace the status quo, as currently used it has a special meaning: "unrealized sources of energy theoretically alternative to sources that already work." As generally considered, alternative energy sources are of two sorts: synthetic fuels, derived by innovative refining of fossil fuels (for example, oil from shale or "synthetic natural gas"† from coal), and solar sources in the broad sense. That is, roughly "hard" and "soft" types of energy.

Despite the massive national commitment made under the Carter administration to a synthetic fuels program, such fuels present very serious problems. However the end product is derived, the process starts with mining. Most of the arguments that can be made against a greatly expanded use of coal through direct burning can be made against the use of coal through indirect burning. In the bargain, the conversion processes are all highly energy intensive. Producing gasoline from coal may make sense for South Africa—a country with no indigenous oil, its back to the wall politically, the coal seams conveniently located in the wilderness, and a labor supply that is, from the point of view of energy exploitation, the next best thing to slavery. We have none of these things going for us (and in most cases must thank God that we do not), and the synfuels program remains a questionable scheme to use up coal for fuel even more intensively than we would through direct burning.

* Not my conclusion alone, but also that of Barry Commoner.[14]

† This bizarre term is necessary to distinguish this product, chemically virtually identical to natural gas, from the quite different manufactured "coal gas" that natural gas long ago supplanted.

Most antinuclearists, to be sure, are also down on synfuels, for some of the reasons I have cited here and also because of what is really the best argument synfuels have going for them, namely, that they are adapted to our present way of doing things and do not require a revolution. Antinuclearists are more inclined to favor the revolutionary path of solar energy. Judged as an energy source, the sun deserves a chapter to itself.

# 4

# The Case for the Atom:
# Considering the Alternative—
# The Promise of the Sun

IN A REAL SENSE, all energy but
that derived from the tides and geothermal sources is nuclear. What we
generally call by that term is derived from the splitting or fusing of atomic
nuclei among the elements left on earth by whatever extraordinary process
created it.

The rest, which we often think of as nonnuclear, is derived from nuclear
fusions on the sun, radiated across space and sometimes stored in such media
as coal, oil, or water, sometimes not. All the fossil fuels are solar in origin,
laid down over very long periods of time and stored in what are essentially
static storage media that require the calculated intervention of man if they
are to be unlocked. (Coal is the most static of these, natural gas the least,
and oil somewhere in between.)

The category of fuels now fashionably called biomass are also derived
from solar radiation stored in the short term in media that are much more
dynamic, which is to say shorter-lived and much more accessible, than the
fossil fuels. The length of storage varies from the single growing season of
annuals to the decades and centuries of trees.

Also solar are the forms of energy that depend upon the weather, such
as wind and hydropower. Here the storage media—air and water—are filled
up and discharged on an erratic and highly dynamic schedule. If humanity

is to make use of either of these forms, it must capture them on their own schedule and use them at once or devise suitable man-made storage media, such as dams or electric batteries.

Finally, there is direct solar radiation, which can be captured directly as heat or converted to electricity. To utilize these forms of energy one must in essence intercept them before they meet such natural storage media as grass or water, and if they then are to be stored it must be in man-made media. This scheme is obviously simplified. Even without human intervention, there can be very complex chains of conversion, as when solar radiation passes through grass to beef cattle to humans to sewage treatment plants to methane converters to end use as heat in a stove burner. Or as when a pumped-storage plant may, in the interest of load management, marry hydraulic force supplied by nature and nuclear electricity midwifed by humanity.

In this connection it is worth noting that the distinction often drawn between "natural" and "artificial" sources of energy is quite pointless. It is an elemental fact constantly ignored in our time that there is nothing in the world that is not part of nature, which means that were we to restrict ourselves literally to the natural, we would fail. The best we could do would be to avoid the man-made. To make the maximum effort to avoid the man-made, we should be forced to return to the good old days before the agricultural revolution changed man from an animal that was merely the most intelligent (if not the most skillful) of predators into something that began to look human. *Homo sapiens* is the only self-improving animal, and if our works are not part of nature, then we are nothing except when we are artificial.

The advocates of the soft path usually distinguish energy sources as either renewable or nonrenewable. This is really a tendentious category that masks another very important distinction. The fossil fuels are nonrenewable precisely because they represent storage of solar radiation over extremely long periods of time. By such storage the comparatively dilute energy available at one moment and at one point on the earth was concentrated and made available to us.

The maximum flow of solar energy is in the best of conditions about one kilowatt per square meter (approximately a square yard). If this is to be concentrated, it must be done over geological time spans, in the case of the fossil fuels, or over immense land areas, in the case of the watersheds that serve hydropower. The comparative inefficiency of these methods of storage is mitigated by two factors: in the case of the fossil fuels, because we were not around when they were being laid down we did not improvidently use them up. In the case of hydropower, the watersheds were already there, essentially useless for any other purpose. Regarding fossil fuels, we do not have time to replicate the process even if we knew how, and regarding hydropower, we do not have the space.

Accordingly, if we are to fall back on the other solar sources we must contend with two facts: The flow of solar energy is dilute and intermittent, and its storage on a large scale difficult and expensive. It is this sort of "solar" energy, renewable but diffuse, that most people have in mind when they use the term and this is the sense in which I shall use it hereafter. It is an energy source now being so oversold that there is danger that its real virtues may be discounted or lost when the solar bubble breaks, as it must eventually do.

The real advantages of solar energy are apparent: It is renewable more or less daily—I say "more or less" because, as I write this, it has been raining for several days—and if it does not fall equally on the just and unjust, it does fall on them both; and it is available to the rich and the poor in substantially greater equity than any other energy source. And although it is far from free and far from safe—in the absolutist sense used by those who demand that nuclear power be "safe"—in the right place and under the right conditions of use it has substantial advantages in cost over most other fuels and is certainly safer than really dangerous fuels like coal.

Solar advocates like Barry Commoner are correct in principle in saying that there are end uses for energy that fit elegantly with solar sources. No one who has ever been to Albuquerque, with its acres of flat-topped, single-story dwellings bathed in sun, can avoid thinking that here if anywhere is a city designed for solar power. And elsewhere as well, *mutatis mutandis,* solar heating of hot water and so-called passive solar design of houses can be better exploited than they have been.

One can also imagine a number of specialized applications for solar energy, requiring comparatively little power and in locations far from existing central generating stations. But not every such application is made for solar power. On March 28, 1980, I attended a birthday party at the national historical site at Three Mile Island. In a field across from the plant some chaps had set up a small solar array and mounted a small radiation counter under it. The counter was happily counting background radiation and nothing else, while connected to a battery apparently unconnected to the solar array. The proprietors explained that the system had been set up to supply intermittent radiotelephone service in, I think, Sierra Leone. This is perhaps a plausible use for a solar array, but looking at the battery that was actually supplying the electricity, I could not help being reminded of the remark of the god Apollo that there is a solar energy enthusiast born every twelve seconds.

But the solar movement is not principally concerned with radiotelephones in Sierra Leone. Solar energy is now being touted as the energy for all purposes. The letters columns of the better newspapers are alive with correspondents comparing—always very unfavorably—other energy sources with solar, on which they ritually confer a magic trinity of attributes: cheapness, safety, and renewability. The authors of *Energy Future*[1] and the Council on Environmental Quality hope we can get 25 percent of our energy from renewable solar sources by the year 2000; and Denis Hayes (who vies with Amory Lovins to be our greatest apostle of the sun) thinks this goal too modest.

Barry Commoner has long been a solar advocate—his *Poverty of Power*[2] was in large part a eulogy of the sun and its potential—and his *Politics of Energy*,[3] which received the supreme accolade of serialization in the *New Yorker*, makes about as strong and detailed a case for a "solar" economy as can be imagined. If he does not make every claim that has been made for solar energy, he is pretty clearly on the leading edge of the popular debate. Commoner's position, then, provides a convenient framework for assessing the promise of solar energy, requiring only supplementary attention to a few solar sources to which he has given only minor consideration.

He is of course fiercely critical of recent national energy policy, which he attacks with a vehemence designed to convince us that his very expensive and constraining proposals are in fact an improvement. It is a familiar tactic among radical Utopians. But even here, Commoner's analysis is little or no improvement intellectually over the objects of his attention. Sometimes his discussion is merely naive, as when he treats as something cast in bronze the computer model developed under the Nixon and Ford administrations to simulate the results of various energy policies. Sometimes the discussion turns downright foolish, as when he notes that "it costs a great deal more to build a nuclear power plant than to drill an oil well with a comparable energy yield."[4] This is gibberish as it stands, for an oil well has no energy yield in the sense that a nuclear plant does. An oil well is a source of primary fuel, useless unless converted to do work. A nuclear power plant is such a conversion device, converting the energy in uranium to the more flexible form of electricity.

Commoner is guilty here of the schoolboy fault of trying to divide oranges into apples. A nuclear power plant can be properly compared only to some other form of conversion device.*

If we make the proper comparison, of a nuclear power plant to an oil-fired one, we will see that a nuclear power plant does in fact cost more than an oil-fired one of the same capacity, and costs more than a similar coal-fired plant as well. But the nuclear plant burns a fuel that is substantially

---

* Or as part of one of two comparable energy systems.

cheaper than coal and very much cheaper than oil; that is, had Commoner compared oil wells and coal mines with uranium mines, he would have discovered that, energy unit for energy unit, it costs much less to acquire uranium than oil or coal. The result is that nuclear electricity is cheaper than that derived from coal in most parts of the country, and much cheaper than oil everywhere. This plain fact is lost upon Commoner, who says "government policy can increase the amount of energy produced per dollar invested, but that would mean favoring oil wells over nuclear power plants."[5]

By way of transition to his own proposal, Commoner then proceeds with a discussion of the economic difference between renewable and nonrenewable energy sources. The latter, he argues, must inevitably increase in cost exponentially as the energy source, be it coal, oil, or uranium, becomes increasingly scarce and therefore hard to exploit. That is, each barrel of oil extracted from the earth makes the next barrel harder—that is, more expensive—to find and produce.

But this fact does not automatically elevate all renewable sources over all nonrenewable sources of energy. One way man has converted solar energy into work is through the horse; it is hard to believe that many people believe it superior for most sorts of transport to a car fueled on nonrenewable gasoline. This is of course a gross example. But, as I shall argue later, there is a strong case for the general long-term superiority of nuclear energy over solar.

Moreover, Commoner's thesis itself is of only dubious validity. He seems not to have noticed that over recent history, the price of oil was declining in real terms until the 1973 oil boycott, and that since then the dramatic increase in the world price of oil has escalated not in response to declining supply but to the manipulations of a cartel. Commoner attempts to exculpate OPEC from blame in the price rise by telling us that OPEC prices are based on anticipations of the domestic price. In the face of OPEC prices that are much higher than domestic prices, it is a little hard to see how this works.

Having established the notion that nonrenewable sources rise more quickly in price than renewable ones, Commoner soon begins to write as if renewable sources are not subject to escalation in price at all. This theory contradicts everything we know about supply and demand. It is merely necessary to consider escalations in the cost of food—a solar energy source if ever there was one—to see that such goods will never be, as Commoner seems to imagine them, inflation proof.

He then turns to his substantive proposal, which is nothing if not grand: a transition, executed over a half century, from our present fossil-based energy system to one based entirely on the sun. Having demonstrated what hardly needs demonstrating anymore, that we cannot rely literally forever on nonrenewable resources, he sets up the alternative possibilities of an energy system based on the breeder reactor* as against one based on solar energy in its widest sense. Since neither system could be set up immediately, he proposes a "bridging fuel" for each. For the breeder system, this bridge is coal, and for the solar system, natural gas.

Not surprisingly, he rejects the breeder-based system, first on conventional antinuclear arguments based on considerations of safety and proliferation. To the conventional arguments he adds the objection that a breeder-based economy would require a major expansion of the use of coal, which he concedes to be a serious environmental, occupational, and public health threat.

The solar scheme would be based on four major developments. The first of these is the rapid implementation of solar technology for water and space heating. Commoner believes that this technology has already arrived, is now competitive, and needs merely be put to work, normally in conjunction with existing systems, rather than as a stand-alone source.

Additionally, there would be a rapid development of photovoltaic technology to allow the conversion of sunlight to electricity through individual installations on houses. This technology Commoner believes to be on the verge of success, requiring only mass purchases by the government in order to become economically competitive with central-station electricity.

Next, we would develop a massive new alcohol industry capable of producing some 50 billion gallons of liquid fuel a year, displacing about half of our present gasoline supply.

Finally, there would be a vast new methane industry, producing that gas from various feedstocks and shipping it around the country through an expansion of the present natural gas network.†

Let us look at this proposal bit by bit.

The provision of water and space heating is the type of solar energy best developed to date. Typically, a large flat collector plate is mounted on the roof of a house and water circulated behind it. Water heated by the sun is carried away into the house, where it is either used directly for washing or radiated through appropriate devices for space heating. Given the best possible environment in which to compete—a maximum of insolation with a corresponding minimum need for space heat, and tax subsidies—such systems

---

* Technically, the fuels used in breeders—uranium and thorium—are nonrenewable, but Commoner correctly assumes that the centuries of power extractable from the two fuels add up to a practical infinity; it would be very surprising if we did not come up with some now undreamed-of replacement before the thorium ran out.

† There would also be increased dependence on wind power and hydroelectric generation. These are both weak reeds to lean on, wind because it is highly capital intensive and visually polluting if heavily exploited and, on the average, unreliable; hydropower because the sites for exploitation are running out, and rivers, even seen merely as damsites, are nonrenewable resources, because they silt up after a century or so. But to be fair to Commoner, these sources do not play enough part in his grand plan to make his reliance on them a fatal objection to it. For further discussion of windpower, see page 176.

are beginning to be competitive with more conventional systems. "Competitive" is not quite the word, because the backup supplies needed for those days—that occur even in the insolated southwest—when there is little or no sun must come from the rival conventional suppliers. When this backup is in the form of electricity, it will be electricity in the most expensive form yet devised by human ingenuity: peak electricity supplied at unpredictable times and inadequately supported by baseload.*

Commoner's analysis is somewhat rosier than the one I have just given, largely because he compares direct solar heating with electric resistance heating, that is, with the most expensive kind. He himself concedes this latter fact but says that nevertheless such heating is "very common." In fact, it accounts for only 13 percent of all residential heating installations. One is tempted 'to suspect that electric resistance heating was chosen not because of its bogus commonness—only coal and wood are less common—but because of its genuine expensiveness. (This is a common tactic with direct solar enthusiasts, perhaps understandable given the cost figures for direct solar heat.)

At least Commoner is aware that direct solar energy is not likely ever to be practical as a total source of heating. But in discussing the economics of an integrated system, he appears to take no account whatsoever of the effect that the subtraction of the baseload would have on the economics of central electricity supply.

Nor does Commoner reckon with real-life experience with solar heating. The solar heating of domestic hot water, which goes back to the nineteenth century, is the best established and simplest solar technology. It is interesting to see what a major consumer magazine had to say on this topic in 1980. In May of that year, *Consumer Reports* issued its first serious discussion of solar water heating.[6] The conclusions of the article should have been quite dismaying to solar enthusiasts.

To begin with the bottom line, *Consumer Reports* found that the average family with electric water heating, given a choice between a solar hot-water installation and three conservation measures (insulation of the hot-water tank, lowering the thermostat temperature to 140 degrees, and putting flow restricters in showers), would save more money a year by adopting the conventional measures, by a ratio of $93 to $69. Moreover, a family with a gas hot-water heater would *lose* $52 a year by adopting solar heating. These figures do not include anything for the opportunity cost of forestalled investment. That

---

* This is an excellent example of how a few direct solar enthusiasts may be able without undue fiscal strain to fit their preferred energy supply into conventional methods, but millions could not be. A hypothetical system in which all houses were fitted with solar installations for heat and light would still require a massive backup installation for electric generation that would have to provide peak supply on a schedule no more predictable than the weather, and without any baseload to serve as a financial underpinning.

is, if a family draws $1,000 of its own cash out of a savings account and "invests" it in a solar hot-water heater, the interest forgone on that investment is properly chargeable against the hot-water heater. The exact amount of an opportunity cost depends on the alternate use an investor might have made of the money. The conventional methods of saving cited by *Consumer Reports* involve little or no opportunity cost.

Even without figuring opportunity costs, however, *Consumer Reports's* figures are all bogus because they depend on the conceit that there is such a thing as a free lunch. That is, part of the "saving" is not really a saving but a federal income tax credit. Whether this credit is really a saving to a particular family depends on which side of the income-transfer the family lives. The article notes the claim of solar enthusiasts that such solar subsidies merely give to solar what nuclear energy has already gotten. It is regrettable that *Consumer Reports* should have passed this claim on without checking it. The current subsidy for a solar water heater costing $3,000 is $800. On the optimistic assumption that the installation lasts ten years, that equals an annual subsidy of $80. If the total federal expenditure on developing light-water reactors were written off in a single year, the share of a family of four would not be $800 but between $60 and $180. Written off over ten years, it would be not $80 a year but between $6 and $18. And written off over the forty-year life of only one generation of nuclear plants, it would amount to between $1.50 and $4.50 a year for a family of four. It should be realized in closing that the current federal subsidy amounts (at maximum) to a little more than 25 percent of the capital cost of a solar installation. The subsidy of the capital cost of a nuclear power plant is, and has been, nil.

But this is the good news. The bad news is that solar hot-water heaters are appallingly unreliable. *Consumer Reports* reported on a test of 100 installations in New England. Forty-two of these had to be replaced within one year. In the same period, thirty more had to be given major modifications. Whether the remaining twenty-eight had an untroubled year or occasional down time, the article did not report.

*Consumer Reports's* own experience was not much more reassuring. Of five units, two were plagued by constant malfunctions. One of these, the article reports, had been inoperative in December 1979 and at press time for the May 1980 issue—presumably at the beginning of April—was still not repaired. These performances should be compared with those of conventional water heaters, notoriously the most reliable of major appliances. Guarantees for ten years are common, and flawless performance for a decade or more is the rule rather than the exception.

*Consumer Reports* found its heaters so unreliable as a group that it had to devise an indicator to tell whether each was actually operating. (Because of the electric backup each required, the supply of hot water—except after sundown—was no indication: It might have been heated by nuclear electricity for all anyone could tell.) Moreover, *Consumer Reports* discovered that solar water heaters do not work very well at night. It is thus necessary, if one is to maximize the savings possible, to use a lot of hot water during the daytime. Needless to say the average family, whose father is at work, whose 1.7 children are probably at school, and whose mother is increasingly likely to be at work out of the house, does not conform to such a pattern of use.

There can hardly be a better example of the comparative inability of direct-solar energy conversion to accommodate itself to the realities of life. The family that can best exploit solar energy for hot-water heating is one that is home all day—that is to say, the family in dire poverty or the family in affluent leisure. The one cannot afford solar hot water, the other does not need it.

It should, finally, be noted that, according to *Consumer Reports,* the typical price of a conventional hot-water heater, installed, is $650, and the typical cost of a solar system is $2,500, not including the backup heating system. That is, a solar system costs ten times what a conventional one does, and because a large proportion of its cost is labor, the price is not likely ever to come down. As is clear from the article, even when differential fuel costs are figured in, solar hot water is no bargain.

This article is a powerful illustration of the grip solar energy has on the fashionable imagination. The article's findings are devastating as to the desirability of solar water heaters. Devices of such unreliability and dubious cost effectiveness would normally earn *Consumer Reports*'s attention only briefly in its scam-of-the-month column called "Once-Over." These solar water heaters, however, are taken quite seriously, and it is suggested that well-designed and constructed ones—that is, ones that work—would be a good idea. One thing that this magazine is normally distinguished for is its ruthless rejection of the phrase "it might have been." Here, however, it goes the last mile for solar power. Indeed, the article was suffused with favoritism from the very start. It was not intended to be a serious test of solar hot-water heaters against *Consumer Reports*'s normal standards. This we know because we are told that the magazine did not intend to make specific buying recommendations. Had it done so, it is hard to see how it could have avoided rating all five heaters "not acceptable," a conclusion that would have made news headlines.

The point is not that *Consumer Reports* is corrupt. No similarly "progressive" journal has anything like an equivalent record of maintaining its intellectual integrity. (The magazine has published reports on fast-food chains showing that their meals are good nutritional value, and it has exposed much, if not all, the fraud in "natural foods.") But solar energy is just now so sacred a cow as to lead *Consumer Reports* into errors not as to the words, or even as to the tune as a whole, but certainly as to the key.

The most impressive promise of direct solar energy is the conversion of sunlight to electricity through photovoltaic cells. The most obvious immediate problem in this technology, Commoner notes, is its extraordinary cost. Currently a cell capable of generating a peak watt* of electricity costs in the neighborhood of $6.00. That is, to provide enough electricity to operate an average color television set at high noon requires $600 merely for the cells. The mounting is extra. So are additional cells to produce peak output under less than peak conditions and storage devices to allow the operation of the set at night.

A typical house with a maximum demand of 15 kilowatts would require nearly $100,000 just for the cells. Commoner does not estimate the cost of mounting the cells or of storage, but we can note that currently suitable batteries for the purpose cost about forty cents a watt/hour, so that the typical house would require $6,000 worth, which would need to be replaced every five years or so.

Commoner is aware that the capital cost of central power generation is between $7,500 and $15,000 for a house that would require upwards of $100,000 for all-solar generation.† But he has a glittering scheme to bring these costs down to more reasonable levels. There has been a Federal Energy Agency (FEA) proposal to require the Department of Defense to purchase, over five years, a total of $440 million worth of solar cells to replace some of the military's small generators.[7] By the end of the five years, according to the FEA study, the cost of photovoltaic cells would have plunged to fifty cents a watt. (This, with auxiliaries, would make the capital investment for a 15-kilowatt house perhaps $15,000, at the high range of the central generating plant cost, and still borne by the consumer.)

One would be more impressed by this scenario if one knew that the manufacturers who estimated these costs had taken firm orders at their estimates. But Commoner suggests that the estimates are conservative because they exclude the additional civilian uses that would be facilitated by earlier price

* A peak watt is a watt generated under the most favorable circumstances: at high noon in midsummer on a clear day with the array oriented due south and tilted at the optimum angle to the sun. If any of these conditions is less than perfect—if it is cloudy, or winter, or dusky, or if the array is mounted unsatisfactorily—a given cell will generate very much less than its peak capacity.

† I have updated his figures to reflect lower costs for solar cells since he made his calculations. He does not note that in the case of the central plant, the capital is scraped together by the utility and amortized to the customer through his bill, in contrast to the direct solar system that would presumably be financed by the customer himself.

drops. For example, he says, when the cells cost $1 a peak watt, they will be economical for streetlights:

Such a unit, mounting a 1,000-watt lamp, might include a vertical panel of photovoltaic cells, about 3 feet by 30 feet, facing south. During the day electricity generated by the cells would charge a storage battery housed in the base of the unit; at night the stored power would be fed into the lamp. There is a potential market for about 60 million to 90 million of such lighting units.[8]

Before proceeding to a discussion of the general prospects of photovoltaic generation for residential use, it is worth analyzing the Commoner Patent Streetlight (CPS) for the illumination it sheds on its deviser's technical capabilities and the kind of nonsense that now apparently escapes the sleepless fact-checkers at the *New Yorker,* not to say the editors at a distinguished publishing house.

To begin with, the proposed collector area, approximately 10 square meters, is grossly inadequate. At high noon in midsummer with optimum orientation, the flow of solar energy is 1 kilowatt a square meter. Assuming cells that are 10 percent efficient—an assumption Commoner makes elsewhere—the array would thus generate approximately 1 kilowatt of electricity, just sufficient to light the 1,000-watt streetlight bulb—at high noon in midsummer on a clear day with optimum orientation.

Let us now return to the world of reality. In this world, the normal energy flow is far from 1 kilowatt a square meter. For example, sometimes it rains. And for half the year, the night is longer than the day, and so even if the sun shone at 1 kilowatt a square meter it would be necessary to provide collectors to store more than 1,000 watts an hour over fewer hours. The sad fact is that in really sun-drenched locations, the supply of sun averages about 5 kilowatt-hours a day a square meter; that is, in such a highly insolated climate, the CPS would require a collector area about three times as large as Commoner proposes, even if the collector were mounted at the optimum angle to the sun, which it is not. The situation is much grimmer in the Northeast, where the mean supply of solar radiation runs, in December, about 2 kilowatt-hours a day per square meter. In mid-December, the nights last about fifteen hours.

When one figures in all additional factors ignored by Commoner—insolation less than the maximum, the length of days, and the inefficient vertical orientation of the collector—the true collector area needed approximates 1,000 square feet. Thus, at the 3-foot width Commoner recommends, a collector about 300 feet high would be required to reliably light a 1,000-watt bulb! Even at a width of 6 feet, the CPS light pole would be fifteen stories high. Such a device would certainly need substantial guy wires, which would presumably be anchored in front lawns and in the streets, or, as seems likely, in the basements of houses via living-room floors.

Moreover, no trees could be allowed to cast shade on such collectors; nor could tall buildings, which would limit the use of such units in urban areas, where many streetlights live. Indeed, the collectors themselves would cast shadows on living space, and depending on the orientation of the street in question, upon one another, requiring that streetlights be scattered farther apart than customary. Although some people have argued that solar energy is more flexible than other kinds, this wider spacing cannot be compensated for by increasing the size of the bulb; that would set up a merciless escalation of bulb size, collector size, and spacing distance. The visual quality of the CPS, whatever its economic problems, is a hideous one, a bizarre regression to the days when utility poles carrying hundreds of lines blotted out the urban skyscape. One wonders what on earth Commoner can have been thinking of.

One wonders this especially when one considers the economics of the CPS. The collector would require cells costing, on Commoner's own price figures, about $5000. The storage problem is something else again. At present prices, simply storing the 15 kilowatts necessary to see the streetlight through a winter night would require batteries costing another $6,000—every five years—and occupying a great deal of sidewalk space. But that would work only on the assumption that it is always possible to store up a night's electricity during the preceding day. The cold fact is that there are days when the collector—designed to work at the mean December insolation, itself higher than the worst case for the month—will be unable to gather enough electricity to last the night; moreover, nothing prevents there being a number of these days in a row.

What one needs, obviously, is enough superfluous storage capacity to hoard electricity from summer for expenditure in winter. And all that will require is many thousands of dollars more and a Chinese wall of batteries running between light poles. This way lies even greater madness than that to which the uncomplicated proposal beckons us.*

But suppose we see what it would cost to build such a streetlight without worrying about it: $13,500 in electronics and let us say—very, very conservatively—another $12,500† for erecting the pole and installing the components.

---

* A more rational proposal would suggest connecting the streetlight to a central power source for such occasions. The supply of such sporadic peaking power would be extraordinarily expensive, but perhaps cheaper than the alternative storage batteries. But Commoner explicitly counts the cost savings made by not having to pay for cables connecting the lights to the electric company.

† In the summer of 1979, Boston flagpole companies were quoting prices of $7500 for seventy-eight-foot flagpoles (the maximum height available).

That is $26,000 an installed kilowatt of demand, and much the highest such figure I have ever seen. As described even by their enemies, breeder reactors cost about a fifth as much. On any reasonable assumptions about interest charges, inflation, and the price of electricity, the CPS could never recover its capital cost before needing to be replaced. Indeed, on the most modest assumptions about storage costs, the amortization of these alone would yearly exceed the value of electricity saved.

To look at it another way, the maximum "market" suggested by Commoner is 90 million streetlights. At $26,000 a shot, that is over $2 trillion. And that is the good news, for it assumes a tenfold reduction in the current price of photovoltaic cells. In short, the CPS is a piece of folly from beginning to end. It is not merely that the nuts and bolts do not fit when looked at closely; the CPS is conceptually foolish, for it matches a demand at its highest—during the long winter nights—to a supply at its lowest—during the short and cloudy days. There is thus a certain irony in Commoner's repeated assertions that solar energy allows us to attain elegant fits between the type of demand and the type of supply.

Much of Commoner's book is concerned not with direct solar devices of the sort I have just been discussing but with indirect methods of converting solar energy on a regularly renewable schedule. Such methods are hardly new to the earth: We have been burning wood on it for a very long time. Whether or not learning to call it "biomass" represents real progress I cannot say. Of the newer sources of such energy, "gasohol" is the one to have reached commercialization first, and the only one that the average citizen might now run into on the street. Although I am concerned to prick the gasohol bubble, there is nothing wrong with the substance itself.

It is often pointed out that all gasoline in Brazil is now gasohol, at 10 percent alcohol.* Brazil's energy policy once called for this proportion eventually to rise to 20 percent. Moreover, Brazil has been planning toward conversion to pure alcohol, and had encouraged Volkswagen of Brazil to produce and sell suitable cars. Brazil's forward-looking policy is often raised as one for the United States to emulate. The conventional answer to this is that we cannot emulate Brazil's low population density (half of this country's, which is itself among the lowest in the developed world) nor Brazil's habit of maintaining a negative balance of trade in food. The fact is that in the United States gasohol competes with food for land, a fact that will be reflected in bread and meat prices just as soon as gasohol becomes popular enough to take off. But in late 1981, Brazil was reported to be reconsidering its commitment to alcohol. As a result of the policy shift, alcohol was becoming

---

* This, I am informed by Petr Beckmann, was also the case before the war in Czechoslovakia. The mix was mandated by the potato lobby, which knew a good thing when it saw it.

difficult to get, and a consequent shift back to petroleum-fueled cars was creating very serious problems for Volkswagen.[9] In late 1981, a number of gasohol producers, led by Texaco, had withdrawn from the market, and it was increasingly hard to find.

The fad for gasohol epitomizes a key fact about alternative energy sources: Even if practical in small doses, especially with substantial tax subsidies, they cannot be scaled up to provide a major source of energy. Thus there is no reason why a farmer cannot divert part of his acreage into the production of alcohol. Mixed with gasoline, it may well be a competitive fuel, especially at the bogus price that results if the state decides to forgive the fuel tax.

The greatest problem with alcohol production has traditionally been its negative energy balance: It takes more—or, if one is optimistic, nearly as much—energy to produce it as it yields in gasoline equivalent.

Commoner dismisses this traditional wisdom of the gasohol skeptics by proposing a major rearrangement of agriculture he has devised in company with four colleagues at Washington University's Center for the Biology of Natural Systems:

Recent investigation . . . has produced what looks like a conjurer's trick: the same acreage that yields grain and hay with a total energy content of 7 quads per year, which is now totally converted into livestock, can instead be made to produce the same amount of livestock plus 8 quads of solar fuel. . . . The present acreage . . . expanded by 15% to include idle land, would be used to plant a rotation of corn, sugar beets, and hay. Most of the corn would be fermented to produce alcohol, and the residue fed to the livestock, together with some hay. . . . This arrangement would yield 5 quads of alcohol . . . the livestock manure and part of the hay would be used to produce methane, yielding about 3 quads. . . .[10]

This scheme has more than just the appearance of a conjurer's trick, for it begins by coolly equating "the same acreage" with the same acreage plus 15 percent. But it would be unfair to cavil were this the only difficulty with the proposal. As it appears in a paper issued by Commoner's research center, it looks very impressive; and it is impressive, as a testimonial to what one can accomplish if one leaves out one or two major variables.

Commoner is quite persuasive in demonstrating that there is enough land to produce the energy yields he cites by the methods he uses. Although he does not adduce any evidence for his estimate that the total capital investment would be on the order of $70 billion, he demonstrates, again fairly persuasively, that the ethanol and methane produced would displace imported oil and gas with a value adequate to pay off the investment fairly quickly. He also adduces evidence that gasohol is an adequate, not to say desirable, automobile fuel. So where is the problem?

For one, he ignores the energy costs of producing equipment for the ethanol distilleries and the methane digesters. In the case of the ethanol, he is talking about a new industry, none of which is now in place, capable of producing 50 billion gallons of alcohol a year. Such an industry will require considerable steel, and steel takes considerable energy to produce. Commoner's examples of the fledgling alcohol industry often use surplus machinery: One of his distillers adapted a gasoline tank from a closed gas station. Commoner appears to believe that closed gas stations will be a significant source of pot stills: He notes that "since Texaco is selling its dealerships, numerous underground tanks in this size range are presently available." (He appears to believe that a dealership sold by Texaco will never again sell gas. The truth is that most will, and many may still sell Texaco gas.) In any event, castoff materials will supply only a tiny fraction of the machinery needed for Commoner's purpose. Moreover, this scheme—like most of the grand solar schemes now being bruited—involves the premature replacement of a substantial proportion of American refining capacity. One cannot do this sort of thing and get away scot-free: Someone is going to pay for it, and it is likely to be the taxpayers.

Commoner also ignores the problem of distribution networks, which will have to be relocated and expanded to accommodate an exceedingly decentralized alcohol industry. (If the alcohol production envisioned in the proposal is carried on at fewer centralized distilleries, it will then be necessary to move the raw materials from farm to distillery by a new and expanded transportation system based on trucks; and trucks, as Commoner ought to know, use oil.) It is clear that this scheme omits major categories of fiscal and energy expenditure necessary to make it go.

But the variable most spectacularly missing from Commoner's calculation is just the one we might most expect him to be most careful about: people. For there is no calculation—not in Commoner's proposal or in either of his two energy books—of the labor needed to operate Commoner's solar proposals. First of all, the rotation of crops needed to produce the feedstocks will obviously require farmers to work a substantially longer part of the year. Furthermore, all those alcohol distilleries and methane digesters are not going to be self-operating. And when farmers are busy growing extra crops they will have little spare time to be factory workers. (The pilot projects mentioned by Commoner typically involve 10 percent of the production his proposal would exact from the average farm.) Doubtless there will be unemployed refinery workers who might be persuaded to move to the farm and retrain as distillers. But Commoner's proposal remains, in employment terms, a chancy one that depends on reversing this century's trends in farm employment.

Commoner's difficulty of seeing agriculture as carried on by real people is not limited to *The Politics of Energy.* In an earlier book[11] he argued that agriculture was once thermodynamically very efficient, depending almost entirely on the sun and requiring little or no external energy. Nowadays, however, farmers have replaced the horse with the tractor—some of them equipped with air-conditioned cabs—and rather than working in the fields from early spring to late fall now plant one short-lived crop. In short, Commoner's grand proposal is the sort of thing that gives theorizing a bad name. The theorizing is not made more reputable by Commoner's use of the term "competitive." He and his associates claim that various tax subsidies (actual state and prospective federal)* make gasohol competitive with this or that grade of gasoline. Gasohol could of course be made free by a federal tax credit equaling the price paid for it. Commoner's writings suggest strongly that he is among those who think there *ought* to be a free lunch, but should it be necessary at this late date to remind him that there is not? On his principle, any device, no matter how inefficient, no matter how noncompetitive, could be made competitive merely by a government decision to yield up part of the tribute normally exacted for its use.†

But if the CPS is a folly, and if gasohol has only a limited place in our future, there is no doubt that under certain conditions one can, or will be able to in the future, provide a certain proportion of residential energy through solar collectors mounted on the roof. It is worthwhile to consider the problems raised by this sort of solar energy even if it is economically plausible—the problems, as it were, of solar success.

First of all, contrary to popular belief, direct solar power generates a great deal of waste—not in the production of power, but in the production of energy sources. A 1,000 megawatt solar plant, Petr Beckmann has noted, needs about 1,000 times more materials than a fossil-fired plant of the same capacity.[12] For example, 35,000 tons of aluminum, 2 million tons of concrete, 600,000 tons of steel, and 75,000 tons of glass would be needed in such a solar plant.

These materials require massive energy inputs for production: The amounts above would total nearly 4 trillion BTU. (That equals about 600,000 barrels of oil, or about 7 percent of one day's imports.) These would all be gotten from sources other than direct solar and would all entail waste products in

---

* The federal tax subsidy proposed equals $16.80 a barrel of ethanol, a subsidy about half the current price of OPEC oil.

† Subsidy is also a key to the solar enthusiasm of Stobaugh and Yergin's *Energy Future,* which is, to do it justice, much more restrained (25 percent of all energy from solar by 2000) than Commoner's works. Their solar chapter decries the inadequate federal tax credit and points approvingly to the 55 percent California credit. One wonders how solar proponents would respond to a claim by nuclear advocates that nuclear power required a direct tax subsidy to each utility equal to 55 percent of the capital cost of every reactor built.

the generating process. Moreover, the industrial processes involved here would generate their own wastes. Commoner, along with many other direct solar enthusiasts, decries large central solar plants, but if 1,000 MW were to be generated by many small residential units, the waste would be worse, as Beckmann points out.

There is, next, another irony in analyzing photovoltaic electricity according to two criteria much used to criticize nuclear power: availability factor and capacity factor. Photovoltaic generators are much the least efficient ways to utilize capital investment to generate electricity. Solar generators are not available after the sun has gone down and so have an availability factor much lower than any type of thermal power plant. Moreover, the weather and the time of day insure that a solar generator, even when the sun is up, generates much less than its rated capacity. Its capacity factor is, accordingly, very much lower than that of a thermal power plant. In an area of maximum isolation, the capacity factor will be about 20 percent. If we were to analyze such a solar generator in the terms customarily applied to nuclear plants, we would point out that a massive capital investment lies unutilized or half utilized much of the time. We might even note that underutilization is an inherent part of the technology and can never be improved by any sort of technological breakthrough short of a photovoltaic cell that generates electricity as a response to darkness—one of the few breakthroughs that can confidently be described as impossible.

Lying just below the surface in most discussions of alternative energy are proposals for reshaping the way we live by controlling the type and amount of energy available to us. Although most direct solar enthusiasts deny that their chosen path will have any such effects, sometimes the mask drops, as when Commoner proposes to acquire some of the vast amounts of steel and glass needed for direct solar conversion by limiting the size and number of cars on the road.

It is indeed worth considering the sorts of constraints implicit in direct solar energy.* One of these affects architecture: At minimum, each house

* One must exempt from the catalogue that follows all proposals to generate electricity from the sun in central locations. The most advanced of these involve the use of the sun to boil water in thermal power plants, which produce electricity that can be utilized in the existing energy system. (A large number of mirrors focus the sun's rays on a boiler mounted on a tower.) Commoner disapproves of such power stations on the grounds that they are centralized, and expensive because there is no economy of scale in the acquisition of solar energy. Hence, he says, because transmission lines are needed, centralized plants cost more than decentralized residential ones. Although if such a solar plant replaced an obsolete, conventional one it would require no new transmission investment, one is tempted to agree with him on the issue itself, for the pilot plant now under construction in California will cost almost as much per peak kilowatt as photovoltaics do now, and has perhaps less prospect of a drastic reduction in price. A more plausible central power project involves replacing the steam supply system of an existing generator with a solar one, making use of existing generation and distribution systems. Commoner

will have to be oriented with its major roof area facing south. It will not matter what is dictated by the lay of the land or available scenery, because these considerations must be subordinated to the simple problem of getting energy. And so ultimately will construction on neighboring lots. The sun comes into North America at a fairly low angle, and if the right of one householder to an all-solar home is to be preserved, his neighbors to the south will not be able to build very high next to him, and indeed their resort to trees may be sharply limited, whether they wish to go solar or not. It is frequently suggested that the truly efficient solar house will have windows only on the south wall, a further restraint on the aesthetic exploitation of a site and on interior design.

This is not a purely hypothetical problem: Since 1980, all houses in San Diego County, California, with a guaranteed access to the sun have had to be built with solar water heating. That is, the architecture of every new home in San Diego County is now to some extent mandated by a governmental commitment to solar energy. Because the collector area needed for a hot-water system is not gigantic, the immediate constraint will not be large. But one wonders how soon similar ordinances will cover not only water but space heating. The eventual possibility for constraint is immense. Some solar projectors have suggested, and at least one has actually built, solar houses underground! Whether we come to this, the higher our use of direct solar energy for homes, the greater the constraint on architecture.

Photovoltaic is far more constraining than water and space heating, not only because it requires more roof area, but because it is important that no part of a photovoltaic collector's area fall into the shade during any part of the day.* Thus, in a photovoltaic economy, trees shading houses will be a remembered luxury from the past. Nor are such constraints, which would fall on householders comparatively unequally as a function of their taste in architecture, be the only ones. Solar collectors need to be kept clean. In the Southwest, this may mean no more than sweeping the dust off several times a year. In the Northeast, it might mean shoveling snow off the collector six times a winter. It need hardly be pointed out that massive utilization of such panels anywhere in snowbelt area would result in significant increases in death by heart attack and by falling.

---

does not seem to be aware of such conversion schemes, one of which is now under way in the Southwest. He also disapproves of satellites in space beaming immense amounts of energy toward earth, and it is not difficult to agree with him. But the book is not yet closed on ocean thermal-energy conversion plants, which utilize the temperature difference between the ocean's surface and the depths to generate electricity. The most serious objection is that the United States has fairly few locations suitable for the technology.

* A portion of the cells in every array is wired in series, and if some members of the series are deprived of light, their internal resistance will rise sharply and they will constitute a serious drain on the efficiency of the rest.

Consider a small disaster scenario: A six-inch snowstorm hits the greater Boston area. Every solar collector in the four-million-person metropolitan area is knocked out simultaneously. Even if these solar collectors supplied merely a portion of hot water and space heat, the resulting spike in demand would almost certainly trigger a massive outage in the New England Power Pool. If, additionally, these collectors were substantial generators of electric power, a blackout over a much wider area would be certain. Even if somehow a massive blackout were to be averted, thousands of old people would find themselves deprived of adequate heat and hot water; I cannot estimate how many of them would die of exposure before their collectors were cleared, but the number would certainly not be zero.

In short, proposals for a transition to solar energy are at best proposals to reverse thousands of years of development by which man, through the division of labor, has made the acquisition of energy increasingly the province of fewer and fewer increasingly well-paid specialists. This is what Commoner and Lovins are decrying when they call for the decentralization of energy sources. A century ago the average American used substantially less energy than he does now, but provided much more of it through his own efforts. Now that anyone can have access to as much energy as he can pay for by pushing the right button, it was probably predictable that some intellectuals would want to play at chopping wood and shoveling the snow off their solar collectors. But we should not expect that real people, as it were, are going to enjoy emulating the lives of eighteenth-century farmers. At worst, as is evident in the proposals for underground houses, the more troglodytic solar advocates propose to take us back well before the eighteenth century.

The other half of Commoner's fossil-fuel replacement program is methane, which is to be generated in immense quantities—twenty quads, which approximates current production of natural gas—by a wide variety of facilities from a wide variety of feedstocks and piped through the land through an expanded version of the present-day natural gas distribution system. Methane is unique as the one primary fuel that exists at present as fossil fuel—natural gas is slightly impure methane—and can also be produced as a solar fuel.

Commoner proposes to exploit methane largely through the cogenerator. Like many others, this buzzword describes a good idea that is being rapidly done to death. Cogeneration is made practical by a simple fact about heat engines. They must always waste a large proportion—typically between 60 and 70 percent—of the energy potential in their fuel as heat. This is why cars have radiators. A cogenerator is a device that uses a heat engine—which may be one of many types, including steam engines and the full range of internal combustion engines—to turn an electric generator, and then uses the waste heat, contained either in the exhaust of a steam engine or the coolant of an internal combustion one, for some other purpose. Typically industrial cogenerators use the waste heat for chemical and physical processes, and residential ones for heating of a number of houses ("district heating"). This last arrangement is used in Europe and is especially widespread in Sweden.

Commoner suggests that cogeneration be brought down to the level of the individual house, and cites a small cogenerator devised by FIAT, based on its standard four-cylinder automobile engine, that would cost $6000 and while running on methane generate 15 kilowatts of electricity for an average home, while providing it with an unspecified proportion of its heat, assuming that it were already equipped with suitable hot-water radiators.

This device would doubtless be useful for the colder parts of the undeveloped world, where a noisy source of electricity and heat subject to fairly frequent down times for unscheduled repair and for scheduled major maintenance would certainly be better than no electricity or heat at all. But it must be understood that the future Commoner holds out for us is one in which our heat and electricity supply will be no more reliable than our car engines.

Commoner proposes that the production of methane from solar sources be gradually increased and mixed in the pipelines with natural gas from wells. He also suggests that certain industries, such as canneries, could be net producers of methane at some times in the year (the height of the canning season) and net consumers the rest. And he says that hydrogen produced by solar means, as from photovoltaic electricity, could be mixed with the methane in substantial quantities and shipped through the same pipeline.

The most obvious operating difficulty of this scheme is the necessity for careful separation of the hydrogen from the methane at the distributing end of the pipeline, and of constantly having to adjust burners to deal with the fluctuating methane/natural gas mix, a problem that would continue until— by Commoner's schedule—well into the next century, when the production of natural gas would finally be phased out.

But these are trivial problems compared to the capital costs implicit in building a massive new energy industry to replace existing natural gas wells. Commoner's book is innocent of any calculation whatever of these costs, which are, by the way, in addition to those implicit in another of his requirements, the near doubling of present-day natural gas production. By his own calculations, existing supplies of "conventional"—a euphemism for "easily and cheaply exploited"—natural gas will not be adequate to see us through the solar transition. We must, accordingly, turn to "unconventional"—a complementary euphemism for "hard to get and expensive"—sources of natural gas. And we must expect that the gas industry will be willing to gear up to produce unconventional natural gas on the clear understanding that just as soon as we can produce enough methane to replace it, bang! goes the market.

One suspects that Commoner does not really think capitalists are as dumb as all that but hopes that the taxpayers are. He ends *The Politics of Energy* by surveying the political problems inhering in the grand transition. One could summarize his argument by saying that solar energy will be good for the Peepul and less good for the bosses, except those who run energy-intensive businesses.

Commoner's discussion begins with one of those examples of naiveté and self-contradiction with which his work abounds. We have been told, he says, that we are running out of oil and natural gas, but this is not so, for Mexico's newly discovered reserves exceed those of Saudi Arabia and we have immense amounts of "unconventional" natural gas. Well, let us assume that the natural gas can be recovered at economical rates. Oil, whatever its source, is just the sort of fuel that Commoner has been telling us we can no longer afford. There is no reason why Mexico should sell the United States oil except at the world price and no prospect that it will. To propose that we rely on Mexican oil is to propose something Commoner elsewhere treats as intolerable, and, back in the real world, to guarantee an exacerbation of the sort of problems we now have with OPEC.

Commoner's main concern here is how we can dispose of the present energy-supply companies once we have erected their replacements. For the electric companies the solution is simple: Competition from photovoltaic electricity will drive them into the ground financially, and we will nationalize them in order to pick up the still useful distribution systems they control. There is no estimate of the total cost—to taxpayers and shareholders—who together will have to pick it up.

For unspecified reasons, Commoner is unwilling to nationalize the oil companies. They will be offered the opportunity to become public utilities. Classic doctrine is of course that the public utility is a form of organization suited to business operations best carried on by one company in an area, that is, the so-called natural monopolies. The inconvenience of having to subscribe to several phone companies is something that comparatively few Americans now remember, but it was once very real; occasionally two electric companies compete in one area, as in Portland, Oregon, but only at the cost of doubling the number of utility poles and lines.

There are no such considerations to make oil a natural monopoly. And that is just why there are so many oil companies. There are many. It is fashionable these days to argue that they constitute a *de facto* monopoly, or cartel. It is surprising that the rise of a genuine cartel has not reminded us of the facts about the oil companies. For before the cartelization of imported oil prices by OPEC, the real price of gasoline in this country had declined steadily for half a century. This is not the sort of price pattern one normally associates with monopolies, *de jure* or *de facto*. Commoner appears to suspect something a little odd in the idea of public-utility oil companies, for he tells us that many of them are run by the kind of entrepreneurs who would rather make extortionate profits while running some risk than have a comfortable life making a profit with a ceiling as well as a floor. Such managers, he assumes, will probably want to take their ill-gotten corporate gains into other industries. He believes that their operations might be picked up cheap on the auction block. Presumably they are to be bankrupted without the benefits even of nationalization. As for their workers, well, let them distill alcohol in Iowa.

In his analysis of the wisdom of nationalizing the electric companies, Commoner's discussion of the railroads is worth a closer look, because it suggests the extreme shallowness of his economic and technical analysis. The railroads, he argues, ought to be electrified and expanded greatly at taxpayer expense so that they can carry a great many more passengers and thus reduce our need for gasoline. He cites the example of Europe, where the railways carry many more passengers than they do here, and operate at a loss as nationalized industries, rather like the post office, only competent. He has been making the same argument for nearly five years now and does not seem to have tumbled to the fact that the airplane is a less effective competitor with the railroad in densely packed Europe, which is essentially one metropolitan area whose railroads in fact are the world's best rapid transit system. The European railroads benefit from an immensely more favorable passenger density. However, they are losing passengers yearly even in the face of generally superb service.

It is also a fact that our present train system has more trains now than passengers who want to ride. Even if we returned to the golden age of the U.S. railroads, or even surpassed it, the evidence is that not many people would ride the trains. Commoner was harsh on the Carter administration's plans to cut back on Amtrak mileage, but the even harsher fact is that most of the trains in question were barely used. The drastic cuts proposed by the Reagan administration and rejected in 1981 by Congress would have wasted many millions in recent capital expenditures on new trains for the western lines. But even the service to be ended by these proposed cuts was on the whole sparsely patronized. Increasing the number of barely used trains would not help the energy crisis; concentrating funds on the lines people actually want to use—such as the Boswash Corridor—would.

Commoner would solve most of the problems inherent in the grand transition by something called "social governance." It is not clear what this is a euphemism for, although by telling us that because we survived Joe McCarthy and Watergate we can probably survive social governance, Commoner does not make it look especially appetizing. There is nothing vague, however, about another key phrase. In his last sentence Commoner calls for us to adopt as a major national goal something called "economic democracy." Although he does not define this term here, he does not need to, for he has already done so in *The Poverty of Power*. In that book, "economic democracy" is explicitly defined as the economic system of such states as China and the U.S.S.R., where, as is well known, economic decisions are all made by individuals and popularly elected assemblies.

It is as a manifesto for Commoner's Citizens' Party—of which he was the presidential candidate in the 1980 election—that *The Politics of Energy* makes the most sense. It is very difficult to see it as a popularization of scientific thought in the honorable tradition begun by the elder Huxley and splendidly continued in our time by such various writers as Isaac Asimov and Lewis Thomas. Commoner probably makes sense best not as a scientist but as a politician. And on that issue, the voice of the people has been heard.

# 5

# Warriors Against the Atom: The Troops

THE ROOTS of the antinuclear movement lie in the civil rights struggles of the late 1950s and early 1960s. But however superficially similar, the two movements are strikingly different. Although a side-by-side comparison would make this quite clear, the contrast is even more stark if we see how we got to the one from the other. It is worth tracing the descent of the antinuclear movement from the civil rights through the anti-Vietnam movements, for the process is exemplary of the degeneracy of mass movements. ("Mass movement" is not really a very accurate term; I use it in the loose sense of a political movement with many thousands of members. The term should not be taken to suggest that antinuclear sentiment has captured a majority, or even a significant minority, of the American people.)

One of the most striking things about the civil rights movement was its devotion to legality. As Martin Luther King, Jr., often pointed out, he and those he led were concerned to test laws of dubious constitutionality through the instrument of the law itself. The United States had, as long ago as the end of the Civil War, committed itself to the proposition that all citizens should be equal before the law. Accordingly the civil rights movement worked to effect a long-delayed implementation of a commitment already enshrined as national policy.

At the time the civil rights movement triumphed in the judicial invalidation of discriminatory statutes and the passage of federal legislation enforcing constitutional guarantees, the Vietnam war presented itself as an issue. The

94

civil rights leadership increasingly joined in opposing the war; followers who had come to work against racial discrimination willingly stayed to work against the war. The Movement—dedicated to the principle of change rather than to one particular change with deep and wide national support—was coming to birth.

Although there was close to a 100 percent overlap in the personnel, both organizational and individual, in the two movements, they were philosophically distinct and even opposed. There was little question but that the Vietnam war was constitutional. Those who opposed it did so on the grounds that it was an unwise, even immoral, use of authority that the government nevertheless certainly possessed. Moreover, for most of the Vietnam war, public opinion polls showed a majority in favor of prosecuting the war. Those who opposed it did so as a clear minority seeking, depending on individual stances, to convert or coerce the majority.

The civil rights movement had proceeded almost entirely over legal paths, violating laws thought to be unconstitutional rather than merely ill-advised, always on the expectation that the laws would ultimately be struck down, and with determination to show respect for the law as a principle by accepting the ultimate legal consequences of disobeying particular laws. By contrast, the anti-Vietnam movement had no legal base and increasingly turned to the use of force and, indeed, on its fringe, savage violence. It thus adopted tactics that had typified not the civil rights movement but rather its more extreme opponents.

A final contrast lay in the fact that although the civil rights movement could fairly have been said to have triumphed in the early 1960s, one could hardly have said then or now that it had achieved all that its followers had hoped for. The most optimistic surveyor of the scene in 1967—or, indeed, in 1980—could hardly argue that black people had received full freedom of opportunity. The legal structures were in place, but the work was still to be completed.

But when at length "peace" came to Vietnam in the shape of American withdrawal and defeat, the *raison d'être* of the movement opposing the war was gone. Some members of the movement doubtless gratefully returned to the quotidian life that had fulfilled them before the rise of activism and from which they had turned out of duty. These mostly belonged to that part of humanity to whom politics is not a pleasure but an obligation that may be very onerous. Others, however, had perhaps never enjoyed themselves so much as in the years between 1968 and 1973. Lives that may have lacked meaning had, for a space, taken on an heroic dimension. Many did not feel the let-down immediately, for Watergate provided a brief and diverting coda to the 1960s.

In the fall of 1974 the campuses first began to see an expressed nostalgia for the good old days of the late 1960s. Students were said to be apathetic, by which was meant that they were primarily concerned with their studies and no longer turned out for rallies or could be mobilized to disrupt the work of the universities. This state of affairs was, extraordinarily, often described as a "malaise" by activists who lamented a golden age that had passed.

These were the amateurs, but there were also professional anti-Vietnam organizations with paid staffs who found themselves facing unemployment when the last mopping-up was completed. This unemployed general staff—and its unemployed troops—were soon to make common cause with another movement that had grown up as a younger sibling of the antiwar phenomenon, the environmentalist movement.

This is not the place to trace the history of that movement, or to separate out the genuine concern for environmental problems from the element of concern about improving the class privileges of the wealthy. The pioneers in this movement sometimes held views that would seem rather strange today: In the 1960s some environmentalist groups were pro-nuclear because they correctly saw nuclear energy as the most benign of all major energy sources.

But in a few years there arose what Petr Beckmann has called "sham-environmentalism," a doctrine in which policies barely supportable on any rational basis were urged on the fuzzy ground that they were "good for the environment." Soon the antinuclear movement as we know it coalesced— a loose alliance among activists (ranging from symbolic protesters to the violent) and "environmentalists" operating largely through the law's delays.

As will I hope become clear, the motivations of the antinuclear movement as a whole are exceedingly diverse and sometimes within groups and individuals exceedingly complex. This is probably because the movement is different from the political mass movements of the past few centuries.

It is common to call nuclear opponents Luddites, after those who opposed—with violence—the introduction of powered looms into nineteenth-century England, but this does an injustice to Ned Ludd and his followers. After all, the Luddites were pursuing their self-interest, for the new machinery they attacked did in fact threaten their livelihood. Although from a Marxist-Leninist point of view it is possible to criticize them for foolishly trying to stop—almost literally—the locomotive of history, they certainly, in the short term, recognized the enemy and presented a direct and lucid antithesis to the thesis of industrialization.

Or consider the antinuclear movement in light of another nineteenth-century English political movement, the Chartists. The Chartists were nothing if not explicit in what they wanted, for they spelled it out in their Charter.

What they wanted, moreover, lay in the power of Parliament to grant them—such things as universal male suffrage and regularly elected parliaments. And, finally, whether or not they should have gotten what they wanted was mired down in a morass of value judgments and conflicting interests. No one debated the claims of the Chartists as if they were to be validated or disproved "scientifically."

The antinuclear movement is without precedent in trying to make policy through a popular consensus as to certain scientific and technical facts. Only recently has it been thought that the public at large could have an informed opinion—adequate to direct policy—on such a variety of highly specialized technical questions. The last time a great technical innovation was seriously debated by nonspecialists was at the introduction of the railway in the first third of the nineteenth century in England. But then the debate was largely limited to the educated few who appeared at the parliamentary hearings on proposed new railway lines, and the opposition was almost entirely quieted within a decade by the successful and peaceable operation of the allegedly dangerous railways.

To be sure, it is a dangerous idea that great decisions ought to be made only by the experts and that the public should stick to those concerns in which it has competence. To avoid that extreme we have developed representative democracy. Ultimately, the decision whether or not to proceed with nuclear power must be taken, in all those democracies where the issue is now being addressed, by the people, through their representatives. And indeed the broad outlines of the technical issues are not beyond the intelligent and concerned citizen. The problem now facing us is that the so-called technical debate is being carried on at a high level of incompetence and mendacity and is aided by a credulous press.

The inactive opponents of nuclear power are those who are troubled by what they read in the newspapers but don't worry about it full time and go on with their lives anyhow. They represent all categories of political opinion, although they are certainly more common left of center. (The Right is the only political tendency where there is a substantial body of pro-nuclear lay opinion.) The active opponents, with perhaps one major exception, are all clearly on the left wing. (The possible exception is the Libertarian Party, whose antinuclear sentiments seem indistinguishable from those of the Left. Whether the Libertarians themselves belong on the left or right is a quagmire I do not propose to enter.)

But although almost all nuclear opponents are leftists, not all leftists are nuclear opponents. In the United States many, but not all, trade-union leaders are pro-nuclear, and that bizarre organization known as the U.S. Labor Party (as well as its Canadian Branch, the North American Labor Party) is frenetically, not to say insanely, devoted to fusion power. The proper location of this party on the political spectrum is nearly as problematical as that of the Libertarians. In general, then, in the United States one normally expects that anyone whose political self-characterization is on the Left will, in some degree, be opposed to nuclear energy. (In Europe, on the other hand, the Social Democrats are, except for their own left-most factions, pro-nuclear.) And for many this opposition will be active and sometimes all-consuming, a phenomenon most marked among students.

Left-wing opposition to nuclear energy is opportunist. There is nothing in any variety of Marxist ideology to lead one to oppose nuclear energy. To the contrary: Marxists have historically been much in love with technological innovations, especially those that deal with large amounts of power. And as a matter of plain fact no ideological gulf separates users of nuclear energy from nonusers. Indeed, the states of the so-called "socialist" world are almost without exception more pro-nuclear than the states of the rest of the world. The Soviet Union has an active policy of developing nuclear power and of exporting it to Finland and to its client states. The director of the Soviet nuclear program has recently suggested that the end of the century will see the capitalist world wracked by energy wars while the socialist world, basking in the warmth of a wisely adopted nuclear option, looks on in comfortable dismay. China has recently been shopping for reactor technology in France and the United Kingdom. When left-wing antinuclear activists in the West are taxed with these facts, they often claim that socialist states can assure safety to a degree not possible under the primitive conditions of a capitalist economy, a claim reminiscent of those made in the 1930s that Soviet agriculture produced crop yields unheard-of under capitalism. It is also an extremely dubious claim, given the fact that until recently Soviet reactors lacked both emergency cooling systems and secondary containments.

The year 1980 saw the rise of serious antinuclear politicians in the United States. This phenomenon had two immediate causes, neither having much to do with politics except in the most narrow and technical sense. The first is that there are some votes to be gotten and few to be lost by taking an antinuclear stance. (There are, in contrast, few to be gained by a pronuclear stance, except locally where nuclear industry is a major employer.) The second—and at this stage much the more important—is that an antinuclear politician can now command support from the movement, a little of it in the form of money but much more in the form of volunteer labor. And this is in fact more precious than gold, for it does not come under the federal limits on campaign spending.

It is common to say that the movement against nuclear energy is part of a revolt against technology. Upon close examination this revolt proves to be nonexistent, or at most highly selective. The attitude in question is little more than a reflex against certain portions of modern technology, the process of selection being on the whole rather obscure. This "revolt" first became apparent about a decade ago in the new pastoralism celebrated by Charles A. Reich in *The Greening of America,* a book that is paradigmatic of the confusions within the revolt. Reich, it may be remembered, regarded neon lights as the ugly creation of technology but Dayglo paints—designed to be neon light in a bottle—as the warm and loving creation of the new consciousness. But contemporary "movement" people embrace technology daily: There is in fact no way to revolt against technology for people whose music cannot exist without electronic amplification. Even more so than superficially more electronic "serious" music, rock music is, in its creation as well as in its reproduction, the music of high technology. Even when antinuclear activists plaster their bumpers with stickers reading "Split wood, not atoms," they use technology to transport and display what seems on the surface an antitechnology slogan.

If the movement has actually declared war on technology, it is a "phony war" with no prospect of a Blitzkrieg to follow. This bogus antitechnologism arises among people sated with a diverse plenty who are attacking the machine that supplies them, quite unaware of the relation they have to the machine. It is not for nothing that New England should be a hotbed of nuclear opposition, for New England's reliable nuclear power plants see it through the winter safely while the Ohio Valley shivers.

We must remember that Americans have become accustomed to thinking of power blackouts as the rare exception, a reason to curse not Fate but the electric company. None of us has had the experience of a regular and cyclical deprivation of power. Electricity is something that is always there. This is perhaps the reason why the sun, in the vision of its most enthusiastic supporters, seems rather like a jolly utility company that forgets to send a bill.

It is a fact of contemporary life that the most reliable and economical public services are those most frequently held to be inefficient and expensive. If there is, for example, a telephone system both more reliable and cheaper in real terms than that of the United States and Canada, it has escaped general notice. Yet there are groups of Americans who organize themselves for the single end of harassing what they conceive to be an oppressive telephone company.

The nearer a large corporation is to filling the role of a parent, by providing an essential service reliably and at minimal cost, the more its exertions will be expected as a right and the more likely the public will be to see it only in terms of its failings, real and imagined. A large proportion of the public seems to view the electric utilities as philanthropic organizations who ought to supply, at convenient rates, electricity generated through politically fashionable means, but always electricity, and as much as anyone wants.

Against such a background it is easy to understand why nuclear power should be widely condemned, indeed why it was certain to be. It could have escaped only by being as unreliable and expensive as it is said to be. Then it would be almost as expensive and unreliable as solar power.

Much antinuclear sentiment is founded on the belief that because nuclear hardware is a profitable line, nuclear vendors sell it and nuclear utilities use it even though they know it is dangerous. At a recent public debate on the nuclear issue, the pronuclear speaker noted to his lay audience that it was obviously not easy for them to choose between the two experts addressing them, men who seemed to agree on scarcely anything, even as to the bare facts. But they might, he suggested, rely on common sense. Was it reasonable, he asked, that thousands of people working in the nuclear industries would deliberately sacrifice the futures of their children simply to make money? The answer, he naively assumed, would be a resounding no! but from around him echoed loud and strong a resounding yes! yes! they would! they do!

This demonological view of the other side, although not linked to any one ideology, is of course an intensely political attitude, commoner among extremists than among moderates and much rarer among politicians than their followers. It poses a very serious barrier to the understanding, for it virtually eliminates common sense as a touchstone for evaluating human behavior. It is also a powerful stimulant to paranoia.

The one political attitude that seems most clearly to animate all antinuclear groups is a deeply held elitism. Public opinion polls have shown a majority of the American people to be supportive of further development of nuclear power, the few and not very striking exceptions having occurred just after Three Mile Island. Even these slight majorities against nuclear power have recently reversed themselves. The position of antinuclear organizations seems to be that the American people do not really know what is good for them.

This position, when taken with regard to *legal* attempts to shut down nuclear power, can probably be defended as ultimately democratic in the sense that the laws and the system by which they are administered are both the result of democratic procedure. But when a minority attempts to impose its will on a majority by force, such as by physically occupying a reactor construction site, the rejection of legality and democracy alike is patent.

Many members of the movement seem unaware of the state of public opinion about nuclear energy. Several years ago I was myself taken to task by a relative for my views on the matter, given the fact that "everyone is against nuclear power." I pointed out the truth about public opinion regarding nuclear power but realized at the same time that probably everyone my relative knew was opposed, if mildly and nonviolently, to it. Her circle was composed almost entirely of well-educated nonscientists for whom the undesirability of nuclear power was as obvious as the undesirability of racism or of war. More recently, a writer in a student newspaper declared, "Of course, Three Mile Island convinced just about everyone but a handful of fanatics that nuclear power is terribly dangerous." And again, as contrary as this vision may be to the reality of most Americans, it probably reflects the writer's reality, and it may not occur to him in what an intellectual ghetto he lives.

The more the antinuclear movement fails, the more it falls back on this sort of fantasy. Speaking in the spring of 1980, a few days before a failed attempt to "occupy" the site of a reactor under construction at Seabrook, New Hampshire, a spokesman for one of the organizing groups explained why she and her colleagues were resorting to what she euphemistically called direct action—what others might call force. The plant, she maintained, was opposed by "the people of New England and New Hampshire," who had tried every legal means to abort it. They had used the courts, the legislature, and the ballot. And yet construction went on. How this was possible in the face of the alleged opposition of an entire region, she did not make quite clear; one suspected that the villain was the invincible power of mighty corporations.

The Seabrook case provides a useful context for examining a few of the key political assumptions that animate the antinuclear movement. Political assumptions are illuminating because they do not appeal to expertise. Presumably most Americans know pretty well what sort of democracy they wish to live in and what limits they would put on the power not only of the government and the majority, but also of the minority to bend the majority to its will. These issues, susceptible of resolution by laymen, would remain to be settled even were the technical and scientific debate over nuclear power to be finally resolved one way or the other.

To begin with, it is plain nonsense that the people of New England have opposed the Seabrook plant. Whatever else they are, those people most assuredly are not a legal entity, and so they cannot have acted against the plant as a group. Nor have they any official spokesman, least of all the direct-action antinuclearists. They are accustomed to speak for themselves as individuals. And even the pollsters, who ascertain their views for the benefit of the media, say that they support rather than oppose nuclear power.

Nor have the people of New Hampshire opposed Seabrook, which is authorized by their laws and sustained by their courts. It is true that an assembly of the citizens of the town of Seabrook once voted against the plant, decisively if not overwhelmingly. Had the people of New Hampshire passed a law giving Seabrook residents the last word, that, for me, would have settled matters. But one doubts that the Clamshell Alliance has any principled belief in local sovereignty. Just before the occupation, activists were in court trying to nullify a Seabrook ordinance regulating camping—so much for local opinion!—and in Massachusetts they have opposed the Pilgrim II plant, which has the resounding support of the people of Plymouth.

The fact is that Seabrook, like all nuclear plants, is being built only after the operation of thoroughgoing democratic process. It has been elaborately authorized by state, local, and federal governments. When the activists are unable to argue or legally compel these authorities to give them what they want, they resort to force, on the apparent principle that they must get what they want.

Antinuclear rhetoricians always present themselves as populists fighting against the forces of elitism, a necessary sham under democracy, which is so satisfactory a form of government that even its bitterest enemies must yield it lip service. But the stand of the antinuclear movement on democratic government is quite clear: They are against it when it comes up with the wrong answers. They do not accept the popular will, expressed through the deliberate process of the legislative and judicial branches. They do not even accept it as expressed through referenda. When, as is usually the case, referenda support nuclear power, the movement is quick to explain that the forces of darkness have outspent the forces of light. That is, the poor dumb public has been convinced by a slick advertising campaign.

The movement is composed largely of elitists who are quite convinced that they know better than the people what is good for them. And those antinuclear activists who resort to force (whether overtly violent or not) are willing to impose their will on the majority through that force. They are authoritarians in the grip of a pervasive and dangerous ignorance about basic science and engineering and an equally pervasive and dangerous certainty as to the absolute truth of their own position. They hold to that truth with religious fervor—indeed, a good deal of the antinuclear movement seems to operate not so much as a political phenomenon but as a phenomenon of faith, and is perhaps best explained in those terms.

This is most apparent in the adulation of the sun that increasingly informs antinuclear sentiment. At the May 1979 antinuclear rally in Washington, one got the impression of an open-air service arranged by unusually uncritical sun worshippers who, having never had to face dying of thirst in the desert, saw their deity as unqualifiedly benevolent.

This is hardly the only religious element in antinuclearism. Nonscientists and nonengineers, for example, perceive radiation in a totally different fashion from scientists and engineers. To those who know what radiation is, it is about as clear a manifestation of materiality as there can be, and one of the most precisely, even exquisitely, quantifiable. But to the average humanist, radiation is a great mystery. It cannot be directly perceived, and even if it is realized that radiation can be measured, the units involved are not only unfamiliar but almost impossible to grasp. It can be known only by its works, and these are understood to involve the destruction of human life in large quantity and through horrible means. Radiation is, in short, Evil. It may even be the Evil One himself. For a generation that has ceased to believe in evil as an active force in the world, nuclear radiation seems to be a very convenient substitute, just as the sun now appears a jovial and undemanding deity for those who have lost their faith in more challenging gods.

For such quasi-religious antinuclearism—which animates a large portion of the activists—rational discourse about the benefits and risks of nuclear energy will be largely wasted. And, indeed, it will be difficult to combat the movement if it is seen as political in the traditional sense. The antinuclear movement has in fact been comparatively ineffective as a political force, having mounted campaigns to abolish nuclear power in seven states and failed in each case.

But consider the way in which these campaigns were conducted. The effect of these referenda would have been to stop the development of nuclear power in six of the states and to close the industry down entirely in a seventh. Had this been because nuclear power proved to be incorrigibly incapable of meeting reasonable safety standards, few could have objected to the referenda beyond desiring a more candid explanation of their purpose. But the referenda would have imposed upon nuclear power safety standards that could be met by no other means for generating electricity.

One provision in the 1978 California referendum hypocritically required that all reactor safety systems, including the Emergency Core Cooling System, undergo tests on an operating reactor. That is, it would have been necessary to initiate a loss-of-coolant accident in an operating reactor, an accident the proponents of the referendum tell us is too dangerous ever to risk.

Another section of the California referendum (substantially duplicated in the other states) required that the legislature certify that no radiation from waste escape with harmful effect into the atmosphere or the land. No coal-fired facility could meet an analogous requirement that no sulfur dioxide escape into the atmosphere. Indeed, no coal plant could meet a requirement forbidding it to emit radiation.

In these seven states, 20 percent of the population of the country had a chance to vote on nuclear power. In discussing the rejections of these referenda, Ralph Nader treated them as victories rather than as defeats. And, indeed, far from being cast down by its failures, the antinuclear movement metastasized. The spring of 1977 saw the sudden development of a new direction to the nuclear debate, the birth of a movement dedicated to stopping nuclear power through the tactics of civil disobedience.

By April 1977 the proposed nuclear plant at Seabrook was already in trouble as the result of environmentalist suits and Environmental Protection Agency (EPA) rulings on its cooling system, which was alleged to be harmful to clams;* on April 30 it became the target of a group of activists under the name of the Clamshell Alliance. Several thousand occupied the construction site, and when about 1,400 refused to move along, they were arrested for trespass. These the State of New Hampshire foolishly refused to release before trial on their own recognizance and held at various locations where there doubtless occurred much effective organization of the antinuclear movement before they were finally released.

Judged in the light of the Zeitgeist that has afflicted us for these past fifteen years, nuclear power is the perfect demon. Kick it and you kick large corporations, the government, and technology, all with one blow. Since almost no one yet understands that his welfare depends on nuclear power—even though the welfare of many already does—moral indignation against it comes unusually cheap.

The movement seems insensitive to the consequences of its positions, for if it were to succeed in shutting down nuclear power, one result would be to sacrifice the lives of coal miners—that is, the actual lives of the actual coal miners who are killed over the decades in their thousands—to prevent the hypothetical deaths of hypothetical people from nuclear power. This indifference to the death of people as long as they are proletarians working deep underground is typical of the environmental movement, members of which often oppose all surface mining despite the fact that it exacts a negligible toll in human life as compared to deep mining. Endangered individuals, especially if they are mere humans, appear to be much less worthy of protection than endangered species. The Seabrook reactor may fall victim to the interests of the clam, and the Dickey-Lincoln hydroelectric project in Maine has been stymied in order to save a few specimens of an otherwise extinct plant called the furbish lousewort, which appears to be, not to put too fine a point on it, a noxious weed having nothing to recommend it but its name.

Because we are in the early stages of such environmentalism, none of those now calling the dance are having to pay the piper, and indeed many

---

* The EPA reversed its regional administrator and approved the cooling system, a decision that was unsuccessfully appealed by the Friends of the Clam. In a related action, some of them went to the site and there deposited a quantity of dead fish and clams, who doubtless were glad to die that other fish and clams might live. It was a scene anticipated a century ago by Lewis Carroll: " 'I like the Walrus best,' said Alice, 'because he was a *little* sorry for the poor oysters.' 'He ate more than the Carpenter, though,' said Tweedledee.' "

may be able to escape altogether, leaving the problems they have created to their descendants.

By May 1980 the assault on Seabrook seemed to be winding down. The movement was unable to mobilize sufficient troops to accomplish either of its announced goals, the occupation or blockade of the construction site. It did not even muster enough force to require the mass arrests that would have been a considerable consolation. As the demonstration sputtered to a close, one of its soldiers was heard to say that they had accomplished the really important thing: being in the headlines for two days without anybody's getting hurt much. Other troops were quoted as saying that the time had come to establish a more broad-based movement, which is to say one involved in other concerns, such as resisting the draft.

Continued failure in referenda—most notably in the failed 1980 Maine referendum to shut down that state's only nuclear power plant—and the blow of Ronald Reagan's election may further dispirit the rank and file of nuclear opposition. The interesting question is what will happen next. Since we are dealing with a movement less political than psychological, less secular than quasi-religious, the answer is not at all foreseeable.*

* By the spring of 1982, much of the energy that had gone into opposing nuclear energy seemed to be turning against nuclear weapons; so single-minded an opponent of the peaceful atom as Dr. Helen Caldicott seemed to have returned to her first love, opposing the warlike atom.

# 6

# Warriors Against the Atom: The Commanders

THUS FAR I have tracked the substantive errors of the antinuclear movement and analyzed the tendencies within it that encourage people to hold such errors. I now turn to the source of these ideas, which are not, by and large, the result of intellectual spontaneous combustion. Animating the opposition to nuclear energy are a number of scientists and near scientists without whose authority the movement would probably recede into the same obscurity now enjoyed by opponents of vaccination and railroads. Their work is the real intellectual scandal to be discerned within the movement, for by it millions of people are constantly misled and often frightened out of their wits.

In the pages that follow I will be harshly critical of a number of prominent antinuclear figures, but not, I hope it is clear, in an *ad hominem* manner. I limit myself to the public statements of the persons in question, none of whom is known to me personally.

I am going to subject their claims to fairly minute dissection and must beg the reader's patience for that. Unfortunately, the only way to understand the unreliability of the intellectual leaders of the movement is to look at their claims very closely.

Few elements in the nuclear controversy are as vexed as the role of scientists in it—or indeed, of science itself. A key element in the problem is the immense respect in which Americans hold scientists, the most eminent of whom have always been public figures with considerable news value. This status is of ancient origin, probably going back to the time when Benjamin Franklin was not only our chief diplomatist but also a scientist of international reputation. The attitude gained fresh currency in the second half of the nineteenth century, as American technologists attained one triumph after another. Final confirmation came at the turn of the century with the conquest of malaria and yellow fever by Walter Reed and William Crawford Gorgas. If there was a slight falling back after 1945, when scientists seemed to have given us a dubious gift in the form of the atomic bomb, things were put right after 1957, when the American public learned that by neglect of its scientists it had allowed itself to be overtaken by the Soviet Union with its space program.

Those now included in the embrace of popular esteem range from laboratory technicians who add the crucial extra fizz to seltzer tablets to the colleagues and heirs of Einstein. The public, although able to rank these by their eminence and perhaps even by their contribution to the public good, is not inclined to distinguish between theorists and appliers of theory—very roughly speaking, between scientists and engineers*—nor to distinguish among scientists in terms of expertise.

This tendency is very marked even among intellectuals. It was a considerable coup some years ago when the American Association for the Advancement of Science admitted parapsychologists to their ranks, a decision the AAAS is said to regret. By this entry into the ranks of Science extrasensory perception was legitimized to an extent that could hardly have been achieved otherwise. Some of the most uncritical views of science are held by humanists.† People who would never assume that being qualified in anthropology qualified one in art history, or even that being qualified in Portuguese qualified one in French, assume that when entomologists speak about nuclear power, they speak with authority.

This attitude may grow out of a belief that scientists are linked by a common methodology known as the scientific method, a notion that seems to be much more common outside science than inside. From this belief grows the idea that because it is possible to find scientists who are bitterly opposed to nuclear energy, there is now a great debate going on among the experts as to its desirability. When one examines the credentials of who says what in this "debate," it becomes apparent that on the whole it is a debate between ex-

---

* In the nuclear industry, the bounds between the two are perhaps not as precise as elsewhere. In this book I generally include both sorts under the term *scientists,* except when there is a need to make the distinction.

† This is not to deny that there is a great deal of ignorant antiscientific feeling among humanists, and even pockets of reasonable skepticism, but when humanists find scientists confirming their prejudices, as in the present nuclear controversy, they tend to believe them to be authoritative in a way they would not if, say, a scientist were proposing the abolition of the foreign language requirement.

perts—who support nuclear power—and nonexperts—who oppose it. It is rather as if a coterie of historians, sociologists, English teachers, and psychologists were to maintain—against the virtually unanimous judgment of French scholars—that Molière was a figure of no importance whatever.

# The Union of Concerned Scientists

No combatant in the nuclear debate has been more astute in exploiting the aura of science than the so-called Union of Concerned Scientists (UCS).

The crucial fact about this organization is that its membership is developed through direct-mail solicitations of the public, and that the only qualification needed to belong to it is a willingness to part with $15.

That is, whatever the concern its members may show, they are not especially scientists, and the union has no way of knowing how many of its members may in fact be scientists. In recent years its executive directors have not been scientists. It should hardly need pointing out that from the ethical point of view there is something seriously amiss in an organization with such a name maintaining such a membership policy. The public is entitled to the assumption that such a name means the members are scientists, and is misled when they are not.

Anyone would see the fraud involved if a general-membership organization, composed almost entirely of laymen and concerned principally with supporting bans on prayer in the schools, were to call itself the Union of Concerned Clergymen. If the Union's dubious practice ended with its name, that would be bad enough, but the sad fact is that its insensitivity over its name is matched by its behavior in the public arena.

Several years ago one of its direct-mail brochures alleged, among other things, that the radioisotopes strontium-90, iodine-131, cesium-137, and plutonium-239 were "among the longest lived substances in nature." It is hard to imagine that even a reasonably competent high-school chemistry student would not see the error in this statement. For radioisotopes are, as a class, the shortest-lived elemental substances in nature. The stable elements, such as the normal isotopes of arsenic or chlorine, are *eternal*. On this scale, any substance that eventually decays away into lead is short-lived. Moreover, the list of substances cited by the brochure consists of three apples and an orange. The orange is plutonium-239, with a half-life of 24,000 years. Although longer-lived than the other three, whose half-life typically is three decades, it is not a waste but an immensely valuable fuel, the substance in all the world richest in energy for a given volume. The apples are the three fission products, genuine wastes but ones that decay away to triviality in several hundred years.

In its next breath, after having described reactor waste as fearfully danger-ous, the brochure cites a government report that supposedly says that by the year 2000 the accumulation of "nuclear wastes" will total a billion cubic yards and be sufficient to pave a coast-to-coast highway several feet deep. But for the following reasons the government study in question covered all nuclear wastes, both high and low level. The first thing to understand about these wastes is that most of them do not derive from nuclear power: The majority are from weapons production and scientific-medical sources. Even more important, the overwhelming majority of these wastes, being low level, are utterly unlike power plant or bomb production waste. Much of such low-level waste is only nominally contaminated: In a hospital where radioac-tive cobalt is used in cancer therapy, it does not pay to check whether a given hospital gown or bedsheet is contaminated. (Even if such cloth is con-taminated, it is radioactive in an extremely minor way.) Whether or not actually contaminated, all this cloth is routinely chucked into a hospital's low-level radwaste disposal bin and ends up as a component in the UCS coast-to-coast highway.

These are errors or overstatements of the kind one comes to expect in the overheated atmosphere of political polemic. They are not typical of the detachment and care that we expect from science, and that presumably under-lie much of the public's respect for science.

But this brochure has an even more dismaying sequel. A colleague of mine made a speech advocating the continued development of nuclear energy, in the course of which he noted that all the waste a nuclear power economy would generate by 2000 could fit in several boxcars. The speech was reported in the newspapers, and in due time he and the UCS received a letter from some members of the public, enclosing the report of his speech and the UCS brochure. Was there any way, he and the UCS were asked, to reconcile these two figures? The UCS replied by citing the government study but re-frained from pointing out its inapplicability to the case at hand. The reply ended by noting that they had no idea where my friend had gotten his figures. He in turn wrote a long letter pointing out a variety of errors in the brochure, citing, where necessary, appropriate chapter and verse in the *Handbook of Chemistry and Physics*. He got no direct answer from either of the other parties, but eventually there was a grudging concession from the UCS in the form of a revised version of the brochure that eliminated the worst of the howlers he had cited.

This action, silent and apparently without any attempt to notify those who had been misled by the earlier version, needs to be judged on the basis of the scholarly notion that the correction of an error, far from being an injury to nurse, is a favor for which to offer thanks.

In this episode the UCS did not behave like a union of scientists, concerned or otherwise. It behaved like an advertiser caught out and compelled to modify an untenable advertising claim. Modified it was, but in such a way as to do the least possible damage to the organization's credibility.

This action is by no means the last discreditable behavior on the part of the UCS. Their direct-mail advertising materials long carried the claim that every time there has been a test of an Emergency Core Cooling System (ECCS) it has failed. This was true in respect to a series of very small-scale simulations done some years ago, but in recent years the government has been developing a larger-scale test reactor in Idaho, known as the LOFT (for "loss-of-fluid test") project.

The reactor, although physically smaller than a commercial light-water reactor, was designed to operate at similar power densities and accordingly to provide a very useful scaled simulation. By December of 1979 it had undergone a number of tests with an electrical simulation of the nuclear core. Some of these had proceeded flawlessly, some had been troubled with procedural difficulties. None of these tests spoke to the question of simulating a loss-of-coolant accident; they were tests of the suitability of LOFT as a test bed. All during these preliminary tests, UCS continued to send out material alleging that all tests of an ECCS had failed and making no reference whatever to the ongoing LOFT sequence.

On December 18, 1978, the LOFT reactor was tested for the first time with an operating nuclear core. It was subjected to a deliberate worst-case loss-of-coolant accident. The ECCS functioned perfectly, keeping the temperature peak in the reactor below the predicted level and bringing the core to a cold shutdown sooner than predicted. A second test the next spring, at higher power density, produced similar results.

It was interesting, shortly after Three Mile Island, to hear these tests reported on by the scientists responsible for them.[1] They did not report them as the triumphs they might have seemed to the outside world. For the operative point of the tests was to prove the accuracy of the computer codes that are used to evaluate the adequacy of the ECCS systems on real-life reactors. Judged by this standard, the tests had yielded a judgment of error in the codes. It was, to be sure, an error on the safe side, but one felt that the men in question disliked convenient errors quite as much as they liked inconvenient ones. That is an attitude typical of real scientists and engineers, to which the behavior of the UCS provides, to say no more, an instructive contrast.

In February, almost two months after the first highly successful LOFT test, the UCS was still sending out material claiming that ECCS tests had been an unmitigated failure. This was not because the UCS was unaware of the December 18 test—indeed, on that occasion the UCS had issued a press release pointing out that because the LOFT reactor was not precisely a full-scale commercial reactor, the test could not be regarded as definitive.

This position itself requires a close look: As long as small-scale tests of the ECCS could be represented as having failed, the UCS was quite willing to cite them in evidence without qualification. As soon as one succeeded, the qualifications came thick and fast. This is the behavior not of scientists but of politicians or worse.

Asked about the brochure, Professor Henry Kendall, the president of UCS, allowed as how they would have to get around to revising those materials some day, and for evidence of the badness of LOFT referred the questioner to an outdated analysis of the LOFT test in an earlier stage—which had been on the whole extremely favorable to it.[2]

The most favorable interpretation of this episode is that the "scientific" and fund-raising activities of UCS are kept so separate that the former has no control whatever over the latter. The next most favorable interpretation is that UCS preferred to use outdated and inaccurate brochures simply because it had already paid for them. The least favorable interpretation is one I will leave to the reader.

In 1980 the UCS was prominent in the controversy over the venting of the containment building at Three Mile Island. Briefly put, the controversy was this: There was a substantial amount of krypton still within the containment building. This is a so-called noble gas, which forms no compounds and so is biologically comparatively inactive. It has a very brief half-life, becoming nonexistent in a day or so. Those responsible for the cleanup at the plant wished to vent this gas to the atmosphere so as to be able to enter the containment building sooner. The levels of radiation exposure at the plant boundary would have been well within federal limits. The UCS joined the generality of antinuclear outcry in opposing the venting and preferring more expensive and time-consuming methods that would have delayed access to the containment building.

By the early summer of 1980 it seemed as if the UCS had finally begun to expend its credibility, for the *New York Times,* which had long called the UCS a "group of experts," published a rebuke to it in its editorial favoring the venting plan.[3]

The UCS, then, presents a collective example of how the notion of science is being misused—in this case, largely by nonscientists—in the war against the atom. But they are not the only ones active in the field. There are a number of individuals who are generally more scientifically confused and shrill than the UCS, and who probably have collectively an even greater impact. Every city with a college or university is likely to have its local example. The preeminent national figures are Amory Lovins, Barry Commoner, Helen Caldicott, John Gofman, and Ernest Sternglass.

The nuclear controversy has, through several distinct means, been largely shaped by television, especially as television has interacted with the widespread diffusion of what now passes for higher education.

To begin with the latter: The expansion of higher education since the Second World War has meant, more often than not, the expansion of half education. This is not an event to be despised, for to be half educated is, in a real measure, to be intellectually half liberated. Someone who is half educated is freed forever from certain intellectual oppressions that are visited on the uneducated. On the other hand, the half educated are subject to new oppressions. They are inclined to have too much respect for the printed word and too much respect for college professors. They are, particularly, likely not to realize that college professors are capable of being as great fools as anyone else, and this not merely in their personal lives but in areas touching their own expertise. (This harsh judgment is shared by many college professors.)

What television has done is to establish a forum formerly unavailable to college professors and kindred intellectuals. To understand this fully, one must go back to the period between the death of Chautauqua and the rise of the television talk show, when to enter the academy was to take vows not only of poverty and bibliography but also of thunderous obscurity. With the rise of television, and especially of talk shows aimed at what used to be called middlebrows, the right kind of intellectual now has a chance for something like fame and can address—in a single appearance on a local show in a major market—more people than would have composed the lifetime audience, before television, of a scholar at the top of his profession.

Of course, one does not often get invited on talk shows to talk about one's scholarly specialty. An intellectual can acquire maximum access to the public only by tying in with some issue that affects an immense number of people and with regard to which his intellectual specialities can be argued, however speciously, to confer some expertise.

# Helen Caldicott

There is hardly a better example of media amplification than the case of Helen Caldicott. Dr. Caldicott is a Boston-area pediatrician born in Australia, where, as she tells us, she was profoundly influenced as a teenager by *On the Beach,* * Neville Shute's fictional chronicle of a nuclear catastrophe.

Dr. Caldicott has considerable stage presence, a certain articulateness, and considerable gifts as an improviser.

More than any other scientifically based nuclear critic, Dr. Caldicott stands on her expertise, which, it must be noted, is not in radiation medicine but genetic diseases. Her basic thesis is brief and to the point: Nuclear power and nuclear war are one and inseparable. Physicians know that nuclear power is, even in its routine operation, horribly dangerous. Whether to use nuclear power is not an economic or political or technical question, but a medical one. As such, it should be left to the doctors, apparently as we leave to them the choice of the best vaccine for measles.

The typical Caldicott lecture in support of this thesis starts out with a quick and lucid account of the various forms of radiation. She then moves to note that it is possible to cause genetic and other physical defects through radiation. From there it is a grand leap to proclaim that nuclear power plants, because they produce radiation, which has been shown to cause various defects, must inevitably cause epidemics of such defects. (There is never any argumentation to suggest how the radiation in a nuclear power plant is to be let loose upon the public so as to cause these defects.) She then notes that although there are unregenerate people who do not agree with her on these matters, such people have never seen a child die and so cannot have any informed opinion on the matter.

From this point on, coherence and evidence begin to go downhill. Sometimes she cites a UCS estimate for the consequences of a maximum meltdown, misrepresenting it as "an official government report of what would have happened if there had been a meltdown at Three Mile Island," and then proceeding to improvise new figures as to the total number of casualties such an accident would have caused.† These, which range from 300,000 to 500,000, are never the same in two speeches running: Indeed I have heard her give a speech in which the total figure had little to do with the individual sums she was citing. When I questioned her about the source of her "official government report," she told me that she had used a UCS "update" of

* This novel is well worth reading or viewing in Stanley Kramer's fine film version. It still has a great deal of power to show how mankind might react to its imminent extinction, but it provides no plausible scenario for what sort of war could have had the effect represented. The chain of events is as inexplicable from the political point of view as it is from the scientific.

† Tufts University Medical School Commencement, May 20, 1979.

such a report. Far from being an update, the UCS document in question (a) was an extended dispute with a government report and had essentially no figures in common with it, and far from validating its authority rejected it on every hand; and (b) did not in any event contain the figure she had cited.

Dr. Caldicott sometimes doubles polemically useful figures. She reports that defense expenditures, currently consuming about 23 cents of every dollar, take up 46. She reports that there are 360 reactors operating worldwide, when there are in fact about half that many.

These may be seen as statistical peccadilloes. More serious is her claim that the enrichment of uranium fuel is so expensive that the federal government pays the total cost of it. When challenged on this, she cited as her evidence a passage from Ralph Nader claiming that because the government enriches uranium at no more than cost (itself an arguable point) the forgone profit amounts to a subsidy. In a rare understatement, she said that viewed in the light of the facts, her statement had perhaps been in error and she would take care to be clearer about the matter in the future.

She also regularly claims that thirty of the airmen who guard missile silos have "by official government records" been certified psychotic. When, in 1979, I asked her for a source for this, she replied with figures indicating that the Air Force's screening programs had kept some thousands of persons variously thought to be less than reliable out of assignments in the Strategic Air Command. Apparently unaware that these data, to the extent that they had bearing on her claim, contradicted it, she put me in my place by noting that the "actual" figure was thus much higher than the conservative one she had quoted. By the spring of 1980, she was again citing the figure of thirty madmen in the silos, still without any evidence whatever.

She seems to have difficulty citing a statistic or quoting an anecdote without exaggerating it. I have heard her say in public that we all know that any undergraduate physics student can make a nuclear bomb. Remarks almost as exaggerated as this are so common that perhaps I had better review the facts. A couple of bright undergraduates have written papers about nuclear bomb construction that are now classified but that qualified observers have said represented "workable concepts." It is a very long way from a workable concept to an actual design, and a still longer way from a design to the finished product. I could probably produce a workable concept for a good camera. I could not, without some years of professional training, produce a design for one, and it is exceedingly unlikely that I could ever make one.

The problem of building a nuclear bomb from plutonium, as opposed to uranium, is especially difficult. Two subcritical assemblies of uranium can be rammed together into superprompt criticality—the weapons designer's jargon for "explosion"—by a comparatively simple gunlike device. But plutonium needs an implosion device—a so-called *lens*—to attain critical mass. It would be considerably easier to make a bomb from high-enriched uranium, but that need not concern us here, for high-enriched uranium is not necessary to nuclear power and is not used in United States light-water reactors.

About the most extraordinary claim she has made is that during the accident at Three Mile Island, every movable patient at Penn State's large medical center at nearby Hershey was evacuated to Philadelphia. Hearing her make this claim for the first time, I rather wondered why CBS and the rest had not picked up this made-for-the-media spectacle. In the next breath she was ready with the explanation: All the participants—patients, relatives, nurses, doctors, the townspeople of Hershey, the Hershey press—were "sworn to secrecy." The one informant was an anonymous medical student who had called her in the night with the scoop.[4] When I later asked her in writing for evidence that anything like this had happened (having satisfied myself by independent research that it had not), the great exodus had shrunk to the moving of a couple of premature infants.

The evidence is, regrettably, that Dr. Caldicott's impassioned speeches frequently have little to do with reality.

There is perhaps a clue to this in an appearance she made at Boston's Arlington Street Church. The occasion was a benefit in the interest of a documentary film being made about her. Addressing herself to the charge that she is overemotional, she argued that emotion is a necessary part of life. She noted that her passion grew out of her own total inability to effect "psychic numbing," a term coined by Robert Jay Lifton to describe a process of controlled ignorance by which man is said to accommodate to the unthinkable. Indeed, presumably some of the good in the world is done by those who cannot accommodate to an unpleasant reality and must insist *"Ecrasez l'infâme!"* But Helen Caldicott appears to be of two minds as to whether she practices such "numbing." Just outside the room where she spoke there were copies of a magazine containing an interview with her. In this interview, having been asked how she survived in the face of threatened universal disaster, she replied: "Psychic numbing." She then explained how she used this device to get through her quotidian life.

In the summer of 1980, a newspaper published for organic food freaks ran an admiring piece on Helen Caldicott. The author assumed that Dr. Caldicott knew what she was talking about. The result was a profile of a heroic scientist-mother devoting her life to saving the children of the world from the ravages of nuclear power. This picture is repeated in similar pieces published in the Northeast about once a month.

Dr. Caldicott's supporters appear to regard her as some sort of saint. Her intentions may well be saintly, but objectively, as the Marxists say, she is a witch hunter. History has judged Cotton Mather harshly for his role in the Salem witch trials precisely because he was an intelligent and educated man. The same rigor ought to apply to Helen Caldicott.

There are some hard truths in this area, truths that must be carefully observed in the public interest. The first of these is that in energy policy it does not matter, if one gets the facts seriously wrong, how committed, how passionate, or indeed how virtuous one is. One must first of all know what one is talking about, and then go on the crusade. The problem with such a figure as Helen Caldicott is that she is frequently—one is tempted to say "usually"—wrong as to her facts. And by wrong I do not mean merely that she takes controversial positions. I mean that she is wrong in the sense of being confuted by basic reference works.

This being so, her speeches serve little purpose but to spread serious misinformation to the American public. And since the object of her speeches, which they must often attain, is to terrify, she terrifies for no good reason. And, finally, because her misinformation is used by herself and by others to encourage the adoption of suicidal energy policies, she is effectively working to hasten a time when this country will suffer, and suffer terribly, from energy shortages and from escalating public health problems growing out of increased reliance on coal.

One presumes she does not intend this, but it does not matter whether she does or not. Since she invariably characterizes her antinuclear activities as preventive medicine, it is hard to understand her indifference to the death toll exacted by fossil fuels. It is not because she is ignorant of this toll (which is not a matter of any serious controversy) for I once took care to point it out to her. Does she care how many coal miners are crushed to death or how many people gasp out their lives suffering from respiratory insufficiency caused by coal?

While it is hard to imagine on what grounds one might forgive Dr. Caldicott for her disastrous campaign of misrepresentation, one can find reasons for understanding it. She is, after all, only one person, lacking any massive research staff, and the narrowness of medical education has attracted increasing criticism and concern within the profession itself. She appears to have been traumatized at an early age by a fear of nuclear warfare.

# Ralph Nader

It is not so easy to make explanations for Ralph Nader, who is possessed of research facilities of his own and who could get advice from the most distinguished physicists and engineers in the nation. If we find Nader bending the facts or the rules of discourse, we cannot, I think, easily relieve him of accountability. Nor, given his cultivated image as the nation's guru on a wide range of issues, can we forgive him simple ignorance when we find it.

He has, perhaps, been put into the shadow by the full-time antinuclear crusaders, and he is less obtrusive than in the days when he was the most prominent antinuclear leader. Back then he appeared to believe that a light-water reactor could explode like a bomb, and he would ask the question, "How many nuclear plants are you willing to have explode? No subtleties, please. Just the number." If a little less evident, he is no less tolerant of subtleties. His magnum opus, *The Menace of Atomic Energy,*[5] written with John Abbotts, serves as a bible even for such other authorities as Helen Caldicott.

The book is a fairly routine syllabus of antinuclear error. Three passages are noteworthy in suggesting just how far Nader is willing to go in pursuit of an ideological point. One of these I have already discussed in chapter 2 for its substantive error: Nader's claim that the cancellation of power plant orders following reduced demand estimates represents a lack of confidence in nuclear power by the utilities.

In their discussion of the vitrification process for disposing of nuclear waste, Nader and Abbotts merely quote an outdated Energy and Research Development Agency (ERDA) press release noting that the version then under development by ERDA would not work for its inventory of weapons waste. The problem has now been corrected by a new process developed at the Hanford facility in Washington. But in any event, Nader and Abbotts omit to note that this problem never obtained with existing or prospective wastes from power reactors. And although they cite the problem as an example of ERDA's inability to manage "its own" wastes, they do not note that the neutralization of military wastes that led to the problem was carried out long before there was an ERDA. It is this sort of passage that raises grave doubts about Ralph Nader's reputation for veracity.

Such doubts are confirmed by another passage, in which Nader and Abbotts engage in a particularly neat bit of footwork:

It should be pointed out that, compared to workers in other energy industries, particularly those in the coal fuel cycle, the numbers of workers injured by the atomic industry are smaller. But it should also be recognized that nuclear power produces much less of the nation's energy than coal power. Moreover, because the occupational dangers of nuclear power include cancers which will not become evident for several years, the full toll of the atomic industry can only be estimated.[6]

This evasion suggests that the numbers of workers killed in the coal cycle are approximately in proportion to the amount of energy produced from coal, and that the occupational hazards of coal mining are limited to those killed in accidents. The facts are quite otherwise. The calculation of the relative health effects of coal and uranium mining is quite simple. One knows the number of gigawatt/hours generated from each source; one knows the industrial accidents causing prompt deaths in each industry. From these two one can calculate the comparative figures, which I have cited.* That figure is, of course, very much to the advantage of nuclear power: about 100 to 1. One can also add in delayed deaths. It would be only proper to add estimates for deaths caused by lung cancer in uranium miners and for deaths caused by black lung disease in coal miners. Can anyone believe that Nader is really ignorant of these health problems, one so grave that the government currently spends more than a billion dollars a year to compensate sufferers? Needless to say, when black lung disease is filtered in, the ratio remains enormously favorable to nuclear power.

Writing a month or so after Three Mile Island, Nader produced an article[7] emblematic of the depths to which he has sunk in his discussions of nuclear energy. It is a brief article, worthy of citation and commentary precisely because of Nader's largely uncriticized reputation as the plumed knight of consumerism.

He begins by citing the 1969 claims made by John W. Gofman and Arthur Tamplin that then current estimates of the carcinogenic qualities of radiation were seriously understated. He represents these claims as a "revelation," and then says that the nuclear industry cast aside these "findings." He does not note that the vast majority of Gofman and Tamplin's professional colleagues also cast aside the findings. He then moves from this omission to downright misrepresentation. He claims, contrary to fact, that the 1972 study of the National Academy of Sciences' committee on the Biological Effects of Ionizing Radiation (BEIR) had been commissioned as an investigation of the "findings." This is a small distortion, but it leads to a larger one, that the BEIR study "generally agreed" with Gofman and

---

* But mining accidents are not the only way miners die. Coal miners are subject to black lung disease, and uranium miners are subject to lung cancer, a consequence of their irradiation not by uranium but by radon, a radioactive gas that is a decay product of uranium. Federal black lung disease law is written on the assumption that any miner, if he works in the mines long enough, will get black lung disease, which is not invariably fatal but often crippling.

Tamplin. It did no such thing. The conclusion as to Gofman and Tamplin was unambiguous:

The conclusion, therefore, is that the figures generated by Gofman et al. are overestimates: The reasons for their overestimates are: (i) An overestimation of the relative risk of solid tumor induction following irradiation of 0–9 year olds by a factor of 4–5, and by a factor of 10 for all other ages. (ii) The unreasonable assumption of a lifetime plateau region following *in utero* irradiation.[8]

In addition to this misrepresentation, Nader makes a hash of the question of radiation limits. He says that the current maximum for exposure of the general public to radiation is 170 millirem. The fact is that this figure refers to the recommended maximum average figure for exposure to the public from man-made radiation, excluding medical uses. There is no point in setting a maximum on exposure from natural radiation, because nature won't obey it, and medical irradiation is in a different class because it is in theory entirely controllable but must be justified on the basis of cost/benefit ratios as determined by professionals.* For while it is clear that in the past X rays have been given indiscriminately, it is also clear that the limits of medical exposure need to be set, under adequate guidelines, by the medical profession. Nonmedical man-made radiation—largely industrial but also from color TV and other minor sources—is the only type for which a specific governmental limit is both possible and desirable.

As far as one can tell from Nader's piece, the nuclear industry may currently be dosing every American with 170 millirem of radiation. The facts, as he must have known, are very different. Nuclear power as a whole contributes far less than 1 millirem a year to the average American.

The 170 millirem figure is, accordingly, at best almost dottily generous, but it does not matter much, for no one is proposing to take advantage of it. The BEIR report does call the standard "unnecessarily high" because that is what it is, like a 3000 mile-per-hour speed limit for cars. But it should be understood that an American who received the average background radiation, the average medical radiation, *and* 170 millirem from nuclear power into the bargain would still be over 100 millirem below the limit of 500 millirem a year set by the International Commission on Radiological Protection. Contrary to the impression left by Nader, the BEIR report did not propose a lower number, but opted for the sensible standard that no increase be permitted in the actual exposure level (a tiny fraction of the 170 millirem limit) without a concomitant benefit.

---

* Whether or not to undergo radiation therapies up to the levels permitted by the doctors is, of course, a decision for the patient.

Having trampled on the truth in the matter of the BEIR report, Nader makes an immediate attempt to surpass his own record:

In 1976, Dr. Thomas F. Mancuso, a radiation epidemiologist, was completing the 12th year of his study of the causes of death among the 35,000 atomic workers at the Hanford Nuclear Reservation in Washington State. The study, commissioned by the AEC, was beginning to show that there was a higher rate of cancer among nuclear workers than would normally be expected. He noted with alarm that there seemed to be a higher than expected frequency of cancer in the most radiosensitive parts of the body.[9]

Nader omits from this passage a number of extremely important facts about the Mancuso study. Until 1975, although Mancuso made annual reports to the Atomic Energy Commission, he published no data whatever from his researches. But it was clear from his annual reports that year after year the study failed to disclose any evidence whatever of abnormal health effects among the Hanford workers. As the years went by, the AEC began to ask Dr. Mancuso to publish some sort of interim report to justify the millions of dollars that were being spent on the study. He refused, unwilling even to publish an account of his methodology. His position was that there was not yet a sufficient data-base—in a study that had, by 1975, thirty-one years of data!—to justify even tentative conclusions. At length the AEC informed him that 1976 was to be the last year in which he would direct the study.

His reaction to this was curious: He fired two of his long-term associates and replaced them with a pair of British epidemiologists who had not hitherto been associated with the study. Dr. Mancuso's next action was even more curious: Using data from the Hanford study, but an entirely new methodology, he published a study.[10] His shyness about drawing conclusions obviously had quite left him, for he now found that the data—which were only part of the data that a year before had been inadequate for conclusions—now supported the conclusion that Hanford workers were dying of cancer at a higher rate than expected. One might wonder whether he had found some new and more sophisticated method, but it is obvious that he had not. Rather, he used a far cruder method that threw out two large bodies of data about control groups.

This needs to be appreciated. In studies such as this, as long as the target population is in a country with adequate health records, finding out what people died of is quite easy. It was, therefore, no great problem for Dr. Mancuso to establish the cancer rate, in some detail, for the Hanford workers. But there remained two serious problems: to isolate confounding factors and to establish a suitable control group. Confounding factors, in a case such as this, are causes of cancer other than radiation. For example, asbestos is a powerful carcinogen, and any Hanford workers who had been exposed to more asbestos than normal ought to show a higher cancer rate than the normal. Dr. Mancuso's first methodology allowed for this problem; his second one ignored it. The reason for a control group is that if one wishes to say that the Hanford workers contracted cancer as often, less often, or more often than could be expected, one must have a precise definition of what group supplies one's expectations. It is that group that will determine the shape of one's conclusions.

For example, if one were to compare the health record of a group of nuclear workers against that of all Americans, one would discover that the Hanford workers got cancer significantly less often than one would "expect." By comparing them to all Americans one builds into the control all those people who contract cancer after retirement, and all those who contract it before normal retirement and cease to work. (Active workers are by definition more healthy than the total population, which includes all those not healthy enough to work.)

Dr. Mancuso's original study included two large control groups against which to compare the Hanford workers. His published study ignored both. Instead he resorted to a comparatively crude method, normally used only in the absence of a control group, known as proportionate mortality. In this technique one computes the proportion of workers who die of each cause and compares that against standard mortality tables. By this method—and by this method alone—the Hanford workers showed a small but significant increase in cancer rate.

Proportionate mortality is an erratic tool for finding the truth: For example, if industrial employers maintain an elaborate program of physical checkups for workers, they will nip a variety of diseases in the bud—the worker who thus discovers that he has high blood pressure may quickly counteract its dangerous effects. Such a population of workers will die of heart disease less often than the total population and will, inevitably, die "more often" of cancer.

Given its failings, it is hardly surprising that Dr. Mancuso's study has been subjected to repeated and devastating criticism and refutation.[11] But it is surprising that Ralph Nader, who is not normally considered a propagandist, should sweep this criticism, as well as the earlier background of Dr. Mancuso's study, under the rug, concealing it from his readers. The question remains as to why he would carry out such a thoroughgoing coverup.

This action is followed by yet another distortion. Dealing with the Rasmussen Report, Nader cited that document's figures for a so-called maximum credible accident—that were slightly revised from estimates made in earlier reports—as if these, rather than probabilities of accidents, had been the point of the study. Nader then misrepresents the NRC's January 1979 statement on the executive summary of this report as if it were an abjuration of the entire report. This misrepresentation is routine among nuclear critics, but Nader takes a new step. He tells his readers that the NRC's advisory panel had reported that the maximum credible accident figures may have been "grossly underestimated."[12] The panel had done no such thing. It had, rather, concluded that the statistical analysis of probabilities in the report could be improved and that sometimes the probabilities had been somewhat underestimated, sometimes somewhat overestimated.

It is not clear that Nader the advocate really pursues the principle of devotion to truth no matter where it leads him. But perhaps it is not surprising that, as a lawyer, he should not. After all, for an attorney to seek the truth rather than his client's advantage would be a seriously unethical proceeding. Short of engaging in the obstruction of justice or the subornation of perjury, the unvarnished truth may well be the last thing an attorney wants to present. And in an adversary system of justice this is entirely proper. But it is not a tactic well suited to develop the technical background for important questions of public policy.

# Ernest Sternglass

Ernest Sternglass is that rare phenomenon, a radiation specialist* who is opposed to nuclear power. He accordingly gets a good deal of press. It would be tempting to dismiss him by noting that he is in a tiny minority in his own profession, and that for every radiation physicist who opposes nuclear power, there are a hundred who support it.

Sternglass has been a prolific student of the health effects of nuclear power. He is, in the neat phrase of the late Michael Flanders, "all right for quantity." The quality is another matter. What is most remarkable about his output is that much of it is simply issued as a press release rather than published in refereed scientific journals, that is, those that screen contributions by sending each submitted manuscript to the author's professional peers, who judge on the basis of its quality whether it should be printed.

This system of peer review—standard among scientists and scholars generally—assures a minimum of methodological soundness without giving editors sole control of what is printed. It is a system of professional evaluation to

---

* He is a member of the faculties of the University of Pittsburgh and Indiana University.

which Sternglass's work has not, on the whole, been submitted. His authority, accordingly, is founded partially if not wholly on his access to a Xerox machine. As we shall see, this is not a purely theoretical problem, for his work has been submitted to the judgment of his peers after "publication," and their judgment has been devastating.

One of his best-known studies deals with cancer and the Millstone Point power station near New London, Connecticut. Noting that the first unit of that complex opened in 1970, he cites cancer mortality figures from surrounding towns for 1970 and 1975. These are, for the years concerned, higher after the start-up of the reactor.[13] (See figure 6–1.)

Does this mean that Millstone causes cancer? In answering that question, we should first note that the plant is near a nuclear submarine base, a fact that Dr. Sternglass does not deal with. Much more important, there is something terribly wrong with his implied assumption that radiation causes cancer mortality within a few months of exposure, a notion that runs counter to

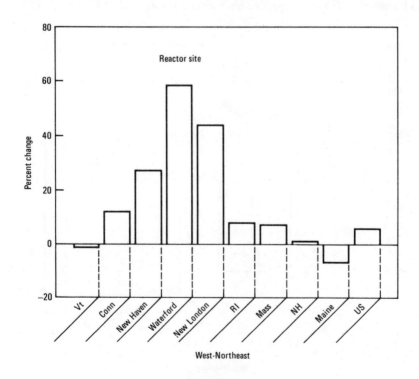

FIGURE 6–1

*Percent of Change in Cancer Mortality with Distance from Millstone Nuclear Plant between Start-Up in 1970 and 1975.*

SOURCE: Jeannine Honicker, *Shutdown: Nuclear Power on Trial* (Summertown, Tenn.: Book Publishing Company, 1979), p. 126.

universally held expert views about the relation of cancer and radiation that not even Dr. Sternglass disputes. For there is always a "latency period" between exposure to radiation and diagnosis of cancer. For leukemia, this is at least five years, and for other cancers at least ten. So one would expect that if Millstone II were in fact causing solid cancers in the citizens of nearby communities, let alone killing them, the fact would not be noticeable for nearly a decade.

But this erroneous assumption on Dr. Sternglass's part is not the most serious difficulty with the study. If one does a similar analysis for two other before-and-after years, say 1968 and 1974 (see figure 6–2), one comes to the reassuring conclusion that the Millstone plant cures cancer!

The problem with Dr. Sternglass's figures is obvious to any tyro in statistics: His yearly sample is too small to be reliable. If one does what any tyro would do, that is, integrate the data from five years before the start-up of Millstone 2 and five years after (see figure 6–3), it becomes clear that there is *no* correlation between the cancer mortality rate and the start-up of the

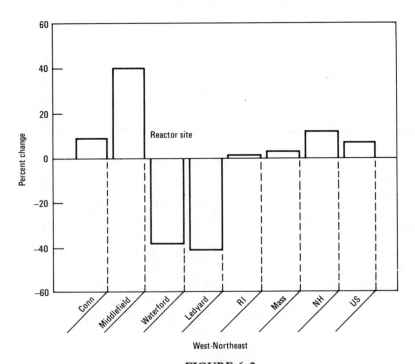

FIGURE 6–2

*Percentage Change in Cancer Mortality with Distance from Millstone Nuclear Plant between 1968 and 1974*

NOTE: Same database as 6–1; different choice of years and towns.

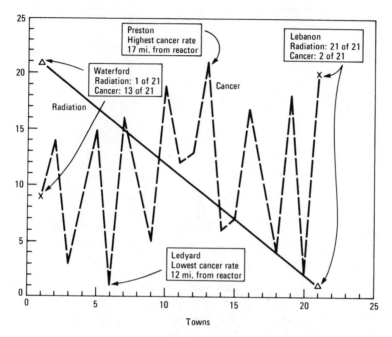

**FIGURE 6–3**

*Radiation Exposure From the Millstone Nuclear Plant and Cancer Rates in Twenty-one New London County Towns, 1965–1975*

NOTE: Same database as 6–1; fuller range of years and towns.

reactor. Most striking is the fact that out of twenty-one towns in New London County, Waterford, the site of the reactor and recipient of the highest dose from it, is thirteenth in its cancer rate, and this town experienced over the decade much less of an increase in cancer than the state of Connecticut as a whole. The town of Old Lyme, third in rank of radiation exposure from the plant, experienced a 19 percent decline in its cancer rate.

We can see the extent to which figure 6–3 is exemplary of the gap between Dr. Sternglass's view and the reality of the situation by considering what it would look like if he were right. If there were an exact correlation between radiation exposure and cancer, there would be only one line on the graph, a diagonal identical to the radiation line on 6–3. If there were merely a close correlation between the two, the cancer line would cling closely to the radiation line, never getting very far from it. What we have in fact is a textbook example of a plot showing minimum correlation, as the cancer line seems to fight to keep away from the radiation line, sometimes shooting above it, sometimes below. Such a chart reminds us that statistical graphics can be as easily founded in fact as in fantasy.

In a similar study,[14] Dr. Sternglass plots the start-up of a reactor—this

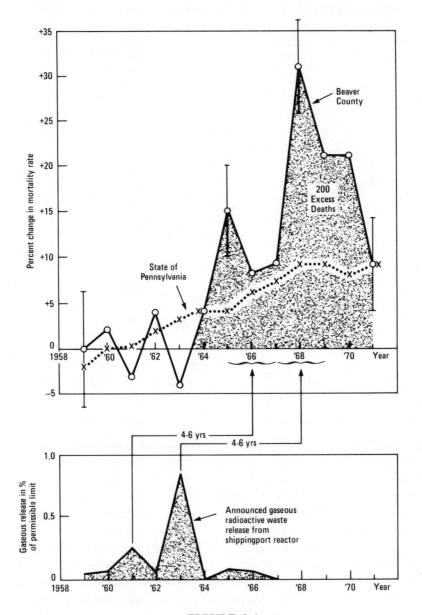

FIGURE 6–4

*Percentage Change in Cancer Mortality Rate Relative to 1959–61, Following Releases
from Shippingport Nuclear Reactor*

SOURCE: Honicker, *Shutdown*, p. 125.

time the one at Shippingport, Pennsylvania—against the statewide cancer mortality rate. (See figure 6–4.) And again, he correlates an allegedly dramatic jump in the cancer death rate as beginning directly with the start of reactor operation. This notion ignores not only the problem of the latency period but also the fact that once cancer is diagnosed, it is treated, and years are likely to intervene between diagnosis and mortality.

Dr. Sternglass treats statistics similarly in yet another Millstone study, this one correlating strontium-90 levels in milk with closeness to the plant.[15] (See figure 6–5.)

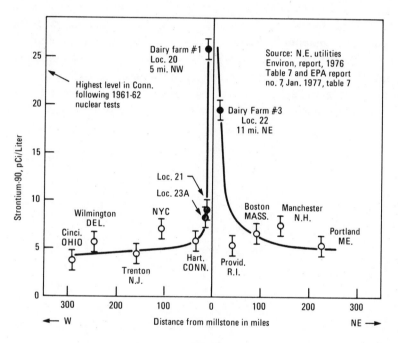

FIGURE 6–5

*Strontium-90 Levels in Milk at Various Distances from the Millstone Nuclear Plant, July 1976*

Source: Honicker, *Shutdown*, p. 126.

Let us first of all consider this as a piece of graphics. An ominous spike hovers over the area of the plant, rising from a plain extending from Cincinnati in the west to Portland, Maine, in the northeast. Cincinnati, mysteriously, is located 300 miles from Millstone Point, whereas the real distance is about 500 miles; and as mysteriously, Wilmington, Delaware, is located about 275 miles west of Millstone Point, whereas it is actually nearer south by southwest.

It should be realized that the spike hovering over Millstone represents a level of radioactivity that is a fraction of that permitted by the EPA, and indeed very much lower than that routinely measured in such everyday substances as salad oil and Scotch whiskey. Why, then, is the spike so ominous? Because Dr. Sternglass made it that way. He did so by the scale he chose for his vertical axis. That is, he determined to fill up the full height of the chart with his highest level, a level well within the most stringent concepts of safety. Had he chosen rather to use for his maximum point the permitted level of Sr-90 activity, comparing it to the highest level he found at Millstone and Portland and Cincinnati (see figure 6–6), it would be impossible on a graph of this size to discern the difference: The plot would appear to be a straight line. Even making the top of the scale equal to the amount of radioactivity in Scotch whiskey (approximately 5,000 picocuries a liter) would result in a graph that would show no discernible difference. If we were to set the scale equal to the radiation in salad oil (about 130 picocuries a liter), it would be possible to distinguish between the reactor and its hinterland, but

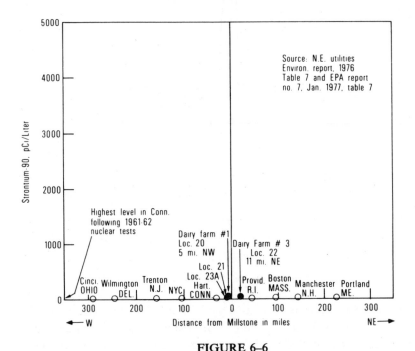

**FIGURE 6–6**

*Strontium-90 Levels in Milk at Various Distances from the Millstone Nuclear Plant,*
*July 1976*

SOURCE: Honicker, *Shutdown,* p. 126.

only barely. Graphics is the most creative branch of the imaginative art of polemical statistics.

But this is only half the story. For the figures that underlie the graphics are no better. As Dr. Sternglass must have known, the milksheds for major cities cover a very much greater area than the cities themselves; milk may come from hundreds of miles away. In short, the EPA figures Dr. Sternglass used for comparative purposes show nothing whatever about ambient radioactivity in the cities in question. They speak only to the level of particular radionuclides in milk sold in the various cities. They are, accordingly, absolutely useless for the purpose he has put them to. They offer no information whatever about radioactivity at various distances from Millstone Point.

Dr. Sternglass limits his sample to three dairy farms and then uses these data to extrapolate doses to a much larger population just as if, as the EPA noted in its devastating review of his work, "they were the only milk suppliers to the population of New London County in Connecticut and half the population of Rhode Island." One of these was a goat farm, and goats produce higher rates of strontium contamination than cows do. Dr. Sternglass simply adds in the figures from the goat-milk farm without compensating for this fact. He then goes on still further to misapply data developed in studies of fetal irradiation to the very different case of Sr-90 doses to bone marrow.

The question still remains as to why Dr. Sternglass is able to find higher levels near Millstone Point. The answer is simple: The level of Sr-90 observed here comes not from nuclear reactors but from weapons-test fallout. That this is so is indicated clearly by the fact that the proportion of Sr-89 in the total strontium was typical of fallout rather than of nuclear reactor effluent. (Moreover, the cesium-137 discussed in Dr. Sternglass's study was not accompanied by Cs-134, as it would have been had it come from a reactor.)

It has become clear, in the decades during which we have studied it, that within fairly small errors fallout is erratic in magnitude. It is not uncommon for neighboring dairies to have sharply different strontium concentrations, nor indeed is it for two cows on the same farm. Nor is this a mysterious fact. For example, differing practices with regard to supplementing pasture with stored feed will produce differences in the amount of fallout that gets into cows and then into milk. Or weather may be differential. As it happens, the Millstone area gets about 33 percent more rain than the Hartford area. In such conditions, rather than using highly selective data as Dr. Sternglass has done, any researcher concerned for the truth would have sought to integrate as many data as possible. He might also, in this case, have tried to verify his estimates of environmental dosage by correlating them with the record of releases from the nuclear plant in question. This Dr. Sternglass does not do.

The bottom line of any critique of Dr. Sternglass's paper is this: The rate of Sr-90 contamination in milk around Millstone Point has remained essentially constant since well before the reactor started up. Q.E.D.

One more example will suffice to show the discreditable and discrediting nature of Dr. Sternglass's work against nuclear power. In a study of infant mortality rates surrounding three reactors, Humboldt Bay in California, Dresden I in Illinois, and Indian Point in New York,[16] he shows increases in infant mortality at all three sites as a result of released radiation. But once again he is highly selective, picking a series of changes apparently for no other reason than that they show increases. When one superimposes this superficially alarming pattern on a complete chart comparing plant activity and infant mortality (see figure 6–7), one discovers that there is no correlation between the two phenomena. For example, a sharp decrease in infant mortality near Humboldt Bay between 1965 and 1966 was concomitant with a substantial increase in released activity. Likewise, between 1966 and 1968 near Indian Point, infant mortality was on the drop while released activity was on the

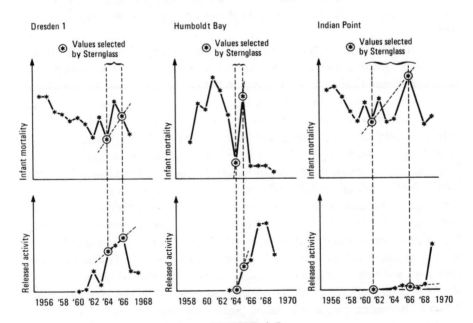

FIGURE 6–7

*Reactor Emissions and Infant Mortality: Dr. Sternglass's Choice of Points vs. the Whole Story*

SOURCE: Petr Beckmann, *The Radiation Bogey* (Boulder, Colo.: Golem Press, 1980), p. 15.

rise. Dr. Sternglass, although in possession of all the facts, chooses to suppress all data but those that support his predetermined conclusion.

In the face of such a performance, it is not surprising that the incumbent president and all living former presidents of Dr. Sternglass's professional organization, the American Health Physics Society, issued a statement rejecting his methodology and conclusions. This is an almost unprecedented action.

Dr. Sternglass is no less unbuttoned when testifying in court. On the witness stand on October 2, 1978, he explained to the court about studies indicating increased cancer deaths in Japan from bomb fallout, identifying the doses concerned as "very small amounts of radiation, typically ten, twenty millirads."[17] He then told the court that these figures were much smaller than the permissible dose from the nuclear fuel cycle—500 millirem to any individual, 170 millirem to the average person. "I now believe," he told the court, "that the present permissible limits will produce a significant increase in the number of deaths among babies, the newborn, and, of course, cancers at all ages."[18] He did not think it worthwhile to tell the court that the actual exposure from nuclear power is not 170 millirem but less than 1. Nor did he produce any scenario to demonstrate how the nuclear industry could get from the present level of less than 1 millirem to 170.

Asked by an attorney whether there were people in the medical field who disagreed with him, Dr. Sternglass replied accurately but evasively: "Sir, there is not a scientific question in which there is not considerable disagreement."[19] But when the court suggested that for every person on Dr. Sternglass's side there was someone else on the other side, he answered:

Not exactly. Today, I believe, the overwhelming majority of independent non-industry scientists would say that low-level radiations probably lead to an increase in genetic defects . . . diseases in early childhood, leukemia and cancer.[20]

This statement is a masterpiece of equivocation. By limiting itself to the vague class of "independent" scientists, it excludes all those who disagree with Dr. Sternglass. But at the root of the equivocation is the term "low-level" radiation. If by this Dr. Sternglass means radiation of the level dealt with in the study under discussion at this point of the testimony, in which the doses were many times those involved in nuclear power and delivered *in utero* in the bargain, then he probably understates his case. There is no significant dissent from the conclusions of this study. But if he means doses of the level attributable to nuclear plants, then the statement is false. Dr. Sternglass's conclusions have been rejected time and again by his professional peers.

How can one explain Dr. Sternglass's behavior? In the summer of 1979

I heard him speak and got a hint of what motivates him. The venue was a meeting of the National Health Federation, which might be described as an organization composed of unconventional healers and their patients, banded together to keep the government from disturbing their oddly symbiotic relationship. It was a wild assemblage, in which people wearing skeletal pyramids on their heads listened to people who told them that cancer could be cured by coffee enemas.

Dr. Sternglass was debating Petr Beckmann on the safety of nuclear power. His message was clearly gratifying to his audience, composed largely of people with polarized political views, united in the belief that someone, whether the communists or the capitalists, was tampering with their precious bodily fluids.

The high point of his presentation came when, in response to a question, he said he did not know what views others might hold, but as for him, he believed in putting people before profits. This sentiment brought the audience to its feet. It is not often that university professors experience the heady experience of moving a crowd, even such a crowd as this, and one wonders whether it is such incense that motivates Ernest Sternglass.

Yet there was a coda to his speech that was both creditable to Dr. Sternglass and confirmatory of the idea that he may be a demagogue. After he was through, a pregnant woman came up. She was, she said, planning several trips to California before delivery. She had heard from Petr Beckmann that airline travel increased one's exposure to radiation. Ought she to postpone her travel? Dr. Sternglass might have been a reassuring family physician. Yes, he said, there was a slight increase in radiation. But it was trivial— only a millirem or so between Chicago and Los Angeles. There was no reason to change her plans and no reason to worry. That is, he was confessing to her what he and the antinuclear movement repeatedly tell us is not so, that there is in fact a safe level of radiation. And since he called "trivial" the 3 or 4 millirem she would have gotten from making the three trips, he was also calling "trivial" the no more than 3 or 4 millirem she might have gotten from a nuclear reactor by living next door to it and standing naked before the fence twenty-four hours a day for a year.

It appeared to me, standing there watching, that although Dr. Sternglass the media figure did not hesitate to terrorize people in crowds with fabrications, Dr. Sternglass the man was incapable of terrorizing an expectant mother face to face and therefore told her the simple truth. It is an old story that individuals are more estimable than the mobs they make up. Perhaps even demagogues are more estimable dealing with people as individuals than as crowds. But Dr. Sternglass is worth examining in some detail. He himself probably represents the nadir in professional responsibility among nuclear critics, and his vogue is an example of the media's inability or unwillingness to view nuclear critics with the same skepticism they are wont to exercise on businessmen and politicians.

# The Honicker Case and "The Farm"

There is a case in which two intellectuals—Dr. Sternglass and Dr. John W. Gofman—have been involved in the role of public experts. This is a legal action growing out of one of the more bizarre claims made about nuclear power, namely that it is unconstitutional. This claim is derived from the argument that the NRC licenses activities that it *knows* will cause deaths, and this is tantamount to licensing murder.

The nuclear industry is different from other energy industries in this regard in that its regulators make clear-sighted estimates of the inescapable deaths that are entrained by any technology for large-scale energy conversion. The figures of deaths per megawatt/hour of electricity derived from such estimates are very much lower for nuclear energy than for competing technologies.

Over the last several years a Tennessee woman named Jeannine Honicker has been pressing a lawsuit to force the suspension of nuclear energy precisely on the ground that it is unconstitutional. In this endeavor she has been aided by a Tennessee religious community called The Farm, which operates its own legal firm.

This community, which is a kind of collective warrior against the atom, describes itself as "a self-sufficient tribal community of 1,200 traditional hippies" and its religious beliefs as being "like Christianity and Buddhism," comprehended by the Ten Commandments and the Golden Rule. The Farm has produced a book called *Shutdown: Nuclear Power on Trial*,[21] the heart of which is a transcript of testimony by Gofman and Ernest Sternglass at an October 1978 hearing on the Honicker petition, fleshed out with some background material.

This includes perhaps the most hysterical and misleading account of Three Mile Island to be seen anywhere, topped only by the hysterical inaccuracy of its accounts of other accidents in the nuclear industry. It features a history of atomic energy and the radiation controversy that is marred by such false assertions as that the 1972 BEIR report had been recalled because it had underestimated the dangers of radiation (a recent updating of this report concluded that the 1972 report had overestimated these dangers) and that the (nonexistent) recall of the Rasmussen Report had occurred because of similar failings over radiation. As anyone who has read as much as a news release on the Rasmussen Report knows, it is not about radiation effects but about reactor accidents. *Shutdown* also repeats most of the standard misstatements that have begun to accumulate like barnacles about the antinuclear case. A concluding statement contains the telling remark that

the overwhelming proportion of the world's people still find their roots in the natural world. If the peoples of the world are to develop free and egalitarian societies, they must keep nature free to support them.[22]

If in fact the overwhelming proportion of the world's people do still depend on something called the natural world, that is the most damning comment one can make on nature and the natural, for it is a fact—not, so far as I know, denied by anyone—that the overwhelming proportion of the world's people are still oppressed by hunger, grinding poverty, sickness, and ignorance. This is the fate to which these American humanitarians would leave them.

The Christian and Buddhist quality of The Farm's output can be judged by a statement in this conclusion:

Today a child born in America has one chance in three of dying of cancer in his or her lifetime.\* Cancer is responsible for the deaths of more children than any other known disease. Yet the American Medical Association, following economic rather than medical considerations, stoutly defends nuclear power.[23]

It is not clear whether the author of this appalling paragraph meant that the AMA supports nuclear power because it is more economical than other energy alternatives, or whether he wishes to imply that the Association supports nuclear power for the purpose of keeping the cancer rate—and therefore profits—up. If the former, it is a position in conflict with all accepted antinuclear wisdom on the economic viability of nuclear power. If the latter, one begins to understand the confusion with which The Farm invokes traditional notions of religious ethics. The statement is especially dishonest since it suppresses the fact that the AMA's position on nuclear power grows out of a careful study demonstrating that such power has the fewest health effects per unit of electricity of any large-scale method except natural gas.[24]

One finally sees the value of The Farm's position by noting a juxtaposition in its history of the radiation controversy. It defends Dr. Mancuso for wishing to delay publication of his research on the ground that "since cancer typically

---

\* The mindlessness that went into this passage is evident in the fact that the author felt it necessary to point out that such persons would die in their lifetimes rather than at some other point. Nor is The Farm quite sure about the cancer rate, for in June 1979 its attorney told the Sixth Circuit Court of Appeals that one out of four Americans contracts cancer, making it quite an achievement for one out of three to *die* of it. Actually, in 1976 cancer accounted for just under one out of every five deaths.

appears twenty-five years after it is actually induced by radiation, Mancuso wanted a few more years to build his data base before drawing any conclusions."[25]

Now, it will be remembered that this ignores two facts: By 1975 Dr. Mancuso had thirty-one years of data, and by 1976 his inadequate data had become suddenly adequate. But leave that aside. If this stand is valid, presumably nothing else in the book is worth anything, since the other authorities cited have drawn conclusions much more quickly than the judicious Dr. Mancuso. It is especially poignant to remember that the equally judicious Dr. Sternglass, in charts reprinted in this very book, regularly discovers that nuclear power plants cause not merely cancer but death by cancer, nearly as soon as they start up. (His study of the Millstone plant purports to show an increase in cancer deaths within two or three years of start-up.) One suspects that Drs. Mancuso and Sternglass are favorites down on The Farm for only one reason—that they are opposed to nuclear power. The contradictions between their two approaches probably would not trouble practitioners of Buddhist Christianity.

# John W. Gofman

John Gofman is the one of the very few antinuclear scientists to have had a distinguished career in the nuclear area. He is, for example, the co-discoverer of the fact that U-233 is fissionable, knowledge that may yet, unless Gofman gets his way, prove of great benefit to mankind. A specialist in, among other things, radiation physics,* he served as the medical director at the Lawrence Livermore Laboratory in California and was its associate director for some years. He is just the sort of figure one would be obligated to take quite seriously were it not that much of what he says is essentially political rather than scientific in nature, and that much of it confounds common sense and the public record alike.

When Dr. Gofman testified for the plaintiff in the Honicker case, he developed two basic theses: one, that there is literally no level of radiation known to be safe—any level might be fatal; and two, the aforementioned argument that nuclear power is unconstitutional.

The transcript of the trial contains some very interesting material. As evidence for the notion that any level of radiation is dangerous, Dr. Gofman

---

* His other major research field has been coronary heart disease, in which he has won a leading reputation and several prestigious awards.

cited the pioneering work of the British epidemiologist Alice Stewart.* Stewart's work dealt with the *in utero* exposure of infants to X rays. In describing these studies, he characterized the doses involved as "very low."[26] And so they were, over the whole scale of possible radiation.

On the other hand, Dr. Gofman, who was given great latitude to present his opinions without having to wait to have them drawn out by counsel, nowhere pointed out that the low-level radiation of nuclear power is lower than the low-level radiation of the X-ray studies by factors of as much as a hundred or a thousand times.

To be specific: The doses in the X rays ranged from 300 millirem to 1,500 millirem, and were delivered to a fetus—that human being most at risk from all forms of carcinogens—in a few seconds. Had Jeannine Honicker stood at the boundary of a nuclear power plant for a year, she would, under federal regulations, been allowed to receive an exposure of 5 millirem, or from 1.6 percent to 0.3 percent, in a year, of the near instantaneous doses in the X-ray studies. And she would have received these doses as a much less vulnerable adult. Note that I said "would have been allowed to receive." The actual dose she would have received would have been a different matter.

For example, had she stood outside the reactor at Shippingport, Pennsylvania, for the entire year during 1964, 1965, 1966, or 1967, she would have received about 0.5 percent of the permitted maximum. Had she made her vigil in the disastrous year of 1963, she would have received 1 percent of the maximum. These exposures would have ranged from 1 percent of 1.6 percent of the X-ray doses to a minimum of 1 percent of 0.15 percent.†

This preoccupation with the amount of radiation Mrs. Honicker would have received at a reactor boundary line (without imposing upon the reader further infinitesimal figures, I should point out that even these tiny figures are 500 times what she would have received from living for a year five miles from a reactor—say, within sight of its cooling towers) is not a quirk of mine. It was literally the legal issue in the trial: Did the operation of nuclear power pose a personal threat to Jeannine Honicker? Extraordinarily, no one asked Dr. Gofman what sort of exposure she faced from nuclear power, or

---

* It should be remembered that no one seriously disputes the fact that radiation can cause cancer, any more than anyone disputes that taken at the rate of a quart or so in an hour, Scotch whiskey is lethal. What the antinuclear forces claim—without experimental evidence to support them—is that very low-level radiation, the equivalent of a swallow of beer, causes cancer in significant amounts.

† If the reader finds such tiny proportions difficult to comprehend, so do I. They are what is usually called "negligible." For comparison, out of a twenty-gallon tank of gas, 1 percent of 0.15 percent would represent less than four hundredths of an ounce, a measure that even at summer 1980 prices came twenty-five for a penny. I do not think anyone will dispute my figures for the Shippingport reactor's modest use of its maximum emissions, since I got them from Ernest Sternglass.

the relative health risks she faced from it. He was, accordingly, allowed to mislead the court on this crucial point. He did admit under cross-examination, however, that there was "reasonable doubt" as to whether a dosage of 3 millirem—much larger than anyone gets in a year from a reactor in normal operation—causes cancer.

He was substantially less candid in dealing with the treatment accorded his work by the BEIR report, saying that "they suggested that my number might be five times too high, but I would consider and so the scientific community considered that that wasn't all that much disagreement. We regarded that as essentially a vindication."[27] It will be remembered (see p. 119) that the BEIR report found—rather than "suggested"—that the Gofman-Tamplin estimates of basic cancer risk were—rather than "might be"—at best five times too high and, in most cases, ten times too high, and that these errors were further exaggerated by errors in extrapolation. An error of more than tenfold is not, *pace* Dr. Gofman, the sort of thing scientists pass over as trivial. It is an error involving an order of magnitude, which is to say one that most scientists would take very seriously. The fact is that the Gofman-Tamplin claims have been repeatedly assessed by their professional colleagues—on the BEIR committee, in the U.N.'s UNSCEAR committee, and at the EPA—and rejected as methodologically unsound.

There is of course no reason why Dr. Gofman should accept such correction, unless he were convinced by it; it would certainly be proper for him to enter demurrers to his critics. What is not proper—what is in fact flagrantly improper—is for him to misrepresent a clear-cut rejection of his claims as a "vindication." That is an unambiguous disavowal of the canons of proof by which a younger John Gofman forged a distinguished career in medicine and physics.

Dr. Gofman's testimony is not the only point at which the sponsors of the Honicker case have attempted to throw dust in the eyes of the courts. At an appeals hearing in 1979, The Farm's attorney told the judges of the Sixth Circuit that "50 per cent of the energy we produce is wasted through inefficiencies that could be easily corrected."[28] He did not provide the evidence for that 50 percent figure, nor any program for its "easy" correction. People who make these claims should be asked to provide both and not be taken seriously until they do. The attorney also continued to ignore deaths from energy sources other than nuclear, and maintained inaccurately that there is no way of separating out cancers induced by radiation from those caused by other things (he did not mention other energy sources). While it is true that one cannot attribute a particular cancer to a particular source, given enough cases and adequate environmental data one can make useful estimates of the proportion of cases attributable to various causes. (See pp. 60–61.)

There is a bit of comic relief in Dr. Gofman's testimony on Dr. Sternglass. Asked whether he regarded Dr. Sternglass's data as reliable, he said, "Ernest Sternglass has published enormous numbers of reports over the past seven years, and you would have to specify which one you want me to answer to." When counsel put the question again with regard to the Millstone study, Gofman delivered the following ringing affirmation of Dr. Sternglass's competence:

I have no reason to regard it as unreliable. I am still in the position of studying that, but I certainly have no reason to regard that as unreliable. I have not seen anyone challenge the actual numbers of the measurements of the numbers of curies of strontium 90, and I am very much interested in the statistics of the cancer rates there. With such matters, there is a way to find out. One watches the cancer rates by year, and I would like to see more data for this year and such, and I have no reason to reject that study at all.[29]

That is, he supported the accuracy of raw data that Dr. Sternglass did not himself collect and suggested a sensible way to test the validity of Dr. Sternglass's statistical manipulations. As the reader will remember, it is the same test that I applied to Dr. Sternglass's work a little way back and by which that work signally failed.

Dr. Gofman was not rigorously cross-examined, but the government's attorney asked him whether he had, while serving at the Lawrence Laboratory, been irradiated by its cyclotron. Yes, he had, Dr. Gofman replied, but "I'm not lethal thereby."[30] Reading the transcript of the trial, I took "lethal" to mean "lethally irradiated," and waited hopefully for the goverment's attorney to pounce. "Aha! Dr. Gofman," I anticipated him saying, "you have testified that there is no safe level of radiation. How do you know, therefore, that you were not lethally irradiated?" But no such question came, and I was forced to play Perry Mason by mail. Dr. Gofman's reply was worthy of Helen Caldicott on such occasions. By "lethal" he meant "dead." This is a remarkable resort to jargon in a man who otherwise uses direct, even graceful, English. It must have been even more surprising in the courtroom. Did the judge imagine that the highly intelligent and forceful John Gofman was telling him, "Your Honor, I am not dead"?

But the fact is that both here and at another point (talking about research reactors) Dr. Gofman plainly conceded that there was a level of radioactivity that was tolerable:

Q. But a small research reactor nonetheless does emit small doses?
A. They do.
Q. Do you regard that as defensible?

A. I think one has to consider the seriousness.

Q. What?

A. I think that one has to consider the seriousness of those.[31]

That is, Dr. Gofman suggested although such reactors emitted radiation, the amount was trivial.

But his neat definition of "lethal" was hardly the only remarkable position he took in his reply to my letter. I had asked him whether, given the health effects, including many deaths, attributable to coal, he would testify for the plaintiff in a suit to prohibit the burning of coal. He replied that I had misunderstood him on this point. His objection to nuclear plants was on the narrow question of licensing, that is, of making legal, operations that would lead to deaths in the general public. By such licensing, the government did not merely permit but legitimated these deaths. That was what made the licensing unconstitutional. Were coal plants similarly licensed, he would probably have similar views on them.

Although courtesy compels one to entertain the possibility, it is hard to believe that Dr. Gofman does not understand that coal-fired plants are licensed by law. There is a mountain of regulatory procedure, federal, state, and local, and each such plant operates only after all these requirements are satisfied. A coal-fired plant pours carcinogens and mutagens into the atmosphere, but its operators have as their defense the claim that they have met all relevant environmental requirements and are licensed by the government to do what they do. There is in this regard no difference between coal-fired and nuclear-fired power plants beyond the fact that nuclear plants are subject to an extra dose of regulation from the NRC.

Hard though it is to believe that Dr. Gofman does not understand this fact, he appears not to. In response to another question from me as to whether he conceded that coal-fired plants emit radiation, he admitted that he did. But, he went on to argue, the total nuclear fuel cycle emitted more radiation than the total coal cycle.

This is a dubious claim. (It is of course certainly not true that the total nuclear cycle emits more carcinogens and mutagens than the total coal cycle—far from it.) But let it stand, and let us evaluate it in the light of Dr. Gofman's assertion—echoed by countless of his colleagues—that there is no safe level of radiation. If we accept this claim, as well as the fact that coal-fired plants emit radiation, then it follows inescapably that coal-fired plants—even forgetting their emission of nonradioactive carcinogens and mutagens—are unsafe on the grounds of being radioactive. The only way to tolerate them is by assessing the relative risks from them and other radioactive sources. This is the one thing that the Gofmans of the world refuse to do. One can understand why they hesitate, given the fact that the radioactive emissions from coal plants are not contained but are shot up the smokestack or buried in unmonitored landfills. They are, moreover, emitted through smokestacks often as not located in the center of cities, and not in the semirural locations of most nuclear reactors.

In midsummer 1979, Gofman published two books. The first of these was curious: *"Irrevy:" An Irreverent, Illustrated View of Nuclear Power.*[32] This is a collection of speeches Gofman gave on various occasions, most of them antinuclear rallies. One of the most interesting passages in this book comes in a speech to a group of antinuclear activists. Having proclaimed the near-certainty of nuclear war, Dr. Gofman made the astonishing statement that he was opposed to unilateral nuclear disarmament because the Soviets are not to be trusted. One thing worse than having nuclear weapons, he said, is not having them when another and potentially ill-willed nation has them. He invoked the lesson of World War II and quoted Andrei Sakharov as saying the West ought to retain its nuclear weapons as the only effective check on the Kremlin.

Now, this is most unusual, for few of those opposed to nuclear power have much good to say about nuclear weapons, and few activists of any persuasion have the integrity and courage to volunteer an opinion so likely to be offensive to their constituencies. Moreover, Dr. Gofman was dignified in noting his awareness that the audience would not approve of his stand and asking not their tolerance but their attention. For a moment he displayed the independence of mind and character one would expect from a scientist of his reputation. But his encomium of Sakharov rings suddenly hollow when one remembers that Sakharov is staunchly in favor of nuclear energy, a fact that Dr. Gofman did not trouble his listeners with.

For the most part, besides developing the familiar themes, *"Irrevy"* is an exposition of village anarchism. Dr. Gofman believes that there is always a ruling class, and ours, swollen in power and privilege, is not that much different from that of the U.S.S.R. And the ruling classes always have their intellectual lackeys, who are, in this country, those who disagree on technical and scientific subjects with John Gofman. (To do him credit, Dr. Gofman at least recognizes and proclaims that the U.S. system has superior freedom of expression.) This is not a terribly original position; the sad thing about it is that for Dr. Gofman it is not a minor eccentricity, living in uneasy truce with his scientific excellence. Unfortunately, he has allowed it to inform and to direct his use of science.

John Gofman's other 1979 book was a reissue of his 1971 *Poisoned Power*[33]—written with Arthur Tamplin—with a new preface and a certain patchwork of new pages to take into account Three Mile Island and the fashionableness of solar power. The base of the book is comparatively routine antinuclearism, a little more casual than some in its political, societal, and technical assumptions, more careful than most in not saying things that would be the laughing-stock of a freshman physics class.

It raises one serious question, namely, why should the permitted average exposure from nonmedical man-made radiation be as high as 170 millirem if the nuclear industry currently supplies less than 1 mrem? The failure of the nuclear industry to provide a good answer to this question—although keeping releases far below the limit all the time—does not in itself validate the Gofman-Tamplin claims, which have been widely rejected by their own professional colleagues. The industry is of course concerned that if the limit is changed, it may well be dropped so low as to be inconvenient. If, for example, nuclear power were to be limited to the exposure given by a single transcontinental jet flight—2 millirem—the industry would presently have little or no difficulty in meeting the new standard. But in thirty years that would become more difficult, and the industry is probably well advised to oppose a new limit as long as its releases are so small a fraction of the old one.

Indeed, the artificiality of the debate can best be seen in the fact that other regulations—those in the Code of Federal Regulations governing reactor operation, which are, unlike the guideline about which Gofman and Tamplin complain, easily enforceable at law—restrict reactors to a level of emissions that insures that the 170 mrem limit for average exposure could never be reached or even approached. In a country where governors on car engines kept the fastest car to 35 mph, who would worry if the highway speed limit were 400 mph?

Particularly noteworthy is Dr. Gofman's treatment of coal. He is too intelligent to deny that it presents an environmental problem. But he merchandises the false idea that we know how to burn it absolutely cleanly—that scrubbers and precipitators end, rather than ameliorate, its death-dealing effluents—and he gives no specifics whatever of what coal does to the public health, restricting himself to calling it "noxious" and "dirty." He does not catalogue the diseases caused by the burning of coal, nor does he offer any estimate whatever of its public health impact per unit of electricity generated. The fact is that had he included such estimates—let us say, the estimates made by the Office of Technology Assessment that by the end of the century "clean" coal will be killing about 50,000 people a year—his whole performance would collapse under its own weight.

But even this suppression of fact pales beside statements contained in the preface he has provided for the new edition. Noting the minor hydrogen explosion that was restrained successfully by the containment building at

Three Mile Island, he tells us it was only chance that a larger explosion did not sunder the reactor vessel. He omits any mention of the NRC admission that there was never any danger whatever of a hydrogen explosion within the vessel and that the fear that there had been one was the result of miscomputation by NRC staff.

Dr. Gofman acknowledges that polls have shown American public opinion still in favor of expanding nuclear power, but he makes the false charge that such polls always presume that reactors will be built elsewhere than in the towns where those polled live. Moreover, he tells us, the pollsters would get a different answer if they asked the right question. The right question, it seems, is rampantly polemical: "If you had proof that neither the government nor the nuclear power industry believes in the safety of nuclear plants, would you still favor going ahead with nuclear power?"[34] The evidence that the government and the industry do not believe in the safety of nuclear power is our old friend the Price-Anderson Act (see pp. 36–37).

Dr. Gofman then takes us through a little exercise designed to show that there may well be several hundred deaths as a result of Three Mile Island. It is, he says, a simple matter to calculate the health effects from a radiation release, and he presents an equation that relates the estimated exposure per hour, the total number of hours of exposure, the total number of persons exposed, and the total exposure necessary to cause one death from cancer. In this case, he assumes that the exposure per hour was 1 millirem, that the exposure continued for 100 hours, that a total of a million people were exposed, and that 300 man/rems* of exposure will result in one cancer death.

Gofman shows conclusively that by taking these assumptions and performing the indicated calculations, the total number of deaths will be 333.† There is nothing wrong with his calculations, but, as we shall see, his assumptions, which he palms off as if they were scientifically noncontroversial, are at best dubious. At worst, they bring to mind an acronymic aphorism of the computer trade: GIGO. Garbage in, garbage out.

These assumptions are worth closer study partially because of what they tell us about Three Mile Island, but much more importantly because they show that Dr. Gofman, the antinuclear movement's most distinguished scientist,‡ is intellectually bankrupt.

---

* A *man/rem* is a unit of total population exposure the equivalent of subjecting 1 person to 1 rem of exposure; it can be achieved by any combination of exposure and exposeds that equals 1, for example, exposing 1,000 people to 1 millirem each equals 1 man/rem.

† Gofman undertakes a similar exercise in the preface to *"Irrevy,"* where he uses somewhat different numbers and comes up with a somewhat higher figure.

‡ There are more distinguished scientists than Gofman in the movement, such as Nobel laureates Hannes Alfven and George Wald, but their qualifications, unlike John Gofman's, are not in nuclear physics and medicine.

By way of preamble, we should consider that estimating public radiation doses is a highly abstract and inferential process. The respect with which Alice Stewart's work is held is in part respect for the empirical solidity of her data. She was dealing with the documented health histories of individuals irradiated *in utero* by medical X rays that had been precisely documented. By contrast, when dealing with public exposures, not only Dr. Gofman but even responsible radiation epidemiologists must rely on a smaller base of hard data and a more complicated calculation from those data. One can use such techniques to make intelligent estimates, but these should not be confused with measured observations.

The way in which responsible scientists deal with this problem is to introduce so-called conservatisms into their models—that is, compensating assumptions that correct for any unrecognized biases elsewhere in the model. Conservatisms introduced in an industry critique of Dr. Sternglass's Sr-90 study are typical:

The critique was based on Millstone 1, the Connecticut reactor with the highest releases of Sr-90 in the state; the critique assumed, contrary to all likelihood, that all the Sr-90 and Cs-137 released from the reactor over several years was available to cows in one grazing season; and the critique picked the dairy farm which, according to weather data, would have gotten the highest proportion of radionuclides released from the reactor. With such conservatisms, one can have considerable confidence in the conclusion that the reactor contributed at most 1/50,000 of the Sr-90 in the milk.[35]

Of similar deliberate conservatisms there is no trace whatever in Dr. Gofman's study.

We can start by realizing that two of the terms treated by Dr. Gofman as independent are in fact reciprocal: average exposure per hour and total number of persons exposed. For the latter figure, he uses the 1 million population of the four-county area surrounding Three Mile Island, a reasonable choice even though the Department of Health, Education, and Welfare (HEW) used the more conservative base of the 2 million people living within fifty miles of the reactor. For average exposure, he used 1 millirem an hour. It is crucial to understand that he got this figure out of a hat. It does not correspond to any figure developed from actual measurement, nor does it represent a reinterpretation of any such figure. It yields an average exposure per person of 100 millirem. This is nearly sixty times the estimate made by HEW of an average exposure of 1.75 millirem for the larger 2 million population. There is no reason in principle why Dr. Gofman should not disagree with the official estimate as long as he is willing to present a rigorously documented and argued defense of his disagreement. He has not done this.

His period of exposure is substantially shorter—more than two and one-half times less—than that used by HEW, which considered that the period of exposure ran from March 28 to April 7. On its assumptions, HEW calculated a total exposure from the accident to the general public of 3,500 man/rems. On his, Dr. Gofman calculated an exposure of 100,000 man/rems, which is, again, an undefended and unexplained increase of thirty times over the HEW figures.

The final assumption used by Dr. Gofman is that 300 man/rems of exposure will produce one death from cancer. This is one-tenth the exposure that is assumed by HEW—as well as by the vast majority of all scientists in the field—to cause one death. So Dr. Gofman ends up with 333 deaths rather than the one death predicted by HEW. Knowing that his figure for the effects of radiation has been rejected by the overwhelming majority of his professional peers, he resorts to a sweeping slander of them all:

As they look at the figures used in our fourth term (one death per 300 man-rems), no doubt some so-called atomic energy "experts" will again say we are overestimating the hazard of radiation. We are proud that we disagree with the "think-alikes" who populate the advisory committees and high government posts in public health. Their jobs, grants, and appointments depend on their minimizing the harmfulness of radiation so that the nuclear industry can go forward as their bosses desire.[36]

One wonders what he will make of the recent Chinese study demonstrating the absence of health effects even at the exaggerated levels Dr. Gofman calculates, and suggesting the presence of a threshold under which radiation has no health effects. Since China had no nuclear power when the study was made, nor has any yet, presumably it is for some other reason that the Chinese scientists sold out.

Having said in effect that he is not like other men, Dr. Gofman proceeds to a bout of self-congratulation:

Our purpose is the objective analysis of the facts at our disposal. Small wonder that there is disagreement! With our degrees, experience, credentials, and proven abilities, we could each be earning $1,000 per day as consultants for the nuclear power industry, if only we were willing to confuse the public, muddy the logic, ignore enough evidence, and say that nuclear power plants make "good neighbors." But we won't take the industry's blood money. You decide whose credibility is higher, when experts disagree.[37]

This, then, is the way John Gofman solves a dispute as to scientific fact. Not by a careful attempt to meet objections by arraying evidence and argumentation against them but by the arrogant dismissal of everyone who has the temerity to disagree with him. He simply proclaims *ex cathedra* that all those who differ with the Gofman-Tamplin estimates are wrong. But more than that, they are liars who ought to be summoned before what Dr. Gofman himself calls Nuremberg-type trials.[38] (There is no suggestion that by this he means some sort of purely symbolic process.)

In his estimate of deaths at Three Mile Island, Dr. Gofman treats as scientifically authoritative assumptions that are either baseless or highly controversial, and represents his derived results as if they were something with which only a few "so-called experts" might disagree. He keeps from his readers the fact that there are competing estimates of the death toll at Three Mile Island. Rather than behaving like a scientist, which is to say, by detailing his disagreements, he has acted like a propagandist.

It is a dreadful misuse of great talents.

# Barry Commoner and Others

From my earlier analysis of Barry Commoner's grand solar scheme, it can be seen what slender credentials he has to be an energy guru. He is worth examining further because he is the most politically active of the environmentalist messiahs.

In the summer of 1979, Commoner was being interviewed by telephone on a Boston radio station. One of his interlocutors asked him the maximum flow of sunlight on a square meter of the earth. This figure is, obviously, the solar enthusiast's equivalent of $E = MC^2$, his governing equation. It is, being approximately one kilowatt per square meter, a memorable number. Astonishingly, Commoner had no idea what the number is. He was calling from his home, he said, but had he been in his office he could easily have found a book with the answer. This extraordinary ignorance goes far to explain some of the weaknesses in Commoner's solar projects.

Commoner's work is studded with passages that make one wonder why anyone takes him seriously. On transportation, much of what he says is more or less a conventional diatribe against the automobile and the airplane. But he begins to display novel failings in talking about the railways. One would have thought it obvious that the major reason for the decline in passenger service in this country is consumer preference for automobiles and airplanes. Commoner discounts this preference, noting that the Europeans have automobiles and airplanes and also tend to ride the trains in much larger numbers. There is, Commoner says, a "specifically American explanation for this effect."[39] His explanation is that the American railroads are in the hands of capitalists who cannot make enough money off of passengers to provide them with attractive service. This explanation ignores the plain fact that when the U.S. railroads ran highly popular passenger trains with a high standard of service, they were no less in the grip of capital, and that such nationalized systems as British Rail are far from immune to sharp declines in ridership. More than that, he ignores the influence of geography, a question I have discussed above. (See pages 65–66.)

And in discussing rail transport Commoner shows in one astonishing passage how little claim he has to be listened to outside the area of his professional expertise. This is manifest in a discussion of the interurban trolley. He alludes to the passage in E. L. Doctorow's *Ragtime* in which an immigrant journeys with his daughter from New York to Boston by a skein of urban and interurban trolleys: They

board the No. 12 streetcar on the east side . . . and three days later are in Springfield, Massachusetts. . . . the fare . . . is a total of $3.40 for both from New York to Boston. Both enjoy the trip, as the electrified cars rocket through the countryside, the sights and smell unobscured by pollution.[40]

Commoner here apparently thinks he is describing the good old days, but it is hard, if one has any sense of time or space, to call a journey from New York to Springfield that takes *three days* "rocketing." And anyone who sees a bargain in a one-way full fare of $2.40 (in the dollars of 1910) for a trip from New York to Boston forfeits all credibility as an economic analyst. This is equivalent to perhaps $200 in present value, and would be enough to pay for a taxicab ride between the two cities. The cost of food and lodging makes the mode of travel so admired by Commoner into even less of a bargain. The whole point of the episode in *Ragtime* is to show the confused and aimless state of the principal character, who starts off irrationally, without the slightest idea of where he wants to go, planning merely to ride each streetcar to the end of the line.

One assumes that Commoner's acquaintance with wage and price indexes must be as remote as his understanding of the realities of travel and, indeed, with the way in which real people live. It is unfortunate that many regard his performance as worthy of a prophet, let alone as any sort of historian.

Commoner's suggestion for improving the thermodynamically inefficient petrochemical industry is to get rid of most of it, except for the necessary plastics used for such purposes as artificial heart valves. He would send us back to cotton and wool for all our clothes and some of us back to being shepherds and cotton-choppers.

How would Commoner enforce such sweeping changes? He thinks that we ought to give socialism a try. It is true, he says, that existing socialist—

that is, communist—states have a bad record on political freedom, but there is no inherent reason why this should be so. It is just a curious coincidence that every single communist state is a repressive totalitarian dictatorship and has been so from its founding.

But the cream of Commoner's jest is the notion that socialist states embody something called "economic democracy," to which one need only add a generous dash of political democracy in order to attain paradise. He ought to try to sell this idea to the Polish members of Solidarity, who could tell him that economic decisions in a socialist state, far from being democratized, are all made by a tyrannical government kept in power by terror. Furthermore, the standard of living in the most advanced socialist states has still to catch up with that of backward capitalist states. (By capitalist states I mean, of course, developed states.)

Most particularly, Commoner does not notice that socialist states ignore his energy prescriptions. The Soviet Union is embarked on an ambitious program of nuclear power development at home and for export to its client states abroad. China has just put in an order for its first two nuclear reactors. We are incessantly told by Commoner and others that it is only the wicked capitalist system that keeps us all from basking in low-priced solar power. But which of the socialist states is attaining—or even striving for—the solar paradise?

Commoner's views are the sort that it is possible to hold only in an extraordinarily rich country, where a glut of everything masks the system that produces it. He really rather resembles that bygone figure of gentle fun, the foolish professor. It is unfortunate that such a figure should be taken seriously on one of the most crucial of the issues facing the world today.

I have already dealt with the pretensions of Amory Lovins to be a theorist of antiproliferation. Soft energy is, to him, renewable and decentralized energy. He has an admitted bias against energy sources that come from distant and, worse, corporate suppliers, preferring local autarky to the regional, national, and international exchange of goods and value. Therefore, most of the technologies comprising the soft energy path are those most amenable to decentralization, such as solar, wind, small thermal installations like backyard diesel generators, cogeneration, and district heating (when excess heat from a generating plant is used for space heating in local homes).

Lovins can be extremely inconsistent: He thinks centralized thermal solar plants, of the sort now under advanced development, are "hard," simply on the grounds of their centralization. Our existing hydroelectric dams are as centralized as any source of electricity we have, and yet Lovins would depend on them for most of the electricity we would need in a world redesigned to his satisfaction, that is to say a world in which electricity is used only for those purposes for which he deems it essential. These include rail transport, electronics, small motors, and perhaps illumination. They do not include space heating or cooking.

Besides being less centralized, soft energy technologies are also alleged to be cheaper, safer, easier to understand and maintain, and nicer. They offer, Lovins says,

jobs for the unemployed, capital for businesspeople, environmental protection for conservationists, enhanced national security for the military, opportunities for small business to innovate and for big business to recycle itself, exciting technologies for the secular, a rebirth of spiritual values for the religious, traditional values for the old, radical reforms for the young, world order and equity for globalists, energy independence for isolationists, civil rights for liberals, states' rights for conservatives.[41]

Soft energy paths do not, regrettably, appear to do anything about fallen arches or dandruff.

It should be obvious that soft energy paths, by making obsolete an extraordinary proportion of contemporary hardware, would force an immense conversion cost on any society, a cost that would be as striking in terms of freedom as in terms of money and, indeed, of energy. Presumably no one would be allowed to purchase, for example, electric ranges. Whether or not those citizens—forming about half of our households—who operate electric ranges would be allowed to continue doing so is not clear. It is even less clear what one is to cook with if not with electricity, since natural gas comes under the curse of its nonrenewability. Wood, perhaps. The same problem occurs with regard to clothes drying. Here, of course, the outdoor clothes line is the soft technology of choice.

Lovins naturally holds nuclear fission severely and strictly to standards based on what has already been accomplished. Yet when he discusses the future of fuel cells, he cheerily says that they "can *in principle* be mass produced in simple modules with short lead times, can readily follow 25–100 percent loads . . . and can use cleanly a rapidly expanding range of fluid fuels."[42] If the standard is one of principle only, then breeder reactors, by using existing stocks of depleted uranium, are essentially devoid of fuel requirements for several centuries and can certainly be made utterly safe "in principle." There is, moreover, a fusion reactor design that "in principle" leaves no radioactive residue whatever and is convertible into electric energy without the use of turbines or mechanical generators. Naturally—and properly—Lovins would call to book anyone who presented this process as a reasonable picture of what may be accomplished in the foreseeable future: Immense engineering problems—greater than for "conventional" fusion—remain to be solved and may never prove soluble.

When estimating the costs of soft technologies and those that might provide a transition between hardness and softness, Lovins is plagued by inaccuracy. Thus he misdescribes a windmill at Tvind, in northwest Denmark, calling it "two-bladed" (it in fact has three blades) and saying that it "costs" $350,000. When I was at Tvind in late 1978, the builders of the windmill put its cost at $1 million. Moreover, this figure obscures the fact that the windmill was built by a socialist commune and that labor costs for the members were booked at subsistence rates. A year after the publication of Lovins's book, in which he speaks of the Tvind windmill as an accomplished fact, it was still undergoing tests, had not been operated at full power, and was a subject of considerable controversy in Denmark, especially over its safety.*

Nor is this the only example of Lovins's substitution of promise for reality. Discussing fluidized-bed combusters (devices for highly efficient burning of coal and other fuels) he describes the virtues of a "currently available" system using gas turbines and such combusters to produce electricity and district heat.[43] Those virtues are so many that one wonders why the system is not being bought by utilities in the hundreds. Well, one problem is that the price is low when compared not to existing operating technologies—for example, nuclear—but to coal gasification, which Lovins estimates would cost, if actually in operation, as much as oil at $40 a barrel.

But there is another problem. Later in his discussion Lovins describes this system as follows: "a detailed design study by Stal-Laval Turbin AB . . . has been developed to the point of cost estimates on which a commercial tender could be based."[44] That is, the system described as "currently available" from Sweden is still in the design-study stage of development. It would be substantially more honest (although still quite false) to call the French Super-Phenix breeder reactor, now under construction, "currently available." One suspects that any bona-fide purchaser not unduly concerned about firm delivery dates might be able to place an order for a Super-Phenix even now.

One suspects that Lovins is printed in such distinguished journals as *Foreign Affairs* because its editors, who would quickly reject a manuscript that placed Vienna east of Moscow, assume that being a scientist, he must know what he is talking about.

* This windmill is a splendid example of the elitist appeal of solar energy. Located in windy northwest Jutland and constructed by devoted and skillful amateurs, it will produce enough electricity each year to supply its owners, a folk high school, for most days of the year, and enough surplus during windy days to exchange with the electric company for backup power on the rare calm day. That is, one windmill's fluctuations can be easily absorbed into a grid. The problem comes—and this is true for this country as for Denmark—when windmills are relied on for major contributions and the power company is reduced to supplying very costly peaking power. Solar energy is solar energy whether trapped directly on collectors or indirectly through the winds: unreliable in the short run, however reliable the sun may be in the very long run.

Karen Silkwood, who has been hailed not merely as the first nuclear martyr but as the first nuclear saint, was a technician at a Kerr-McGee plutonium-reprocessing plant in Oklahoma. She died on November 13, 1974, when, driving to an appointment with a union official and a *New York Times* reporter, she ran off the road into a culvert. She was allegedly carrying with her papers documenting safety violations at the plant. Within the movement, the universally held view of her death is that she was forced off the road by agents of darkness, presumably in the service of her employers.

This version of her death (which is the only version reported by the media) omits several key facts: The dents on the back of her car—allegedly put there by a vehicle that forced her off the road—were not noticed until several days after the accident, after the car had been pulled out of the ditch by the rear; her blood was found to contain the widely abused drug methaqualone, in a concentration between the therapeutic and the fatal; the fatal accident was her second accident in two weeks, and in the earlier one—recorded by the Oklahoma State Police—she had run her car into a ditch; and, finally, her friends and associates testified to the police that she had left on the last drive exhausted and, in their opinion, in no condition to drive.[45]

The suppression of these last three facts—the drugs, the earlier accident, and the fears of her friends—is essential to the antinuclear claim that it was not likely that she had run off the road through her own fault.*

I cannot proceed, as has been my custom in this chapter, to show the error of Karen Silkwood's antinuclear views, because the record does not show that she had any. She was, after all, in real life not exactly a warrior against the atom, having chosen to work in a plant that fabricated nuclear fuel. She was certainly at the least highly suspicious, and perhaps convinced, that occupational safety regulations at her plant were being flouted.† But that would not have made her antinuclear any more than an employee at U.S. Steel, having found what he or she thinks are violations of the Occupational Safety and Health Administration (OSHA) regulations, must thereby be opposed to the manufacture of steel. The movement, however, has exploited her memory so as to enlist her posthumously in its ranks, serving, now that she is conveniently dead, as a rallying point.

Let us next consider a comparatively minor imposition on the public's credulity, instructive because it caused a great deal of unnecessary anguish

---

* For a brilliant analysis not only of the Silkwood accident, but also of the media cover-up, see the articles by Nick Thimmesch in the November and December 1979 *Saturday Evening Post*. This is investigative reporting of the highest order.

† Silkwood's urine and apartment both proved to be contaminated with traces of plutonium. It has been alleged on one side that the forces of evil arranged this, on the other that she did it in order to gain publicity. The truth is not likely to be known, and the present state of uncertainty does not bear on this discussion.

to a number of people and also because of the machinery by which the imposition was made.

There is a navy shipyard at Portsmouth, New Hampshire, and part of the work done there involves the repair of nuclear submarines. A young Boston physician named Thomas Najarian published a study showing that workers employed on the nuclear side at Portsmouth had a very much higher death rate from cancer than the general population. The first interesting thing about the study is where he published it. Not in the distinguished *New England Journal of Medicine,* where researchers have typically made major announcements, nor even in a less prestigious but no less professional medical journal. His forum was, rather, the Boston *Globe.*[46]

There was something distinctly unusual in a daily newspaper serving thus as a primary source of medical research. And indeed one might well wonder whether the Najarian study was subjected to the sort of peer review obligatory in scholarly journals. One might indeed wonder whether the *Globe* in its turn wondered why the Najarian study had not appeared in the *New England Journal* or some other professional forum.

A hint came some months after the original story when Dr. Najarian, testifying before a committee chaired by Senator Edward M. Kennedy, conceded that most of his conclusions had been based on inadequate data and had proved to exaggerate the facts seriously. To Senator Kennedy's credit, he berated Najarian thoroughly for his irresponsibility. And it is to the *Globe*'s credit that it gave Dr. Najarian's exposure nearly as much prominence as his original study. Needless to say, however, this discredited piece of work is still being quoted as authoritative by such people as Ralph Nader, and probably will continue to be quoted even though a National Institute of Occupational Safety and Health report[47] has further devastated the Najarian study.

One story about Paul Ehrlich, the biologist and population control advocate, is typical of the apparently deliberate and certainly cynical manipulation of the public carried on by such men of science. According to Dr. Ehrlich, radioactive waste in levels "thought to be safe" had been dumped in a southern river, the practice having ceased only with the discovery that oysters living at the mouth of the river had begun to glow in the dark.

This tale is itself typical of radiation scare stories, purporting to illustrate by some sensational and highly unnatural occurrence either the gross incompetence or serious dishonesty of the experts. The trouble with the story is that it is at best grossly improbable. To effect such a physical change in living tissue through radioactive bombardment would require radiation powerful enough almost to disintegrate the tissue. The notion of a living animal made phosphorescent by radiation is scientific nonsense, and one would have thought a biologist of Ehrlich's distinction would have known that. But it is a common layman's apprehension that radioactive bombardment makes things glow, and Ehrlich appears to have been willing to pander to this delusion. Asked by another scientist to document the story, Ehrlich replied that it had been told him casually many years ago by an unidentified scientist who might have been exaggerating, but even if he had been, it didn't make any difference. This is the sort of remark for which "cynicism" is an inadequate category.

These scientists are best understood in the light of the health effects of coal, effects they inadvertently strive to intensify and spread more widely. We do not have terribly precise figures for deaths caused by coal because we know less about the hellish broth of carcinogens and mutagens than we do about radiation, having studied them much less long. Let us remember the estimate of the Office of Technology Assessment that over the rest of the century, burning of coal—principally for the generation of electricity—will kill about 50,000 Americans a year. That adds up to 1 million deaths by 2001. If we were able—as we are not—to replace overnight all our coal-fired capacity with nuclear-fired capacity, 1 million lives would be saved.

Do the Caldicotts and the Commoners and the Sternglasses and the Gofmans and the rest know this? The short answer is that they ought to know it and if they do not, they are, given their backgrounds, inconceivably ignorant. To use no stronger term, the behavior of these and other prominent antinuclear advocates raises exceedingly grave questions of professional responsibility.

# 7

# *Nuclear Energy and the Public Imagination*

## Nuclear Energy and the News Media

THE NUCLEAR INDUSTRY'S image is formed, first and foremost, by the coverage it has received in the various news media; it has suffered badly from that coverage. To say this is not to blame the messenger but to observe merely that nuclear power has, especially since Three Mile Island, been in the limelight of highly selective coverage. Although it is possible to quarrel with the media practice of allocating space according to subjective, not to say intuitive, judgments of newsworthiness, the fair observer must admit that nuclear power has recently been the big story and that accidents are better copy than no accidents. Most of the energy news coverage not devoted to nuclear energy or to breaking stories on other forms, such as when Congress passes a synthetic fuel bill, has been devoted to newly fashionable solar energy.

A careful analysis of television news coverage of nuclear energy is disturbing. A study by the Media Institute[1] shows that before Three Mile Island, coverage of nuclear energy was so small as to be nearly invisible. In the decade before the accident, the three networks broadcast a total of 182,688 minutes of weekly news coverage. Nuclear energy occupied a total of 472 minutes, or 26/100 of 1 percent of that time. A closer analysis shows astonishing gaps: NBC carried *no* coverage during the last five months of 1968 and a grand total of 15 seconds during 1969. Moreover, 94 percent of the coverage appeared in the last two-thirds of the broadcasts—that is to say, on the middle and back pages.

The Media Institute considers that before Three Mile Island, over 80 percent of the stories were neutral in tone, but that after, this figure dropped to 47 percent. One of the hardest issues to argue is tone, and I shall not attempt the feat here. Any observer of the press knows that a major article on a well-known human being will attract letters praising the publisher for (a) finally exposing the swine and (b) having been viciously unfair to a saint. For what it is worth, the Media Institute's standards in this seem fair enough to me.

What is more persuasive is a tabulation of the top ten sources quoted by the networks before Three Mile Island. These are for the most part unambiguously for or against nuclear power—for example, Ralph Nader or the Atomic Industrial Forum—and the scorecard shows that the "antis" got 72 percent of the time.

The most serious flaw revealed in the study is simply the inadequacy in the amount of coverage, a fault that presumably both sides of the controversy would deplore. The technical thinness of the coverage is something else again. It probably derives from an unwillingness or neglect to have reporters who are well versed in energy questions. Acquiring such knowledge is not impossible but, given the demands on a journalist's time, it is probably very difficult for anyone for whom energy is not a full-time assignment.

There are a few striking examples to the contrary—one is Jules Bergmann, whose scientific coverage has always made ABC news worth watching; another is Stuart Diamond of *Newsday;* and there are doubtless local exemplars not known to me—but the majority of journalists are not very knowledgeable about science and technology, and they tend to listen to those whom they recognize as the experts—who are, more often than not, the Union of Concerned Scientists.

The competition to the UCS, Scientists and Engineers for Secure Energy (SE$_2$), which numbers among its membership seven Nobel laureates in physics, is not so often heard, partially because it does not, out of scientific conviction, play the media as skillfully as its rivals.*

My own rough surveys of the print media suggest that television news may be substantially better in its coverage than its rivals. Newspapers have been especially remiss in covering nuclear energy abroad, feeding the extraordinarily parochial nature of the debate within this country; for example, breeder reactors are almost always discussed solely in the context of the failed experiment at Fermi I near Detroit and the proposed reactor at Clinch

* Recently the Nuclear Regulatory Commission invited testimony from so-called public interest groups and accepted testimony from UCS but not from SE$_2$!

River in Tennessee. One would not often find coverage of the thriving British and French nuclear programs, or even the troubled Soviet breeder program. That a small breeder has been operating in Idaho since 1964 would be news to most Americans and to most journalists as well.

Moreover, journals of opinion have almost without exception covered nuclear energy as if it were a classical political question, so that conservative and neo-conservative journals have been fairly well informed about it and generally in favor, while everyone else has been fairly ignorant and opposed.

But even with all allowances made, it is surprising that the portion of the media most devoted to investigative journalism has not turned a little attention to the dangers inherent in nonnuclear energy. It is odd, one might think, that a press that covered the disputed issue of the harm done to Karen Silkwood should be so blasé about the undoubted deaths of a hundred or so coal miners a year.

This is a little less inexplicable when we consider that the death toll in the mines does get covered, but almost never as an energy story. It is covered as a crimes-of-capitalism story. The fact is that most Americans, newsreaders and news suppliers alike, are indisposed to believe that there is ever ultimately bad news about anything, and to cover the mining of coal honestly as a news story, it would be necessary to say finally that while there can be improvements in the safety of coal mines, the industry can never be absolutely safe. A certain number of men must die each year in order to provide us with coal; we may substantially reduce the number from what it is now, but we are unlikely ever to reduce it to zero.

The most striking example of this general inability to face up to bad news is contained in Naderite writing on automobile safety, a phenomenon that is worth exploring here for the light it sheds on related attitudes toward nuclear energy. Nader's own two books on the subject are full of horror stories, but the one story they never contain is about irresponsible drivers. It is always irresponsible manufacturers and their irresponsible products. When accidents happen, they are always seen as caused by cars—indirectly by the manufacturers—and the cars themselves are treated almost as possessing volition.

The sad fact is that while we ought to take all reasonable precautions to make automobiles as foolproof as we can, there is no possibility whatever of making them finally and utterly foolproof. Few would argue that this fact compels us to abolish cars. While there are many who would argue that cars ought to be denied to some or many, depending on how close they are to so-called mass transportation and whether they have properly refined uses for a private car, such ascetics do not go off the deep end: They usually end up allowing, at least by implication, cars for the happy few.

The parallel with energy is close. It is very difficult, among those who are convinced the world can be substantially improved in the next fiscal year or two, to admit that the mobility demanded almost as a right by Americans means that a certain number of them must die in the attempt to achieve it. It is even harder to admit that the proximate cause of this state of affairs is not Detroit's unexampled rapacity but rather the cussedness, and even the incompetence, of the human race. It is equally hard to admit that we need to produce coal and that coal cannot, even under the best of conditions, be produced without deaths.

The media, at any rate, have been remarkably uninterested in widely based investigative reporting of the energy story. In the course of doing research for this book, after I had gotten sufficient data to impugn the competence of figures like Nader, Commoner, Caldicott, and the rest, I wrote Mike Wallace, Walter Cronkite, and Mary McGrory, suggesting that there was a real story in the manipulation by such people of the media and public opinion. The first two did not think the idea worth an acknowledgment. The third, Mary McGrory, responded promptly and courteously, saying that I had obviously made some serious charges and seemed to have evidence for them but that she was not able to judge between me and my targets.

And there the matter rests. In June 1981, faced by Israel's attack on an Iraqi reactor with a very big story that was partially about energy, the media performed at best erratically.

The reactor in question was not a nuclear power plant, nor was it even convertible to one of useful size (if it were to be converted—at great expense—it would produce about 3 percent of the electricity available from a plant such as that at Three Mile Island). Moreover, unlike most power reactors, it operated with highly enriched uranium fuel that would be directly usable in nuclear bombs.

Yet this research reactor was repeatedly described as a "nuclear power plant" by both major wire news services, by two of the commercial television networks, by the Public Broadcasting System, and by heaven knows how many local stations and newspapers.

As will be clear to readers, this was more than a technical error. For if Israel had destroyed a power reactor in the hands of an enemy because the Israeli government thought the plant was a nuclear bomb source, that would have been almost definitive evidence that nuclear power was a source of nuclear weapons proliferation, an argument that was being made publicly a week after the attack. It is an argument based on a flat error, but even now, how many Americans, misled by the media they trust, still believe that Israel sent its aircraft against a dangerous power reactor?

Some of the media published or broadcast corrections—sometimes labeled with the blessed and comfortable word "clarification," and even these continued suggestively to call the reactor a "nuclear plant." There was a striking contrast with the case of the *Washington Post*'s bogus Pulitzer Prize story. On that occasion, however serious the reporter's misbehavior had been in terms of journalistic procedure, the story did not seriously mislead the public about the problem of heroin addiction. In the case of the mythical Iraqi power reactor—which might well have been named "Little Jimmy"—there was probably no intent to deceive but great deception nevertheless.

# Nuclear Energy and the Book

NONFICTION

Nuclear power has become the subject of a good deal of popular literature, both fiction and nonfiction, although the difference is not always easy to see. It is probably the first scientific and technological issue to have achieved such treatment, and the results have generally been very unhappy.

John G. Fuller's *We Almost Lost Detroit*[2] purports to discuss an accident at the Enrico Fermi reactor near Detroit in 1966. The Fermi reactor, a demonstration fast breeder, suffered a coolant-pipe blockage that seriously damaged it and kept it out of action for two years. It did not, as Fuller claims, undergo a "partial meltdown." Meltdowns are either full or nonexistent, and there were not enough fission products in the Fermi reactor at the time to have led to a meltdown in any event. In a plutonium-fuel reactor there is a theoretical possibility of a small nuclear explosion, which the containment building is designed to withstand. This did not occur at the Fermi plant. Had it done so, it would hardly have been the end of Detroit or even of Lagoona Beach, where the reactor was located.

Fuller's sensationalizing ignorance is perhaps best illustrated by his belief that liquid sodium is thick and slow-flowing (actually it flows more freely than water) and that it remains dangerously radioactive for years (its principal radioactive isotope, which has a half-life of fifteen hours, had decayed away to essentially nothing a week after the reactor was shut down). Fuller paints an awesome picture of many drums of this allegedly dangerous sodium, which allegedly no one was willing to cart away, marooned as it were at the reactor site. He is apparently unaware that it had been given to and accepted by the Clinch River Breeder Project in Tennessee, and was stored at the Fermi site pending that reactor's need for it.

But this is hardly his only serious technical error. He puts forth as the measure of the threat to Detroit a study done at the University of Michigan, without noting that the study assumed that two tons of high-burnup fuel were to be released as a gas to the atmosphere, an assumption ignoring the existence of the reactor's containment building, which was designed not only to hold a meltdown but to restrain the sort of low-grade nuclear explosion that might have occurred had the total fuel load melted down into a pair of subcritical masses and joined to make one critical mass. The remoteness of such an explosion can be gauged by the fact that at most 1 percent of the fuel at Fermi I melted, that this fuel was of very low burnup, and that its melting did not damage any of the many containment barriers around the core. Even on the worst possible assumption, that all of the fuel had melted to form a critical mass, the explosion would have had the force of about 1 percent of 1 percent of the atomic bombs used on Hiroshima and Nagasaki—that is, an explosion of a few hundred pounds of TNT equivalent.

Fuller is no more competent in dealing with a 1957 Atomic Energy Commission (AEC) study known as WASH-740, nor with a 1965 update of it. He seems quite unaware that neither of these attempted to assess probabilities but dealt rather with what would happen if every one of the multitudinous safeguards built into a reactor were to fail. He repeatedly suggests that the AEC and the industry had hoped that the update would come up with more optimistic conclusions than the original study in light of improved safeguards. Since each study assumed, for the purposes of estimating the maximum credible accident, that the safeguards, whatever they were, had all failed, one wonders how closely Fuller could have read either.

One could go on and on listing the technical absurdities of this silly book, in which reality is constantly distorted and vulgarized to serve a practiced journalist's need for sensation. For example, Fuller describes a difficulty in "scramming" the Fermi reactor: "All the rods went down into the core normally except one. It stopped six inches from the full 'down' position. This was no time to take a chance. A second manual scram was activated. The reluctant rod finally closed down fully."[3] The suggestion here is that there would have been some risk in leaving a bit of one rod uninserted. The fact is that the engineered redundancy of the Fermi plant was such that a single control rod would have been enough to shut down the chain reaction.

For another example, Fuller at one point says that the radiation level "had not yet reached intolerable limits outside the containment shell."[4] The "yet" suggests that it did at some later time reach such a limit. One would never guess from this book that radiation releases did not reach accident levels; they stayed well within operating limits. The radiation inside the containment building never reached a level sufficient to cause a serious problem of meeting weekly occupational radiation limits.

And finally, in suggesting that the removal of the fuel elements was especially hazardous, Fuller says: "each fuel unit was on the verge of becoming critical, even in the cooling water."[5] That last phrase about the cooling water is a measure of Fuller's cosmic ignorance about a topic on which he claims competence. For water serves as a moderator and increases the possibility of criticality in that which it cools. For that reason, assemblies to be stored in water must be so arranged as to be far from subcritical in mass. If an accident were to deprive stored fuel of its water, the chances of criticality would be sharply reduced. (Lacking water, recently extracted fuel would begin to melt, but that is another problem.)

Fuller's book was originally published by the Reader's Digest Press, a sponsorship that many readers must have taken as assuring at least a certain level of technical editing and freedom from gross exaggeration.

Another seriously defective book, Robert Jungk's *The New Tyranny*[6] contains many ideas from other sources—he is a convinced Lovinsian and repeats the usual falsehoods about the NRC and the Rasmussen Report, and Karen Silkwood—but he has some original material. His pessimistic account of life at the Cap La Hague reprocessing plant in Normandy would be difficult to verify or disprove without an extensive visit to the site, but the chapter is so shot through with inconsistencies as to raise grave doubts about it. On the one hand, the French government hires thugs to beat up farmers who will not sell it land and uses an almost totalitarian power to control opposition to the plant. On the other hand, numbers of named workers at the plant have allegedly provided Jungk with endless details as to its malfunction. On the one hand, the plant threatens the health of its workers. On the other, it employs repressive techniques to maintain radiation protection, techniques that the cleverly heroic workers constantly circumvent.

The aim of the work is to verify that the development of nuclear power requires the establishment of a totalitarian regime. This claim is supported by an apparently ill-organized and almost totally undocumented melange: allegations of various alleged breaches of rights, including the charge that the United Kingdom Atomic Energy Authority screens those who work in its installations; dark allegations of conspiracy, including the claim that the German nuclear power program is run by Nazis; bizarre suggestions, including a proposal that a fund be set up to buy antinuclear testimony from nuclear scientists and engineers, and the idea that one threat to American fast breeder reactors (of which only one now exists) is kamikaze attacks by Japanese aircraft.

It is a measure of Jungk's competence that while he frequently mentions the fast breeder reactor as a concept, the only actual installations he deals with are the uncompleted reactors at Kalkar in Germany and Creys-Malville in France. The two operational breeders at Dounreay in Scotland and Marcoule in France do not seem to have taken his fancy, possibly because they work and would have been very inadequate grist for his mill.

He closes with a plea for the soft path, with an appeal to authority that as much as anything symbolizes his naiveté: "Those who make do with less may be laughed at today; but, according to the Stanford Research Institute, by the turn of the century (at the latest) they will serve as the role model for all of us."[7]

There is something almost touching in the author of a book so ferociously convinced that intellectual elites are corrupt to the core citing a bastion of the U.S. intellectual establishment quite as if it were a single authority with a single view.

The work has garnered the plaudits of predictable figures, including Dr. Benjamin Spock and Professor George Wald. But then what antinuclear book does not gain their endorsement? Professor Wald has even been willing to confer the luster of his Nobel Prize on Helen Caldicott's scientifically weak and aptly named *Nuclear Madness*.[8]

Perhaps the most extraordinary thing about Jungk's work is the subtitle of the American edition: *How Nuclear Power Enslaves Us*. This, in Orwell's memorable formulation, is a piece of nonsense so bad that only an intellectual could believe it. It is perhaps not Jungk's own devising, but it is worth speculating on the state of mind of the person responsible for it. Did he really feel himself to be enslaved, and by nuclear power?

The most striking example of the depths to which even respectable publishers can fall, even in treating nonfiction, appeared recently on the back of a book published by W. W. Norton. The Soviet dissident geneticist Zhores Medvedev, exiled in Britain, in 1976 published an article[9] arguing that in 1957–58 the Soviet nuclear program suffered a major accident at a site in the Urals as a result of which there were many deaths and widespread and serious contamination of land. No one—except the Soviets—now disputes that Medvedev is on to something. He uncovered a spate of articles in the open literature dealing with radiation effects on a wide variety of flora and fauna that made sense only if the experiments alleged to have lain behind the articles were in fact some sort of major accident. Medvedev believes that the accident was caused by careless storage of nuclear wastes, and in his book on the topic, published by Norton, he was careful to point out that these came from nuclear bomb production rather than from nuclear power plants. He observes that at the time the Soviet power program was in its infancy and stored its wastes elsewhere.

These facts about Medvedev's theory are necessary background for understanding the blurb describing that theory put on the back of his book when it was published in late 1979.[10] This is worth quoting in full:

The danger inherent in the use of nuclear energy has been with us now for decades and, in spite of many popular efforts to curtail its spread, governments persist in expansive programs for its use while telling their people that little or no threat exists. The radiation leakage at the Three Mile Island nuclear power plant in Pennsylvania is the most recent example of the potential for disaster. Even as massive amounts of radiation were being released into the surrounding atmosphere, people were told it was a "controlled leak" and that there was little danger. At the same time, a spokesman for the Soviet Union declared that the possibility of such a disaster has never existed in his country because of their superior precautions. In this timely and important book, the governments of both nuclear super powers are caught in their own deceptions. Zhores A. Medvedev's *Nuclear Disaster in the Urals* is a chilling and sobering revelation of the terrifying path we are being led down.

For every reader who reads the book and discovers that this statement has nothing to do with the book it purports to describe, a dozen browsers are likely to be taken in by it. It is a sign of declining standards that a distinguished publisher can print on one of its books a summary that appears to be so far from its contents.

NOVELS

We live in an age of disaster novels, and nuclear energy has been the subject of more than its share of these. Most are negligible even as trash fiction, but they are still worth considering for the light they cast on the ethical and intellectual state of the American publishing industry.

The best of the lot, artistically and technically, is *The Prometheus Crisis,* by Thomas N. Scortia and Frank M. Robinson,[11] called on its jacket with no doubt unconscious irony "the new big superthriller about the most incredible disaster of them all." In an afternote, its authors are at pains to point out that nuclear reactors cannot explode like bombs, and they note a number of places at which their scenario differs from contemporary engineering practice. One of these, which they attribute to a desire for a more dramatic effect, creates a nuclear plant with four very large reactors enclosed in a common containment building. Such a construction is beyond credibility in the real world of engineering, but it is necessary in the novel not merely for high drama but to provide the lynchpin of the plot, which is that a minor problem in one reactor quickly leads to failure and meltdowns in all four. Such a course of events would not be possible at any real-life multiple installation, where each reactor, for very good reasons that are adequately illustrated by the plot of the novel, gets its own containment building. Given this trifling adjustment of reality, Robinson and Scortia are able to spin out a superficially convincing scenario that results in the apparent destruction of much of California.

In doing so, they manage to libel the nuclear industry by suggesting that such gross irresponsibility in design and construction would be permitted. This is not to suggest that the industry and its regulators are incapable of error, but neither has been guilty of errors of this magnitude, which destroy through the grossest incompetence the integrity of a key reactor defense.

The authors are less careful with regard to the oddities of their on-site fuel reprocessing plant, where bomb-grade plutonium (which is not produced in power reactors) appears to be stored in casks sized for a single man to carry away and in which there are no security measures whatever to keep him from doing so. This also seriously conflicts with reality, and yet serves as a springboard for another important part of the novel, whereby a disaffected plant employee is supplying unspecified clients with bomb material.

The novel offers a reasonably good read, as long as one assumes that little of the technological *mise-en-scène* has anything to do with reality. It is fair to say, however, that Scortia and Robinson appear better informed and more responsible than some antinuclear authors who purport to write nonfiction.

One cannot say as much for Lawrence Huff's *Dome*,[12] which, if not the worst of the lot, must be the most preposterous. The mechanical villain of the piece is a huge breeder reactor located on an island in Lake Pontchartrain near New Orleans; it is planned that all the electric power needed by Louisiana shall be generated from the one plant, and that all existing plants will be shut down as soon as it goes on line. This is a pretty good indication of how Huff treats reality, for such a scheme would be financially plausible only on the exceedingly unlikely assumption that all the other plants were of an age and at the end of their useful lives.

Equally unlikely in concept is his 8 gigawatt (8,000 megawatt) breeder power plant. Although commercial breeders will probably be somewhat larger than the largest light-water plants, no one imagines that they will be of this size. The more one looks at the plant, the crazier it seems. On the one hand, it has (as it would have to) heat exchangers in which the hot sodium is piped through boilers in order to generate steam. On the other hand, the sodium is also sent many miles through underground pipelines to provide heat for various New Orleans suburbs and industrial uses. It does not appear to have occurred to Huff that such pipes would radiate immense amounts of heat into the subsoil (as well as the waters of Lake Pontchartrain, through which they run) and that little would be left at the other end. Not that this is the real problem with the pipes, for it is inconceivable that any engineer would design, any company build, or the government license, a nuclear plant in which key parts of the cooling circuit were not accessible for constant monitoring. To judge from the jacket of the book, the reactor is also equipped with at least one cooling tower, but a close examination of the novel suggests that this is no more than the illustrator's mistaken concept of the containment building.*

Even more unlikely is the series of accidents that strike the plant, as which have been predicted by an Apache nuclear physicist named Slayer. (He is an Apache, apparently, simply to allow extended discussions on the corruption of white society.) Slayer's thesis, based on mathematics so abstruse that only the best minds can understand it, is summarized for a layman by one of his associates as meaning essentially that the more safety systems a nuclear plant has, the greater the risk of an accident because each of the systems has its own element of risk, and it all adds up.

Now of course in a general sense it is true that the more complicated a mechanism is the more things there are to go wrong with it. But this has application as increasing risk in a nuclear reactor only with regard to nonre-dundant systems. And it is precisely the case that the elaboration of systems in a nuclear reactor—in real ones as well as Huff's—is to provide duplicative ways of providing the same safety. If one of four ways to put out a fire is not available, that does not increase the risk of fire in the least; having only three ways to put the fire out to begin with would lower, rather than increase, the level of safety. Huff argues that having four fire extinguishers rather than three raises the risk of fire.

The principle of redundancy in reactors is much more sensible than Huff makes it seem. To take only two examples: Every nuclear reactor has four auxiliary sources of electricity in order to maintain control even if its own generators are shut down. Two of these are from other power plants (which must be far enough away not to be affected, say, by the same hurricane that might have knocked out the plant in question). And two of these are diesel plants on the site. One is there in case the other one does not start. By the Slayer thesis, these precautions increase the risk of a loss of power.

The other example involves instrumentation. Data from key sensors in the reactor are typically brought into the control room over four independent circuits, and in order to trigger an alarm the signal must have come in

---

* The hyperbolic cooling towers at Three Mile Island have been fairly regularly confused with the containment buildings, which are comparatively invisible. And people almost universally imagine that such towers are a peculiarity of nuclear power. Everyone I know who has ever been near Oxford, England, tells me about the gigantic nuclear plant one passes by on the railway. Gigantic it is, but nuclear it is not. In Britain, one should note, with the exception of one or two experimental plants, the possession of such towers is proof that a plant is nonnuclear, for the British nuclear plants are all on the sea and have no need of cooling towers.

over two of the four. This requirement lowers the risk of a false alarm. The odds are astronomically against three of the four lines going out at the same time, or against two of them sending a false signal at the same time.

The final lunacy in this novel is the method the heroic Slayer uses to avert a threatened nuclear explosion in the reactor. He and a colleague enter it, quickly fabricate a nuclear bomb from plutonium on the site, and blow the reactor up, causing a more benign pattern of release than would otherwise have happened.

It is hard to know where the greatest grotesquery lies. The plutonium produced in nuclear plants is not particularly adaptable for bombs, and in any event it is not kept in a form suitable for quick fashioning into a bomb. Even if such plutonium were available, it is beyond belief that such a team could improvise such a bomb. Certainly no one would have used the gloriously dotty design provided by Huff: Two masses of plutonium are positioned above a container surrounded by liquid sodium. When the temperature in the containment building becomes great enough to melt the plutonium, it will flow down through zirconium pipes into the sodium-cooled container where it will be cooled into a solid mass and go boom. Perhaps the most obvious problem here is that there is no provision whatever for containment of the nascent chain reaction, without which an explosion is impossible.

But the most hilarious feature of this design is the use of liquid sodium. Sodium boils at a temperature slightly below that of water. Accordingly, any sodium that is liquid is dangerously hot, and in any environment cooler than that of boiling water it is solid. Huff's treatment of liquid sodium suggests overwhelmingly that he does not understand that it is liquid only because it is very hot, and that it can cool a fast breeder reactor only by being circulated rapidly through the core and then to heat exchangers. It is an excellent medium for the transfer of heat, but it does not have what Huff clearly thinks it has, a normally liquid state and inherent cooling qualities.

We are all richer for imaginative fiction, and certainly a free society must allow the publication even of such wretched twaddle as *Dome*. Such novels, however, are not always taken as imaginative, but rather as speaking the truth, in this case about the dangers of nuclear power. As such, they seriously miseducate the general public on an issue of great importance. This may not be intentional, but that does not matter. Is it not too much to ask that Pocket Books might have sent the manuscript of *Dome* to a nuclear physicist or engineer for review? Any such review would have uncovered the fact that the novel as it stands is infused with dangerous ignorance. Such a review would certainly not have converted *Dome* into a pronuclear tract. But it might have produced something less destined to befoul the public understanding.

One of the most recent, and by far the slickest, disaster novel is *The Dorset Disaster,*[13] by Alexander Sidar III. This work perverts a device recently used by General Sir John Hackett in his *The Third World War,*[14] that of providing a work of speculation about a future event with a great deal of "evidence" adapted from existing photographs. I say that Sidar perverts the technique of *The Third World War* because it is not Sir John Hackett's thesis that the events he "chronicles" are certain to happen, either tomorrow, or in 1985, or ever. Rather, his is a cautionary tale of how a war with the U.S.S.R. might be won by the West if NATO would finally get its act in order. Sidar, in contrast, presents his scenario as something likely to happen soon, and just as he presents it.

This disaster in this case is a so-called ATWS without RPT*—a simultaneous failure not only of the turbine but also of the system for plunging control rods into the reactor core, and also the failure of the trip mechanism designed to lessen the consequences of a scram failure. Sidar's primary concern in the novel is apparently to show what might happen were an operating reactor to blow up and discharge most of its inventory of fission products into the atmosphere. And the consequences are as grim as in any other nuclear disaster novel, or indeed any scenario for assuming that all the safety devices on a reactor fail, made in this case more piquant by Sidar's having provided us with the reactions of the late Governor Grasso, Governor Carey, and Mayor Koch, as well as a photograph of a grim Jimmy Carter walking to the Oval Office to break the bad news to the nation.

But this disaster is just like all the others in requiring a wildly unlikely concatenation of bad luck and reactor failures. It also requires a lurid overestimate of the amount of steam energy available within the reactor vessel. And so the novel is but one more example of how the antinuclear impulse, denied a genuine disaster by the safeguards engineered into nuclear reactors, must satisfy itself with fictional disasters. This novel is unusual in its claim to be nonfiction, that is all.

# Nuclear Energy and the Movies

A neat coincidence has insured that one antinuclear production out of Hollywood will be well-known for a long time. Columbia Pictures' *The China Syndrome* did good business before Three Mile Island and better after. On March 16, 1979, when the film was released, the corporation's stock closed at 21⅝; on the Monday after Three Mile Island, it stood at 26⅞.

* *Anticipated Transient Without Scram* without *Recirculating Pump Trip.*

The film stars Jane Fonda, Jack Lemmon, and its producer, Michael Douglas. The fable is simply told: Fonda plays a light news reporter for a Los Angeles television station, assigned to do a series on energy. While visiting a nuclear plant in the company of her hip cameraman, played by Douglas, she witnesses an accident that begins rather like Three Mile Island but that proceeds to an uncomplicated shutdown, not without an immense amount of implausibility and downright inaccuracy.

The cameraman films the scene in the control room during the accident, and the two rush back to the station with their scoop, which consists largely of shots of the reactor's shift supervisor, played by Jack Lemmon, behaving like a Jack Lemmon character whose wife has come back from her vacation early and whose mistress is in the bathroom. The station's news director suppresses the story and orders the film locked up. The chairman of the operating utility, fearing financial disaster if the accident delays start-up of a recently completed reactor for even a few weeks, orders the plant superintendent to do what he can to cover up the accident. The superintendent and the NRC cooperate in a whitewash, and an implausibly early restart is scheduled for the reactor.

But the shift supervisor is not fooled, and after a little research discovers a leak of radioactive water from a cooling pipe. The superintendent pooh-poohs this very ominous discovery, noting that it would cost a good deal of money if the plant were shut down to investigate. The supervisor next discovers that the plant's X rays of some its welds have been faked. He tracks down the construction company employee who had approved the bogus X rays and announces his intention to go to the NRC; for his pains, his life is threatened.

Meanwhile, back at the station, the cameraman has stolen the film. The reporter, sent off to look for him, runs into the shift supervisor in a bar near the reactor, where he makes an impassioned defense of the nuclear industry and its safety standards. The next day she discovers that the cameraman has taken the film to the licensing hearing for the new reactor, where he has shown it to a couple of antinuclear academics. The same day she learns the story of the bogus X rays from the supervisor; he promises to supply the evidence to be brought out at the hearing, delivered there by the cameraman's sidekick. The reporter goes to the hearing and finds the cameraman deep in conference with the academics. "You're very lucky to be alive," they inform her, "and so is most of Southern California. They came very near to the China Syndrome."

Back in Los Angeles, the supervisor turns the X rays over to the courier. On the way to the hearing, a truck runs the courier off the road and he is seriously injured; the X rays turn up missing from his car. The supervisor goes to his plant and seizes the control room, demanding television time to expose the whole fraud. At length the utility's executives have him cut off the air and machine-gunned, not before he has made himself look like a madman and they have contrived another near disaster for the plant.

This film, which has been widely praised, resembles less a documentary than that meretricious type of *roman à clef* in which actual persons, having been sketched with just enough authentic detail to identify them, are then subjected to savage misrepresentation. The touches of authenticity here include a plausibly elaborate mock-up of a reactor control room and real technical jargon that the characters sling about with more enthusiasm than accuracy.

The film's master misrepresentation is the notion that it is in the financial interest of an electric utility to ignore and cover up a serious malfunction in one of its reactors. Although the utility in question is said to be facing serious cash-flow problems if its reactor is not gotten back in service quickly, in real life, when a reactor is temporarily out of service, the principal cost to the utility is that of replacement electricity. This is a charge borne not by the utility but by its customers, and accordingly it is no threat to corporate greed. What would threaten not merely the health but the existence of the entire nuclear industry would be a catastrophic accident, such as an uncontained meltdown, that posed a potential threat to large numbers of the public. Thus the rational self-interest of utility officials—even of such moral monsters as those in *The China Syndrome*—would lead them to be maximally careful, not implausibly reckless.

The picture given in *The China Syndrome* should be compared to the real-life incidents surrounding the NRC's early 1979 shutdown of five plants over faint doubts as to their earthquake-proofness. In this actual case, it is instructive to note who blew the whistle: not a little band of journalistic heroes, but officers of one of the affected utilities and of the firm that built all five plants.

Almost as fantastic as the film's economics is the course of the accidents it purports to record. The first of these is, in certain respects, eerily like the Three Mile Island accident, although it is treated with grotesque inaccuracy. It begins with a so-called "turbine trip,"* an event in the nonnuclear part of the power station that makes it necessary to shut down the turbine, the generator, and the reactor. Since the steam circuit that drives the turbine is integral to the system by which the reactor is cooled, the reactor cannot operate unless the turbine is working. The problem is analogous to the over-

---

* In the jargon of the industry a "trip" is an automatic shutdown of a component made necessary by safety or operating considerations.

heating that follows when a water pump fails on an automobile engine. In either case, the remedy is to shut off the major source of heat: in the car, this is the engine; in the power plant, the chain reaction.

In the accident the film describes, an unexplained turbine trip leads to a computer decision to "scram" the reactor. As this automated process gets underway, there is a sudden indication that water levels in the reactor core are rising dangerously. This very notion is so much nonsense: The reactor, from its outward appearance and the diagram used by its public relations man, is clearly a pressurized-water one, and it would have had no gauges to indicate water level in the core.* The shift supervisor agitatedly says that they've got to find where all this extra water is coming from, because the water has gotten almost to the steam pipes. This is another bit of nonsense: There are no steam pipes in the reactor vessel of a pressurized-water reactor. Suddenly someone else notes that another indicator shows the water level falling below normal. (This indicator is placed at another location in the control panel, although in real reactors—specifically the Trojan plant in Oregon that the film takes as its model—the two types of indicator are adjacent.)

The shift supervisor taps the glass cover of the recording graph, and the stylus falls precipitously. It is never explained how it got above normal before sticking to begin with, but the shift supervisor, now dealing with the problem of inadequate coolant, is apparently too busy to wonder about this. The new problem is even more preposterous than its predecessor. There is only one cause for such a drop in reactor coolant: either a major venting of water from the primary circuit, as happened at Three Mile Island, or a serious leak in the primary cooling circuit, the equivalent of a ruptured water hose in a car. In either case, the cause of the drop in reactor coolant would have been immediately apparent as water and steam gushed into the containment building. The reactor's Emergency Core Cooling System (ECCS) would have sprung into action to replace the lost water, as it did at Three Mile Island. In the fantasy world of the film, the shift supervisor, after being told that the primary ECCS system is down for maintenance,† appears to

---

* Technical advice for the film came, from among other sources, three nuclear engineers who several years ago, having joined the para-religious and antinuclear organization Project Survival, itself a stepchild of the so-called Creative Initiative Foundation, resigned from the General Electric Company. Their experience at GE was with boiling-water reactors, and this may have led them astray. Alternatively, the film's producers may not have realized that the schematic diagram they placed in the hands of the plant's PR man, showing a pressurized-water reactor, did not describe the plant as set forth in the script. Or—perhaps most plausibly—they may not have cared much about accuracy.

† Operating with an entire ECCS system out of commission would have been a very serious violation of NRC rules. The real-life NRC threatened to revoke the operating license for Three Mile Island for a somewhat less serious offense, but in the film it confines itself to a mild remonstrance.

activate a backup ECCS manually, after which action he turns to prayer. Following an unexplained delay, the water level begins rising slowly (the real-life ECCS functions quickly) and the reactor's computer informs a relieved shift supervisor that the scram is complete.

The film treats the sequelae of this accident even more unrealistically. When the film was made, a loss-of-coolant accident had never happened in a light-water power reactor. Had such an accident happened, as the film clearly claims it did, it would have caused a sensation. It is instructive to contrast what happens in the film with what happened after Three Mile Island. Not only would the NRC have conducted a lengthy investigation before even attempting to repair what would have been perforce a severely damaged reactor, but antinuclear activists would have seized on the accident as the ultimate proof that nuclear power is unsafe. In fantasyland, however, the NRC conducts a perfunctory investigation and the reactor is returned to service in less than a week.

The second accident is a confused emulation of the first. By now the shift supervisor has seized the control room and is demanding television time to tell the terrible truth about reactor safety. The bad guys start interfering with the security systems guarding the control room—a reasonable action even for good guys, given the hysterical behavior of the man at the controls—and when he realizes this, he threatens to flood the containment with water, and says that if he does, "God help the power company." The audience is left to speculate as to what horrors the threat entails. In reality, the most a man in the control room could have done would be to spray the containment with water designed to cool it down and counteract the effects of leaking radiation.

Undaunted, the bad guys decide to shut the reactor off without using the control room. Their technical experts tell them that there *is* a way to do this, involving bypassing a variety of connections in the bowels of the reactor. Their minions repair thither, attempting to scram the reactor behind the shift supervisor's back. After an hour's effort, they succeed. (This sequence too is fantasy: When I asked a shift supervisor at a very similar reactor how hard it would be to scram his reactor without access to the control room, he replied that he could think of about a dozen ways right off, of which the easiest would be to disconnect the generator from the grid by tripping the main circuit breakers of the distribution system. This could be done in a few seconds and a scram would follow.)

In the film, when the villains finally succeed, another accident begins— one heralded by a shaking of the control room and containment building that would be unlikely even in a major earthquake and that could not be caused by a loss-of-coolant accident—followed by the failure of a small pipe connected to what is presumably a steam generator.* There is a loss of coolant, and after appropriate nail-biting the reactor scrams and the China Syndrome is once more postponed. This chain of events corresponds to no known or technically envisionable reactor accident. It appears to have been confected for its dramatic effect alone.

Yet even if we were to concede that Hollywood showing a reactor accident in 1978 is no more interested in technical accuracy than Hollywood in 1938 was in showing the court of Elizabeth I, there are other and more meretricious flaws in this film, extending well beyond the technicalities of reactor operation.

One nonnuclear example is its bizarre picture of television news, which is presented as being reticent about prompt publication. The spectacle of a station manager refusing to run sensational footage "until we know exactly what this means" is counter to everything we know about the way television works, as is the suggestion that television stations are timorously unwilling to run the risks of libel actions from public corporations in a world in which such actions have been effectively ruled out.

Another serious distortion is apparent in the film's treatment of plant security. We see a total of three security guards, two of whom are elderly buffers at the gate, drawn from Central Casting's sheriff's-deputy pool. The other is a wimpy guard in the control room itself whose general alertness is insufficient to keep him from being disarmed by a stock Jack Lemmon character. This picture, as anyone who has visited a reactor can testify, is very far from the truth. There are formidable-looking armed guards everywhere, and the security checks even for friendly visitors seem to be derived from practice at maximum-security prisons. These facts, if represented, would not have been helpful to the film's message.

Much more serious is the film's flagrant misrepresentation of the licensing process. Early on, the public relations man says that the utility hopes to put its new reactor on line shortly. "We're having the licensing hearings next week," he notes. As represented in the film, the "licensing hearings" consist of citizens addressing a panel of what are presumably NRC commissioners or their deputies.

One pro-nuclear witness appears: Identified in an interview outside the hearing as a health physicist, he tells the television audience that he believes the new plant should be licensed because he believes that *any* large source of energy should be licensed; that is apparently the extent of the case for nuclear power. Once before the panel, he announces his special concern with

---

* I say "presumably" because the hodgepodge of locations used in the film makes it hard to judge just what is really being represented. The turbine room is that of a smaller oil-fired plant; the "steam generator" is reported to be a bit of plumbing in a Southern California hydro-power plant, and is not very convincing.

the problem of radioactive waste. He then states the view that he has come to oppose: the conventional (and false) claim that we have no idea how to deal with the problem of waste storage, a claim already made by two other characters in the film. The camera then leaves him and does not return until he has finished his testimony. The film thus neatly censors the view that solutions for radioactive waste storage have already been found—a bit of manipulation that is necessary in order to leave unchallenged one of the central myths of the antinuclear movement.

We see two antinuclear testimonies, both theatrical exercises. In the first, a group of mothers hold up pictures of their children—who presumably must be protected from nuclear power—while one of their number reads names and ages. In another, a group of people wearings gags stand before the tribunal while a young man says that since in all the licensing hearings held heretofore the NRC has never denied a license, there is no point in talking. He then gags himself and his group waits until their five minutes are up.

The film thus puts forth an unambiguous account of how nuclear plants are licensed; in brief *pro forma* hearings in which the NRC ignores all critical testimony, which testimony has in any event been reduced to upper-middle class guerrilla theater. The truth is of course very different: Typically, nuclear reactors are subject not only to federal but to state and local licensing arrangements. The federal requirements are not merely those of the NRC, but also of the Environmental Protection Agency (EPA). The NRC requires licenses not only for the operation but also for the construction of nuclear power plants. The EPA requires a massive environmental impact statement; state requirements vary, with California's being as tough as or tougher than the federal standards. The total number of licenses and permits can exceed 100, and it is possible for a plant to lose ground during the licensing process as governments impose new requirements faster than old ones are met.

Decisions made by administrative bodies can be taken into the courts by so-called intervenors. A reactor put on line in 1981 will have gone through a licensing process lasting not a few days but years. Typically a construction license is granted two years after application, and typically a utility applies for an operating license four years before it expects to be able to operate. The total time between a decision to build a nuclear power plant and the generation of electricity is now over twelve years. During this period, the design and construction of the plant would have undergone repeated modification in response to the objections of nuclear opponents. A study by a group at the Harvard Business School and M.I.T. concludes that delay in the licensing period is the single most important cause in increasing the cost of nuclear plants.[15]

There is an unpleasant term for what the film does in this respect, but its unpleasantness should be no bar to its use: The film lies. It lies, moreover, to the public, and on an issue of great consequence.

But even this does not exhaust the mendacity of *The China Syndrome*. It shows the nuclear industry as being on two occasions willing to commit murder in order to suppress inconvenient facts. On the second occasion, the character played by Jack Lemmon is machine-gunned to death by a county sheriff's SWAT team. Perhaps in the inflamed imaginations of those who produced this film such events are possible; given their comic-book view of businessmen, they may just have thought they were depicting something that could happen.

The first murder (which is only attempted) is rather different: It is based on an actual case and has been distorted in a fashion that makes clear the cool way in which the film's perpetrators have "improved" reality whenever it was insufficiently horrific for their ideological purposes.

The attempted assassination appears to be modeled on the antinuclear movement's version of the death of Karen Silkwood. I have already discussed* a number of facts that devastate this version. None of these facts is built into the film's emulation. And there is a further improvement of the evidence. The altered X rays in the Silkwood case, unlike those in the film, did not involve misrepresentations of welds; rather, an analyst had touched up scratches in the background of otherwise usable negatives rather than reshoot them; there was no falsification of evidence about the welds themselves. Improper activity, to be sure, but a far cry from representing an X ray of one weld as an X ray of many.

*The China Syndrome* is, in sum, a consistent act of fabrication. It is a slick disaster film, generally superior to the run of such films because of the performances of actors who have been used to bamboozle the American people. This is, of course, not behavior substantially different from what we have been led to expect from Hollywood. Who ever expected Tinseltown to cover complex and highly politicized issues with either penetration or accuracy? Miss Fonda and her associates have been widely regarded as heroic purveyors of a truth suppressed by other media types who are motivated by a base desire for money.

Jane Fonda, Jack Lemmon, and Michael Douglas, at any rate, will be able to giggle all the way to the bank. If they are wise, it will be a Swiss bank, for Switzerland pursues a rational energy policy, and when the lights begin going out in America, even in Southern California, adequately provident antinuclearists can opt for a comfortable exile among the atomic gnomes of Zurich.

* See p. 150.

# Nuclear Energy as a Moral Issue

Antinuclearism in its most fashionable form claims that the nuclear industry is manned by moral monsters to whom profit is all and human life nothing. Sometimes the claim is made with amazing explicitness. The key to much antinuclear thought, as it is indeed to most extremist thinking, whether left-wing, right-wing, or merely antitechnological, is a profound belief in the innate viciousness of the other side, and especially in the innate viciousness of its leaders. Speaking in a backyard in sight of Three Mile Island on the first anniversary of the accident, Barry Commoner claimed that the proposed plan to vent radioactive krypton gas (carried out in the summer of 1980) would pose a serious health hazard and had been chosen simply because it would cost less and thus protect the profits of the contractor. The implication was that the contractor had made the choice quite aware of the serious health hazards, and that the NRC and the Commonwealth of Pennsylvania had knowingly gone along.

Now, such criminality—on the part of one group of executives—is *possible,* in the sense that one could not reject outright a carefully documented claim that such behavior existed. But Commoner made no such documented claim. Rather, he cited the a priori criminality of businessmen and government officials as his evidence.

He is not alone in this view of the opposition as beast. Helen Caldicott, after a reasonably civil television debate, burst out that I and a colleague were "merchants of death." She appears utterly unwilling to imagine that those with whom she disagrees on a key issue might be decent, if mistaken, folk. George Wald has taken this sort of view about as far as anyone is likely to take it. Admittedly, he was talking in the context of nuclear weapons rather than nuclear power, but he would probably be the first to tell us that the two are hopelessly entangled. The capitalist class, he said, would not find a nuclear war any problem, for all they cared about was profits.

On the presumption that he really believed what he was saying, it is hard to know which is the more appalling idea: that he really believes business management would not find a nuclear war troublesome so long as their dividends could be maintained, or that he really believes those dividends could be maintained in the face of a nuclear war.

One gets the impression that in private Professor Wald may well be a nice man, and that he would never utter so vicious a slander against someone he knew personally. But he has apparently come to regard the capitalists—for which read a large proportion of his fellow Americans—as heartless monsters of whom practically anything may be believed or said.

This sort of approach to the opposition, besides indulging one's aggressions, is also a convenient and easy substitute for thought. It may be comparatively easy to identify one's opponents and their errors. To analyze the source of their errors is substantially more difficult. In an age that has begun to deal with fairly sophisticated issues through comic books, it should not be surprising that a lot of people don't want to work that hard.

The tendency to deal with opponents in the shortest way exists on both sides of the nuclear controversy. (Although it is fair to say that among educated pronuclear people it is much rarer than among educated antinuclearists.) Every so often I find myself trying to explain to some helpful supporter that no, I don't think that all active opponents of nuclear power hold commissions in the KGB. This sort of stereotyped attitude toward dissent is usually recognized for what it is by people who hold all the proper views on large social questions. They are less apt to identify it among themselves.*

It should be clear that people who enter the nuclear debate freighted with such assumptions about the industry and its regulators are seriously blinded. Although it has not been much noticed, there can hardly be a better example of public blindness pandered to by a half-seeing intelligentsia than the case of Columbia University's TRIGA reactor.

The case of this research reactor is well worth examining. This type of reactor, developed and produced by the General Atomic Corporation, grew out of a project of Edward Teller, to produce a small research reactor that should be *inherently* safe rather than safe through engineered safeguards. The distinction is important: Elevators are an example of devices made safe— extraordinarily so—through engineered safeguards. The machinery that brakes and then locks a falling elevator into place is kept from acting by the tension of the cable that holds the elevator up. Once this tension is lost, the brakes automatically set without further intervention by either humans or control devices. An analogous system governs the setting of the Westinghouse air brake on railway trains.

But as clever as these systems are, they depend on intelligent conception and faithful execution of human schemes. They insure a remarkable degree of safety, but they are not infallible. It is otherwise with inherent safety, in which natural law provides the margin, as in the case of the laws of physics

---

* Among the educated and liberal, support for nuclear energy does indeed constitute a tiny minority position. At my son's school, antinuclearism comes as close to being an established religion as is possible in an institution that values freedom of thought. One of his friends, noting that a certain person didn't care for him much, reported as the ultimate evidence of his hostility: "He even said you were in favor of nuclear energy!" Needless to say, that support for nuclear energy is a minority position held only by dissenters gives it no cachet whatever among intellectuals, who value only those forms of dissent that everyone they know joins in.

that prevent a light-water reactor from exploding like a bomb. The TRIGA was provided with a graphite moderator that has immense capacities for absorbing heat. But beyond this line of defense, it was designed so that its power production is inversely proportional to its temperature.* That is, if it starts to overheat, its inherent response is to shut down.

Freeman Dyson, in a recent memoir,[16] recounts the dedication of the prototype TRIGA at the General Atomic plant. Niels Bohr, after the death of Einstein the most distinguished living physicist, made the address. After he finished, the TRIGA was started up, its power output shown on a large meter on the rostrum. Suddenly all the control rods were pulled out, an action guaranteed to produce a massive excursion of power. As the crowd watched, the power rocketed up and then suddenly tumbled to nothing, quenched in obedience to the laws Bohr had been fundamental in discovering.

In the years that followed TRIGA research reactors were sold to various colleges, universities, and other institutions. One of these was Reed College, where the TRIGA was located in the midst of one of the better residential sections of Portland, Oregon. The reactor building was a few blocks from my own house, and I do not believe I gave a second's thought to the possibility that it might act up until some time in the late 1960s during a dust-up between students and faculty, when it was rumored that certain students planned to seize the reactor and threaten to blow it up were their demands not met.

At the time a colleague in physics explained to me how, even were a team of technicians from the AEC to try to blow it up, they could not succeed. I count this experience as something of an inoculation that later made me skeptical when I heard Ralph Nader and others talk about nuclear reactors blowing up.

Another TRIGA was sold to Columbia University. But it has never been used. Antinuclear hysteria in the community kept delaying the start-up, and finally after Three Mile Island Columbia announced that it had decided not to use it.

Here reason confronted the witch doctors and fled the field. The administration of Columbia University, if it was advised by its experts in nuclear technology, can have had no doubts about the safety of its reactor, but rather than stand up for the truth and attempt to educate the community on this vital issue, it receded before the witch doctors.

This incident is testimony to the extent to which misinformation about the atom, fed originally by irresponsible scientists and then amplified by

---

* This state of affairs also obtains with the allegedly dangerous liquid-metal-cooled fast breeder reactor.

the press, the publishers, and their less educated followers, has damaged our ability to see technical reality. Columbia University is an extraordinary storehouse of intelligence and dedication. We will never know what problems of mankind, whether in energy, food, or medicine, its throttled research reactor might have helped us to solve, had it been made available to that dedicated intelligence.

# 8

## *The Atom and the Future of Energy*

ON THE ASSUMPTION that we owe a primary obligation to ourselves and our immediate posterity and a very strong secondary obligation to our more distant posterity, let us consider some imperatives for our future use of energy.

The first should be that man is not made for energy but energy for man. We do not live for the purpose of using any particular energy system or manifestation of it. That means we should be willing, should the opportunity ever arise and it seem desirable, to let the Arabs keep their oil. Nor should anyone be required to feed a wood stove unless he wants to. Nor, indeed, does nuclear energy, however well established it might be, have a right to exist except as it satisfies the nation's energy needs in a fashion suitable to it.

The second imperative is that we owe to our posterity access to petroleum, coal, and natural gas not merely as fuels* but as chemical feedstocks. That is, we cannot justify burning any of these as fuels except on the ground that some very serious harm may come to us otherwise. This fact lies heavy on coal whether burned directly or through synfuels.

The third is that the continued importation of OPEC oil is economically— and, more important, politically—deleterious to the welfare of the United States. Import of any oil whatever affects the balance of payments; such

---

* It seems fairly unlikely that our distant posterity will want to use fossil resources as fuels, but our immediate posterity will have to. If they know what's good for them, and for their own posterity, they will do their best to lessen their dependence.

imported oil as does not hold us up for political ransom is still damaging economically. OPEC oil will continue to be politically damaging until such times—not in sight—as the Arabs no longer dominate OPEC (or a successor group) or there are no longer any serious political issues between this country and the Arab world. Although we must continue to import OPEC and other foreign oil, we should not regard the practice as tolerable indefinitely.

Fourth, even if we could regard our coal as a resource properly to be burned, even in the best of circumstances, in the foreseeable future its use will be occupationally dubious and environmentally disastrous. Although in pursuit of the second goal we must burn not only coal but more coal, this reliance, over the long haul, is as intolerable, if for different reasons, as the use of OPEC oil. Although coal is somewhat less dangerous when converted to and used as synfuel, it is not harmless and should come under similar constraints.

Fifth, although the various "alternative" sources of energy roughly groupable as "solar" can make some contribution to our energy needs, neither severally nor singly are they an answer to our problem. And even when successful some of them are unsuitable under the dictates of the first imperative.

Sixth, when we use fossil fuels, we ought to use them in the most reasonable fashion. For example, we have devised or are devising substitutes for petroleum in all types of transportation other than aircraft. This should lead us to such programs as the electrification of railways to be run on electricity generated from the atom, as well as projects to electrify as much of our automobile use as possible. Such conversions, it should be realized, are proposals to save fossil resources that will almost certainly be needed by our remotest imaginable descendants and to spend nuclear resources that those descendants would find a patrimony literally of lead. Similarly, natural gas, burning as cleanly as it does and comparatively so easy to transport, is so well adapted to certain uses—such as cooking—that its use should be discouraged outside those areas.

The inference to be drawn from these principles is that nuclear energy, far from being a pariah among resources, ought to be the energy source of choice for all uses for which electricity is a suitable intermediary. It does not matter whether electric generators waste heat if they waste heat derived from abundant and otherwise useless thorium. Wastage is, after all, the misuse of something that could be better used otherwise. On the long haul, any use of oil to generate electricity is entirely waste. But thorium, essentially incapable of being used elsewhere, can be wasted only through disuse. The same is true for uranium and plutonium, unless we regard bomb explosions as a more provident use than power reactors.

It is important to realize that an end use of energy does not necessarily have the same value as its primary source. When used to spin motors, electricity has an extremely high mechanical efficiency, much higher than the thermal generating plants that produce it. Trolley cars are coming back into their own because they are said to be nonpolluting. And so they are, but the same cannot be said for the coal-fired plants that may produce their electricity for them.

There is no point in converting to electricity except as a means to exploit a superior means of generating it—that is to say, to increase the use of the atom as a primary energy source. At the moment, we burn residual oil in power plants. This is a fuel that can be reformed into synthetic crude and then into gasoline. But we not only need to convert existing coal- and oil-fired power plants to nuclear energy, but to convert energy demand now directly satisfied through coal and oil to nuclear electricity.

An example of this problem is to be found in current programs to develop cars powered by electricity. The most affectionate user of the gasoline- or diesel-powered car must concede that just now it has two serious drawbacks that must be balanced against its many virtues. It is, first of all, a very serious contributor to air pollution, and especially to that most noxious form that is not merely lethal but also unpleasant to smell. And, second, it burns a politically and economically disastrous fuel. At least for use in urban areas, electric-powered cars present a substantial promise of improvement.

But the promise will not be fulfilled by replacing millions of internal-combustion-engine–powered cars with millions of electric cars and then generating their electricity by burning coal or oil. To begin with, the changeover replaces one set of heat engines with another, ensuring efficiency problems. (Advantages of scale in central generation and the high efficiency of electric motors make this additional reduction less serious than it might be, but it is still there.)

The plain fact is—and it is not often recognized by electric car enthusiasts—that a massive conversion to electric cars would require a massive new source of electricity, which would have to be generated by entirely new power plants. There is no more absurd spectacle than those who argue out of one side of their mouths that we ought to replace the internal combustion car with the electric car and out of the other side that we do not need to increase our generating capacity.

Moreover, if these plants are run on fossil fuels, much of the advantage sought in the conversion will be lost. There is one source of electricity in very large amounts that preserves the advantage: nuclear power, which neither pollutes nor increases our servitude to OPEC. The same, *mutatis mutandis,* is true of converting railways to electricity. We could convert a substantial portion of present long-distance truck traffic to the rails, substituting otherwise useless uranium and thorium for valuable oil.

Looking still further ahead, we could convert a substantial portion of our airline mileage to high-speed electric trains, which could run from Chicago to Los Angeles at 300 miles per hour. The technology for these has been well advanced in Great Britain and France.

Now, it is not the case that we can derive infinite new supplies of electricity merely by building more light-water reactors. Such reactors waste most of the uranium put into them, for most of it is neither fissioned directly nor transmuted into plutonium. This is not a serious problem at the moment, given world uranium supplies, but any serious expansion—or, indeed, prolongation—of the present light-water program would lead to difficulties of supply.

What is remarkable in most discussions of energy alternatives is that they never deal with alternatives in nuclear energy, an energy technology that is uneasily suspended between tradition and innovation, never receiving the easy benefit-of-the-doubt extended to coal or the glister of the new and different. As it happens, there is an alternative form of producing nuclear energy that is as near commercialization as most of those we have been surveying, and nearer than many.

This is the High-Temperature Gas-Cooled Reactor (HTGR), which already operates in a major demonstration project in Colorado and for which commercialization strategies are now being drawn up. In such a reactor the liberation of energy is accomplished by a chain reaction like that used in contemporary light-water reactors, but that is about the only close resemblance. In an HTGR, the fuel is a mixture of uranium and thorium, the latter an element so plentiful that estimated world reserves equal the energy content of all other known fuels, fossil and nuclear. Thorium-232, the most common isotope, is not fissionable; but when exposed to a chain reaction fueled by uranium, atoms of thorium are transmuted into U-233, the uranium isotope best suited for reactor operation. These atoms in turn begin to take part in the chain reaction.

The HTGR is a so-called converter reactor: Although it cannot, like the breeder reactor, produce more fuel than it consumes, it can produce almost as much as it uses. It thus requires very little natural uranium to start with, and once U-233 is reprocessed from spent fuel, an HTGR system becomes independent of uranium mining, existing on thorium and transmuted U-233. Moreover, U-233, which plays a role analogous to plutonium in the most common breeder cycle, is much less toxic than plutonium and is produced in association with U-232, which is a powerful emitter of gamma rays. This makes the spent fuel substantially more dangerous and therefore harder for a band of terrorists to steal.

The HTGR is superior, however, in more than its fuel cycle. Small grains of the fuel are encased in tiny spheres of carbon and graphite, which serve as miniature pressure vessels encasing the highly radioactive fission products created by the chain reaction. These encapsulated grains are then mixed in graphite blocks. Graphite serves as the neutron moderator and has the great advantage that it grows stronger as it grows hotter, and cannot melt—it has no liquid phase. The chain reaction is cooled by circulating helium gas. Unlike the sodium used to cool breeder reactors, helium is highly inert, and unlike the water used in the light-water reactor, it is not made radioactive under neutron bombardment. And the pressure vessel of an HTGR, which is made of prestressed concrete lined with steel, encloses not merely the core but also the entire primary system of the reactor—that is, everything that would be inside the containment building of a pressurized-water reactor such as Three Mile Island.

The power density—that is, the heat per unit of core volume—of the HTGR is the lowest of any modern reactor design. This means that cooling it is comparatively easy, and should the helium coolant be lost and the chain reaction be shut down, air at normal pressure can be circulated as a coolant sufficient to carry away the decay heat. The core, moreover, contains much less fissionable material than that of most other designs. On the other hand, the burnup—the proportion of atoms in fuel that can be fissioned before reprocessing—is unexcelled by any other reactor design. And, finally, the thermal efficiency of an HTGR is much better than any other electric generator, nuclear or not, and can in some designs exceed 50 percent.*

This energy system is not, like so much proposed by Barry Commoner, a statement of theoretical possibilities left for the engineers to chew on. Rather it is a working device already brought near commercialization. The first HTGR was designed and operated in Britain; the next was operated with great success as part of Philadelphia's power supply and has now been decommissioned at the conclusion of the test program of which it was part; and now a demonstration plant, with about a third of a modern LWR in output and embodying a number of important advances, is generating power at Fort St. Vrain in Colorado. Like any first-of-a-kind device, it has not been without problems, but almost all of these have been in the nonnuclear part of the plant. The only major problem in the nuclear part has been a small and controllable but unexplained fluctuation in the temperature of the coolant.

One of the Colorado HTGR's most endearing features is the minuscule amount of its occupational radiation exposures; its owner is unable to provide

---

* The design I have just been describing is more efficient and safer than the light-water reactors now in use, but I do not want to be misunderstood here: I am not varying the view I have expressed elsewhere that the LWR is superior, in terms of economics and safety, to any nonnuclear source of megawattage.

the NRC with radiation readings at a number of stipulated locations because there are no instruments sensitive enough for the job. The General Atomic Company, builder of the Colorado plant and the principal home in this country of HTGR technology, designed and put on the market a larger plant based on the Fort St. Vrain model for which it received ten orders. Price escalation and regulatory delays eventually made the contracts for these plants financially disastrous for the company, and it exercised a buy-out option and cancelled the contracts. While it is not currently vending power reactors, its research program goes on unabated.

In company with the Department of Energy, it has turned its attention to two important modifications of the HTGR. One is the development of a power reactor in which a gas turbine is spun directly by the helium coolant, eliminating steam generators and making it possible, with the use of dry cooling towers, to site the plant in arid locations. Such a plant—for which the basic mechanism, the fuel core and the fuel cycle, have already been developed for the earlier steam-generating HTGR—would be cheaper, simpler, and even better contained than the Fort St. Vrain plant.

The other proposal is for an even higher-temperature gas-cooled reactor to produce not electricity but industrial process heat. If this country does become involved with synthetic fuels in a big way, it is going to need vast new sources of heat to convert oil shale or to liquefy or gasify coal, and such a reactor would provide them without requiring a massive start-up supply of fossil fuels for initial heat.

The HTGR is especially adapted to live in symbiosis with other types of reactors. For example, four existing light-water reactors burning uranium could provide plutonium sufficient for the core of one plutonium-uranium-thorium fast breeder. This reactor would be a net consumer, not producer, of plutonium, for it would annihilate plutonium in its core and breed U-233 from thorium in its blanket. This U-233, with appropriate amounts of thorium, would fuel ten HTGRs.*

Let us assume that each of these reactors generated 1,000 megawatts (MW). The breeder and the HTGRs would produce 11,000 MW of electricity from fuels artificially transmuted from the otherwise almost useless U-238 and Th-232. This is not something out of nothing, but it is a pretty good approximation, requiring no societal dislocation to turn the trick.

There is a potentially even more attractive reactor in the wings, the Canadian "Slowpoke." In contrast to the 100-ton cores of some power reactors, this reactor has a very small core, containing only a few pounds of uranium. The Slowpoke core is surrounded by beryllium reflectors that act as mirrors

* This model has been proposed by Peter Fortescue, Technical Director of the General Atomic Company and the pioneer of HTGR development in this country and in England.

to reflect neutrons shooting out of the core. In more conventional reactors, a neutron that escapes from the core without shattering an atom is a neutron lost forever, but in Slowpoke, such neutrons carom back into the core for another try. The result is that a very small core can sustain a chain reaction.

In a Slowpoke reactor, cooling water never gets above 80 degrees C., and there can never be a loss-of-coolant accident. Even if there could be, the reactor's tiny core never builds up enough fission products to produce a meltdown. It is so inherently safe that it has been said that although a Slowpoke is always very safe, it is safer with its operators off duty than on.

The Slowpoke is not a fantasy or a promise: Atomic Energy of Canada, Ltd. (AECL), now sells Slowpoke II as a research reactor, and is assessing Slowpoke III as a source of hot water for apartments and for district heating. By a clever use of beryllium reflection—originally devised for plutonium bombs—AECL has domesticated the nuclear reactor and made it useful for an immense energy load that is now carried by oil, gas, and coal.* Such a development ought to remind us that technology is full of surprises. Three days before the first flight of the Wright Brothers, the *New York Times* editorially concluded, on the basis of S. P. Langley's failure, that manned flight was impossible; in 1941, after both the British and German jet fighter projects had proved successful, a blue-ribbon American commission decided that the gas turbine would never be efficient enough to power an airplane.

It is a measure of the confusion with which we deal with energy policy that we are more likely to base our energy system on the constraining and inflexible source of the sun than to develop such exceptionally efficient and almost benevolent alternatives.

Further in the future are fusion reactors. We may yet find out that these devices will give us essentially unlimited energy (a consequence feared by Amory Lovins, who does not believe that we can be trusted with it). Or we may yet find out that operable fusion reactors can never be made to be economic or indeed to function. They remain a glittering promise, development toward them is proceeding on schedule (or ahead of it, in some views), but we would be very unwise to consume any kilowatts from them before we have them.

More important than settling on any one means of exploiting the energy of the atom is realizing its potential for humanity. At present, this is not

---

* Such use of small nuclear reactors for district heating has already been tried. A Swedish 65 MW reactor supplied heat to a suburb of Stockholm in the decade before 1973 and was closed down as uneconomical just before the oil embargo. In light of current oil prices, a Finno-Swedish consortium is developing a 200 MW heating reactor. France is developing a 100 MW reactor of similar design. The Soviets have one 5 MW heating reactor and others in development, although these, being pressurized, are not inherently safe like Slowpoke and its cousins.

easy: The controversy over the wisdom of nuclear energy is fueled by a variety of organizations whose good faith is open to doubt and whose accuracy leaves everything to be desired, magnified by media that are generally ill-equipped to transmit, let alone participate in, the discussion. Moreover, this is a country so rich in energy and so accustomed to getting it cheaply that it seems plausible that energy sources be chosen for such qualities as "decentralization" or indeed "naturalness" ahead of such qualities as "affordability" or "operability." After seven years of price rises, Americans still pay little more than a third as much for gasoline as, say, Danes.

But we cannot long pursue a frivolous energy policy. Ultimately we must come to grips with the fact that our society is energy-dependent, that it is so because we preferred it that way, and that if we are to maintain ourselves, we must take an unsentimental view of how best to fill our energy needs. Moreover, the only hope for the nations of the developing world is to become similarly energy-intensive. For if human beings do not have electrical and other energetic servants to work for us, we will have no option but to cut out much of our activity, and, in the remainder, do for ourselves.

The least constrained practical source of energy on a large scale remains nuclear energy. Not all the cries of the warriors against the atom can efface that fact, and if we are very fortunate we will come to our senses on the matter, and quickly. If not we will survive to leave a posterity to curse us for our improvident folly.

# Notes

## Chapter 2

1. Updated, unpublished file version (1965) of WASH-740, "Theoretical and Possible Consequences of Major Accidents in Large Nuclear Power Plants" (Atomic Energy Commission, 1957).

2. C. S. Forester, *Captain Horatio Hornblower* (Boston: Little, Brown, 1948), p. 22.

3. This report, issued in 1979, is one of a series produced by the National Academy of Sciences-National Research Council (Washington, D.C.) under the title *The Effects on Populations of Exposure to Low Levels of Radiation*. It is known colloquially as BEIR-II.

4. This is the 1980 update of the preceding, known as BEIR-III.

5. *New York Times,* 30 April 1979, p. 1.

6. Estimates vary considerably: D. J. Rose, P. W. Walsh, and L. L. Leskovjan, "Nuclear Power vis-à-vis Its Alternatives, Chiefly Coal" (unpublished, M.I.T., December 10, 1975), estimate between twenty and one hundred excess deaths from respiratory disease caused by coal-burning plants; the estimate embodied in W. Meyer, M. R. Rollins, and R. W. Williams, "Estimates of the Effects of a Five-Year National Nuclear Moratorium" (unpublished, University of Missouri, 1975) is forty to one hundred excess deaths; similar estimates have been calculated by L. Lave and E. Seskin, *An Analysis of the Association between US Mortality and Air Pollution* (Pittsburgh: University of Pittsburgh, 1971); R. Wilson and W. J. Jones, *Energy, Ecology, and the Environment* (New York: Academic Press, 1974); and the office of Technology Assessment, *The Direct Use of Coal* (Washington, D.C.: Government Printing Office, 1979), p. 217.

7. *Times* (London), 22 November 1957, p. 6d.

8. Personal communication from staff of National Radiological Protection Board (U.K.).

9. High Background Radiation Research Group (Ministry of Health, Beijing), "Health Survey in High Background Radiation Areas in China," *Science,* vol. 209, 22 August 1980.

10. W. J. Schull, M. Otake, and J. V. Neel, "Genetic Effects of the Atomic Bombs: A Reappraisal," *Science* 213 (4513), 11 September 1981, pp. 1220–27.

11. *New York Times,* 11 December 1978, p. 14.

12. See bibliography, under Kemeny.

13. WASH-1400, *Reactor Safety Study: An Assessment of Accident Risks in U.S. Commercial Nuclear Power Plants* (Washington, D.C.: Atomic Energy Commission, October 1975).

14. Ford Foundation, *Energy the Next Twenty Years* (Cambridge: Ballinger, 1979), p. 437.

15. Personal communication with Petr Beckmann.

16. John G. Fuller, *We Almost Lost Detroit* (New York: Ballantine, 1976).

17. *New York Times,* 20 November 1978, IV, 1.

18. Personal communication from staff at Jersey Central Power & Light.

19. Nuclear Regulatory Commission, NUREG/CR-0130, n.d.

20. Personal communication from staff of South of Scotland Electricity Board.

21. The $38 million estimate is contained in a prepublication draft (January 1981), Joseph Bowring, *Federal Support for Nuclear Power: Reactor Design and the Fuel Cycle,* Analysis Report,

Department of Energy, Office of Economic Analysis, Assistant Administrator for Applied Analysis, Energy Information Administration. This was released to the press without peer review. After peer review, the figure was lowered to $12.8 million, and the report was officially issued in February 1981 under the same title and the number DOE/EIA-0201/13.

22. Charles T. Rombaugh and Billy V. Koen, "Total Energy Investment in Nuclear Power Plants," *Nuclear Technology* 26 (1975):5–11.

23. Charles Komanoff, "Doing Without Nuclear Power," *New York Review of Books,* 17 May 1979, pp. 14–17.

24. Atomic Industrial Forum, "INFO," February 1981, n.p.

25. Ibid.

26. A. D. Rossin and T. A. Rieck, "Economics of Nuclear Power," in Milton R. Copulos, ed., *Energy Perspectives* (Washington, D.C.: Heritage Foundation, 1978), pp. 67–83.

27. Reliability of the various forms of power generation nationally is tracked in the annual reports of the Availability Task Force of the Edison Electric Institute, New York.

28. Ralph Nader and John Abbotts, *The Menace of Atomic Energy* (New York: Norton, 1977), p. 217.

29. Personal communication from NRC staff in Washington, D.C.

30. Personal communication from staff at the Public Service Commission of New Hampshire.

31. "High-Powered Fish Farmers," *Newsweek,* 14 July 1980, p. 61.

32. Amory B. Lovins, *Soft Energy Paths* (San Francisco: Friends of the Earth International and Cambridge: Ballinger, 1977), p. 16.

33. Amory B. Lovins and L. Hunter Lovins, "Nuclear Bomb and Nuclear Power," *Foreign Affairs* 58 (Summer 1980):1137–77.

34. *New Republic* 76 (28 May 1977):10.

## Chapter 3

1. H. Hurwitz, Jr., "The Indoor Radiological Problem in Perspective," General Electric Technical Information Series, February 1981.

2. J. E. Martin et al. "Comparison of Radioactivity from Fossil Fuel and Nuclear Power Plants," 91st Cong., Joint Committee on Atomic Energy, Hearings on Effects of Producing Electric Power, vol. 1, 1969, pp. 773–809.

3. Office of Technology Assessment, *The Direct Use of Coal* (Washington, D.C.: Government Printing Office, 1979), p. 217.

4. D. J. Rose, P. W. Walsh, and L. L. Leskovjan, *Nuclear Power vis-à-vis Its Alternatives, Chiefly Coal* (Cambridge: M.I.T., 1975).

5. Ibid.

6. Petr Beckmann, *The Health Hazards of Not Going Nuclear* (Boulder, Colo.: Golem Press, 1976), p. 107.

7. *New York Times,* 25 July 1977, p. 43.

8. Petr Beckmann, *Access to Energy,* April 1977.

9. W. Meyer, M. R. Rollins, and R. W. Williams, "Estimates of the Effects of a Five-Year National Nuclear Moratorium," (unpublished, University of Missouri, 1975).

10. Beckmann, *Access to Energy,* December 1976.

11. Beckmann, *Health Hazards,* p. 159.

12. Beckmann, *Access to Energy,* October 1976.

13. Beckmann, *Health Hazards,* p. 127.

14. Barry Commoner, *The Politics of Energy* (New York: Alfred A. Knopf, 1979), p. 48.

## Chapter 4

1. Robert Stobaugh and Daniel Yergin, *Energy Future* (New York: Random House, 1979), p. 211.

2. Barry Commoner, *The Poverty of Power: Energy and the Economic Crisis* (New York: Alfred A. Knopf, 1976).

# Notes

3. Barry Commoner, *The Politics of Energy* (New York: Alfred A. Knopf, 1979).

4. Ibid., p. 9.

5. Ibid.

6. *Consumer Reports* 45 (May 1980):322–27.

7. "Preliminary Analysis of an Option for the Federal Photovoltaic Utilization Program" (Washington, D.C.: Federal Energy Administration, 1977).

8. Commoner, *Politics of Energy*, p. 36.

9. *Economist*, 24 October 1981, p. 65.

10. Commoner, *Politics of Energy*, pp. 42–43.

11. Commoner, *Poverty of Power*, pp. 159–60.

12. Petr Beckmann, *Why "Soft" Technology Will Not Be America's Energy Salvation* (Boulder, Colo.: Golem Press, 1979), p. 6; see also K. A. Lawrence, "Review of the environmental effects and benefits of solar energy technologies," Solar Energy Research Institute, Golden, Colorado, 1978.

## Chapter 6

1. Presentation by L. P. Leach at the Workshop on Reactor Licensing and Safety, New York, May 13–16, 1979.

2. Personal communication from Henry Kendall in February 1979.

3. *New York Times*, 16 May 1980, p. 30.

4. Address at the 1979 Commencement of Tufts University Medical School.

5. Ralph Nader and John Abbotts, *The Menace of Atomic Energy* (New York: Norton, 1977).

6. Ibid., pp. 62–63.

7. Ralph Nader, "The America Syndrome," *Family Health*, July-August 1979, p. 6.

8. The original (1972) BEIR report, now known as BEIR-I, p. 188.

9. Nader, "America Syndrome," p. 6.

10. Thomas F. Mancuso, Alice Stewart, and George S. Kneale, "Radiation Exposure of Hanford Workers Dying from Cancer and Other Causes," *Health Physics*, 33 (1977):365–85.

11. T. W. Anderson. "Low-Level Radiation and Cancer Deaths," *Health Physics* 38 (1980):716–17; T. W. Anderson, "Radiation Exposures of Hanford Workers: A Critique of the Mancuso, Kneale and Stewart Report," *Health Physics* 35 (1978):743–50; G. B. Hutchinson et al., "Review of Report by Mancuso, Stewart and Kneale of Radiation Exposure of Hanford Workers," *Health Physics* 37 (1979):207–20; E. Gilbert and S. Marks, "Comment on 'Radiation Exposure of Hanford Workers Dying from Cancer and Other Causes,' " *Health Physics* 37 (1979):791–92; E. Gilbert and S. Marks, "An Analysis of the Mortality of Workers in a Nuclear Facility," *Radiation Research* 79 (1979):122–48; J. A. Reissland, "An Assessment of the Mancuso Study," National Radiological Protection Board, Report NRPB–79 (September 1978); L. A. Sagan, "Low-Level Radiation Effects: The Mancuso Study," Electric Power Research Institute (Palo Alto, California), 1978; and B. S. Saunders, "Low-Level Radiation and Cancer Deaths," *Health Physics* 34 (1978):521–37. I cite all these articles to show the extent of the critique of Professor Mancuso's work. These are never mentioned by antinuclear writers. The pro-Mancuso literature is slimmer: J. W. Gofman, "The Question of Radiation Causation of Cancer in Hanford Workers," *Health Physics* 37 (1979):617–39; K. Z. Morgan, "Cancer and Low-Level Ionizing Radiation," *The Bulletin of the Atomic Scientists* 34 (September 1978):30–41; and J. W. Rotblat, "The Risk for Radiation Workers," *The Bulletin of the Atomic Scientists* 34 (September, 1978):41–46.

12. Nader, "America Syndrome," p. 63.

13. E. J. Sternglass, "Cancer Mortality Changes around Nuclear Facilities in Connecticut," paper presented at a Congressional Seminar on Low-Level Radiation, 10 February 1978.

14. E. J. Sternglass, "Radioactive Discharges from the Shippingport Nuclear Power Station and Changes in Infant Cancer Mortality," 8 May 1973.

15. E. J. Sternglass, "Strontium-90 Levels in the Milk and Diet Near Connecticut Nuclear Power Plants," privately circulated, 27 October 1977.

16. Petr Beckmann, *Access to Energy*, May 1980 (reprint of chart from H. Boeck, *Naturwissenschaftliche Rundschau*, October 1974, p. 411); Sternglass discussion in *Proceedings of the*

*Sixth Berkeley Symposium on Mathematical Statistics and Probability* (Berkeley: University of California Press, 1972).

17. Transcript of 2 October 1978 hearing in Federal District Court, Nashville, in Jeannine Honicker, *Shutdown: Nuclear Power on Trial* (Summertown, Tenn.: Book Publishing Company, 1979), pp. 118–20.

18. Honicker, *Shutdown,* p. 120.

19. Ibid., p. 121.

20. Ibid.

21. Ibid., pp. 118–20.

22. Ibid., p. 175.

23. Ibid., p. 174

24. "Health Evaluation of Energy Generating Sources," in American Medical Association, *Proceedings of the House of Delegates,* 127th Convention, 18–22 June 1978; Report C of the Council on Scientific Affairs, American Medical Association, pp. 286–89.

25. Honicker, *Shutdown,* pp. 164–65.

26. Ibid., p. 38.

27. Ibid., p. 67.

28. Statement of Joel Kachinsky, Esq., appearing before the Sixth Circuit Court of Appeals in Cincinnati, Ohio, 7 August 1979. Quoted in *Shutdown* (this is to be distinguished from the book cited above and below; it is the newsletter of the Plenty Shutdown Project) 1(2):1980.

29. Honicker, *Shutdown,* pp. 104–05.

30. Ibid., p. 110.

31. Ibid.

32. John W. Gofman, *"Irrevy": An Irreverent, Illustrated View of Nuclear Power* (San Francisco: Committee for Nuclear Responsibility, 1979).

33. John W. Gofman and Arthur R. Tamplin, *Poisoned Power* (Emmaus, Pa.: Rodale Press, 1979).

34. Ibid., p. xii.

35. Northeast Utilities, "Northeast Utilities Response to E. J. Sternglass' Report on Strontium-90 Levels in Connecticut Milk," Hartford, Conn.: n.d. [1978?], pp. 5–6.

36. Gofman and Tamplin, *Poisoned Power,* pp. xvii–xviii.

37. Ibid., p. xviii.

38. Ibid., p. ix.

39. Barry Commoner, *The Poverty of Power: Energy and the Economic Crisis* (New York: Alfred A. Knopf, 1976), p. 191.

40. Ibid., p. 189.

41. Amory B. Lovins, *Soft Energy Paths: Toward a Durable Peace* (San Francisco: Friends of the Earth, 1977), p. 23.

42. Ibid., p. 144.

43. Ibid., p. 48.

44. Ibid., p. 118.

45. Oklahoma State Police report as reprinted in Jacque Srouji, *Critical Mass* (Nashville: Aurora Publishers, 1977), p. 358.

46. *Boston Globe,* 19 February 1978, p. 1.

47. This study by Robert A. Rinsky et al., "Epidemiologic Study of Civilian Employees at the Portsmouth Naval Shipyard," U.S. Department of Health and Human Services, December 1980, is as yet unpublished but is available from the National Institute for Occupational Safety and Health at 4676 Columbia Parkway, Cincinnati, Ohio 45226; a summary discussion can be found in Robert A. Rinsky et al., "Cancer Mortality at a Naval Nuclear Shipyard," *The Lancet* 8214 (1981): 231–35.

## Chapter 7

1. *Television Evening News Covers Nuclear Energy: A Ten Year Perspective* (Washington, D.C.: The Media Institute, 1979).

2. John G. Fuller, *We Almost Lost Detroit* (New York: Ballantine, 1976).

3. Ibid., p. 201.

# Notes

4. Ibid., p. 200.
5. Ibid., p. 233.
6. Robert Jungk, *The New Tyranny* (New York: Warner Books, 1979).
7. Ibid., p. 205.
8. Helen Caldicott, *Nuclear Madness* (Brookline, Mass.: Autumn Press, 1979).
9. Zhores Medvedev, "Nuclear Disaster in the Soviet Union," *New Scientist,* 30 June 1977, pp. 761–64; also available in Alan Roberts and Zhores Medvedev, *Hazards of Nuclear Power* (London: Spokesman, 1977). The title of this work is misleading in that the Medvedev essay never mentions nuclear power.
10. Zhores Medvedev, *Nuclear Disaster in the Urals* (New York: Norton, 1980).
11. Thomas N. Scortia and Frank M. Robinson, *The Prometheus Crisis* (New York: Bantam, 1976).
12. Lawrence Huff, *Dome* (New York: Pocket Books, 1979).
13. Alexander Sidar III, *The Dorset Disaster* (New York: Grosset & Dunlap, 1980).
14. General Sir John Hackett et al., *The Third World War* (New York: Macmillan, 1978).
15. I. C. Bupp, Jean-Claude Derian, Marie-Paule Donsimoni, and Robert Treitel, "Economics of Nuclear Power," *Technology Review,* February 1975, p. 14.
16. Freeman Dyson, *Disturbing the Universe* (New York: Harper & Row, 1979).

# Selected Bibliography*

Atlantic Council of the United States, *Nuclear Power and Nuclear Weapons Proliferation: Report of the Atlantic Council's Nuclear Fuels Policy Working Group,* vol. 1. Boulder, Colo.: Westview Press, N.D.

Beckmann, Petr. *The Health Hazards of Not Going Nuclear.* Boulder, Colo.: Golem Press, 1976.

> This is still the most enlightening discussion of nuclear energy in print, written by one who has rightly been called a national resource. The tone is polemical, hotly so, for Beckmann is God's angry man. This fact should not be allowed to obscure the coolness with which he treats the immense volume of facts at his disposal. It is probably difficult to obtain, but it is available from the Golem Press, Box 2298, Boulder, Colorado 80306.

———. "The Radiation Bogey." Boulder, Colo.: Golem Press, 1980.

> This is number 8 in a series of Beckmann's pamphlets under the general title *Different Drummer.* Most are on energy, and all are worth reading.

Behrman, Daniel. *Solar Energy.* Boston: Little, Brown, 1976.

Berger, John J. *Nuclear Power: The Unviable Option.* Palo Alto, Calif.: Ramparts Press, 1976.

> Distinctive primarily for its fictional account of an accident at the "Santa Bonita" nuclear plant, which can be profitably compared with what really happened at Three Mile Island.

Bergman, Elihu, Bethe, Hans A., and Marshak, Robert E. (eds.). *American Energy Choices Before the Year 2000.* Lexington, Ky.: D.C. Heath, 1978.

Bupp, Irvin C., and Derian, Jean-Claude. *Light Water: How the Nuclear Dream Dissolved.* New York: Basic Books, 1978.

> An interesting study of American success in generalizing one form of nuclear technology almost to the exclusion of others. It is not convincing in arguing that this success is tantamount to the failure of nuclear energy.

Cohen, Bernard L. *Nuclear Science and Society.* New York: Anchor Books, 1974.

> Although outdated in a number of areas, this is a superb book by a nuclear physicist whose work has illuminated the nuclear controversy in a wide range of areas.

*Commoner, Barry. *The Poverty of Power: Energy and the Economic Crisis.* New York: Alfred A. Knopf, 1976.

*———. *The Politics of Energy.* New York: Alfred A. Knopf, 1979.

Congress of the United States, Office of Technology Assessment. *Application of Solar Technology to Today's Energy Needs.* Washington, D.C.: U.S. Government Printing Office, 1978.

> An essential text for understanding the true promise no less than the true constraints of solar energy.

Copulos, Milton R. (ed.). *Energy Perspectives.* Washington, D.C.: The Heritage Foundation, 1978.

> An extremely useful collection of essays and reports, by no means limited to nuclear energy but invaluable in understanding the controversy surrounding it.

Entries prefixed with an asterisk are discussed in the text.

# Selected Bibliography

Crabbe, David, and MacBride, Richard. *The World Energy Book: An A-Z, Atlas and Statistical Source Book.* Cambridge, Mass.: The M.I.T. Press, 1979.
>    If one were to be allowed only one reference book about energy, this should be it.

Croall, Stephen, and Kaianders. *The Anti-Nuclear Handbook.* New York: Pantheon Books, 1978.
>    Much the best of the Pantheon cartoon series, because genuinely witty and beautifully drawn. But this work is terribly ill-informed about the simple facts and distorted by what Marx used to call "infantile leftism."

Dau, Gary J., and Williams, R. F. *Status of Commercial Nuclear High Level Waste Disposal.* Palo Alto, Calif.: Electric Power Research Institute, 1976 (EPRI NP-44-SR).

Department of Energy. *Inventory of Power Plants in the United States.* Washington, D.C.: Department of Energy, December 1977 (DOE/RA-0001).
>    An essential work for anyone who wants to understand the present electric generating capacity of the country in terms of actual—one is tempted to say "living"—machines rather than vast blocks of megawatts.

Edison Electric Institute. *Report on Equipment Availability for the Ten-Year Period, 1966–1975.* New York: Edison Electric Institute, 1976 (EEI 76–85).

Faulkner, Peter (ed.). *The Silent Bomb: A Guide to the Nuclear Energy Controversy.* New York: Vintage Books, 1977.
>    Snippets from most of the best-known critics. This work is almost unique in having a bipartisan list of information sources.

Ferrara, Grace M. (ed.). *Atomic Energy & the Safety Controversy.* New York: Facts on File, 1978.
>    Useful chronological treatment.

Francis, John, and Abrecht, Paul. *Facing up to Nuclear Power: Risks and Potentialities of the Large-Scale Use of Nuclear Energy.* Philadelphia: Westminster Press, 1976.
>    The outgrowth of a 1975 World Council of Churches (WCC) "hearing" on nuclear energy. While one can reasonably disagree with much said by the writers in this collection, the overall quality is high and an interest in discovery rather than polemic is obvious. The WCC, many of whose members live daily with serious energy insufficiency, has been substantially more reasonable on this issue than the purely American National Council of Churches.

*Gofman, John W. *"Irrevy:" An Irreverent, Illustrated View of Nuclear Power.* San Francisco: Committee for Nuclear Responsibility, 1979.

*———, and Tamplin, Arthur R. *Poisoned Power: The Case Against Nuclear Power Plants Before and After Three Mile Island.* Emmaus, Pa.: Rodale Press, 1979.

Gyorgy, Anna, et al. *No Nukes: Everybody's Guide to Nuclear Power.* Boston: South End Press, 1979.
>    Superficially an extremely thorough discussion of the nuclear question, containing much not found in other antinuclear books. But this work is full of careless errors in detail in addition to all of the generic errors of the antinuclear case.

Hewlett, Richard G., and Duncan, Francis. *Atomic Shield: A History of the United States Atomic Energy Commission,* vol. 2, 1947–1952. Washington, D.C.: U.S. Atomic Energy Commission, 1972 (WASH-1215).

Hocevar, Carl J. *Nuclear Reactor Licensing: A Critique of the Computer Safety Prediction Methods.* Cambridge, Mass.: Union of Concerned Scientists, 1975.
>    The author critically analyzes and casts doubt on the methods that appear to have been vindicated both by the LOFT tests and by Three Mile Island.

Honicker, Jeannine. *Shutdown: Nuclear Power on Trial.* Summertown, Tenn.: Book Publishing Company, 1979.

*Huff, Lawrence. *Dome.* New York: Pocket Books, 1979.

*Jungk, Robert. *The New Tyranny: How Nuclear Power Enslaves Us.* New York: Warner Books, 1979.

Kemeny Commission. *The Report of the President's Commission on the Accident at Three-Mile Island: A Need for Change: The Legacy of Three-Mile Island.* Washington, D.C.: U.S. Government Printing Office, 1979.

Kendall, Henry W. *Nuclear Power Risks: A Review of the Report of the American Physical Society's Study Group on Light Water Reactor Safety.* Cambridge, Mass.: Union of Concerned Scientists, 1976.

————, and Moglewer, S. *Preliminary Review of the AEC Reactor Safety Study.* San Francisco: The Sierra Club and Union of Concerned Scientists, 1974.

This and the preceding work are two of the more respectable critiques of the *Reactor Safety Study;* although the Nuclear Regulatory Commission's withdrawal of the executive summary of the *Reactor Safety Study* has been claimed to vindicate these two studies, the LOFT program and the reactor's performance at Three Mile Island can more justly be said to have vindicated the *Reactor Safety Study.*

*Lovins, Amory B. *Soft Energy Paths: Toward a Durable Peace.* San Francisco: Friends of the Earth, 1977.

*————, and Lovins, L. Hunter. *Energy/War: Breaking the Nuclear Link.* New York: Harper & Row, 1980.

Text discussion covers condensation published in *Foreign Affairs,* Summer 1980.

Media Institute, The. *Television Evening News Covers Nuclear Energy: A Ten Year Perspective.* Washington, D.C.: The Media Institute, 1979.

Medvedev, Zhores. *Nuclear Disaster in the Urals.* New York: W. W. Norton, 1979.

Although it has in fact nothing to do with nuclear power, this is a superb piece of reconstruction of fact as glimpsed through the interstices of the Soviet security grid. While few U.S. experts agree with Medvedev's diagnosis of the cause of the disaster, few doubt that such a disaster occurred.

Munson, Richard (ed.). *Countdown to a Nuclear Moratorium.* Washington: Environmental Action Foundation, 1976. [An earlier version of Stephenson, cited below, which see.]

Murphy, Arthur W. (ed.). *The Nuclear Power Controversy.* Englewood Cliffs, N.J.: Prentice-Hall, 1976.

*Nader, Ralph, and Abbotts, John. *The Menace of Atomic Energy.* New York: W. W. Norton, 1977.

Novick, Sheldon. *The Electric Wars: The Fight Over Nuclear Power.* San Francisco: Sierra Club, 1976.

A curious book, containing some useful raw material, but barely edited, almost as if the Sierra Club feared any editorial attention would interfere with the ecology of ideas. For example, the author feels it necessary to document the idea that a corporation is legally a person with a considerable discussion of the Dartmouth College case and a full-page portrait of John Marshall.

Nuclear Energy Agency, Organisation for Economic Co-Operation and Development. *Objectives, Concepts and Strategies for the Management of Radioactive Waste Arising from Nuclear Power Programmes.* Paris: Nuclear Energy Agency of the OECD, September 1977.

Nuclear Regulatory Commission. *Reactor Safety Study: An Assessment of Accident Risks in U.S. Commercial Nuclear Power Plants.* Washington, D.C.: U.S. Nuclear Regulatory Commission, October 1975 (WASH-1400).

————. *Investigation into the March 28, 1979 Three Mile Island Accident by Office of Inspection and Enforcement.* Washington, D.C.: U.S. Nuclear Regulatory Commission, 1979 (NUREG-0600).

————. *TMI-2 Lessons Learned Task Force Status Report and Short-Term Recommendations.* Washington, D.C.: U.S. Nuclear Regulatory Commission, 1979 (NUREG-0578).

Oregon, State of. *Transition: A Book on Future Energy: Nuclear or Solar?* Portland: Prometheus Unbound, Specialty Books.

It answers its own question—"solar." Notwithstanding, it is so crammed with intelligently displayed data and so open in its argumentation as to put it in a class of its own. This work is highly useful even if ultimately mistaken.

Pape, Gordon, and Aspler, Tony. *Chain Reaction.* New York: Bantam Books, 1978.

A better-than-average thriller about Quebec nationalism, less concerned with nuclear affairs than the title might suggest. But nuclear energy, badly misdescribed, serves as a spring of the plot.

Patterson, Walter C. *Nuclear Power.* Harmondsworth, England: Penguin Books, 1976.

The best book on nuclear power by a nuclear critic. Patterson, a Canadian nuclear physicist now an activist in Britain, knows a lot more about nuclear energy than the other critics, and he is better at separating polemic from report.

Phillips, Owen. *The Last Chance Energy Book.* Baltimore, Md.: The Johns Hopkins University Press, 1979.

One of the most clear-sighted (and certainly the most charming) of the books arguing that we can work our way out of the energy crisis by conservation, simplified living, and the exploitation of new technologies even more exotic than nuclear energy.

Post, Roy G. (ed.). *Waste Management '75: Proceedings of the Symposium on Waste Management at Tucson, Arizona, March 24–26, 1975.* Tucson: The University of Arizona, 1975.

Roberts, Alan, and Medvedev, Zhores. *Hazards of Nuclear Power.* Nottingham, England: Spokesman, 1977.
Contains Medvedev's original article on the disaster in the Urals, keeping odd company with an essay attacking nuclear power plants.

Sawhill, John C. (ed.). *Energy: Conservation and Public Policy.* Englewood Cliffs, N.J.: Prentice-Hall, 1979.

Schmidt, Fred, and Bodansky, David. *The Fight Over Nuclear Power.* San Francisco: Albion Publishing Company, 1976.
A thorough and enlightening discussion by two physicists with the right credentials.

Schurr, Sam H., et al. *Energy in America's Future: The Choices Before Us.* Baltimore, Md.: The Johns Hopkins University Press, 1979.

*Scortia, Thomas N., and Robinson, Frank M. *The Prometheus Crisis.* New York: Bantam Books, 1975.

*Sidar, Alexander III. *The Dorset Disaster.* New York: Grosset & Dunlap, 1980.

Srouji, Jacque. *Critical Mass: Nuclear Power, the Alternative to Energy Famine.* Nashville, Tenn.: Aurora Publishers, 1977.
In terms of failure to edit, the pro-nuclear equivalent of Novick, cited above. Srouji, a reporter and editor for the Nashville newspapers, began as a critic and changed her views in response to what she learned. Amid a good deal of naiveté and trivia—such as astrological data on people she interviews—there is much worth reading, including the most complete documentation of the Silkwood case generally available.

Stephenson, Lee, and Zachar, George R. (eds.). *Accidents Will Happen: The Case Against Nuclear Power.* New York: Harper & Row, 1979.
A fairly complete conspectus of the antinuclear case, contained in snippets from the leading critics.

Stobaugh, Robert, and Yergin, Daniel (eds.). *Energy Future: Report of the Energy Project at the Harvard Business School.* New York: Random House, 1979.
An immensely influential book ("The Harvard Report"). It is uneven in quality; the chapter on coal is especially informative, that on nuclear energy especially tendentious—its footnotes cite no authors in favor of nuclear energy. This work is best known for its highly optimistic forecasts of what can be achieved by conservation.

Sutton, Antony C. *Energy: The Created Crisis.* New York: Books in Focus, 1979.
One need not accept the basic thesis that the energy crisis is a hoax to profit from much useful data.

Williams, Robert H. (ed.). *Toward a Solar Civilization.* Cambridge, Mass.: The M.I.T. Press.

Willrich, Mason, and Lester, Richard K. *Radioactive Waste: Management and Regulation.* New York: The Free Press, 1977.

Wohl, Burton. *The China Syndrome.* New York: Bantam Books, 1979.

Workshop on Alternative Energy Strategies. *Energy: Global Prospects 1985–2000.* New York: McGraw–Hill, 1977.

World Health Organization. *Health Implications of Nuclear Power Production.* Copenhagen: World Health Organization, 1978.

Yager, Joseph A., and Steinberg, Eleanor B. *Energy and U.S. Foreign Policy.* Cambridge, Mass.: Ballinger, 1974.

193

# Index

# Index

# Index

Friends of the Clam, 104
front end processes, 9–10
fuel: for CANDU, 8; for gas-cooled reactors, 8, 180; for light-water reactor, 6–7, 9, 69; during melt-down, 27; nonrenewable, 72; plutonium, 239 as, 5, 53, 108–9; production of, in breeder reactor, 8; renewable, 69, 76; and reprocessing, 10, 38; and uranium for Slowpoke, 182
fuel cladding, melting of, at TMI, 27, 30
fuel cycles, and antinuclear argument, 10, 11–13
fuel rods: damage to, at TMI, 25; effect of waste products on, 38; meltdown of, in nuclear accident, 20; optimum life of, 10; uranium dioxide and, 9; *see also* spent fuel rod
Fuller, John G., *We Almost Lost Detroit*, 36, 157–59
fusion energy, 97–98, 148, 183

gamma ray, 4, 180, *see also* x ray
gas, *see* natural gas
gas-cooled reactor, 8; *see also* HTGR; Magnox reactor
gaseous diffusion, uranium enrichment, 9
gas hot-water heat, cost of, and solar heating compared, 77
gasohol, 83–84, 83n, 86, 86n
General Atomic Company, 182n; and TRIGA reactor, 174–76; *see also* HTGR
General Electric Company, and boiling water reactor, 168n
genetic effects, from radiation, 19–20, 113
geography; and energy consumption, 64, 65, 66; and railways in U.S. and Europe, 66, 146
Germany: Jungk's thesis on nuclear power of, 159, 160; Kalkar nuclear reactor, 160
gigawatt, 162
glass, for solar plants, 87
glassified nuclear waste, 39
*Globe* (Boston), on Portsmouth Shipyard study, 151
Gofman, John W., 112, 135–45; on carcinogenic nature of radiation, 118, 119; on coal for energy, 139, 141; on disarmament, 140; on HEW officials, 144; and the Honicker Case, 133, 135, 136–37, 138; and irradiation by cyclotron, 138; *"Irrevy": An Irreverent View of Nuclear Power*, 140, 142n; as Livermore Laboratory Director, 135; on Millstone Point reactor studies, 138; *Poisoned Power*, 140–42; reply to BEIR report, 137; on safe levels of radiation, 135; on effect of smoking on lung cancer in uranium miners, 51; on Three Mile Island, accident, 141–42, 143–45
Gofman-Tamplin report, 119, 137
Gorgas, William Crawford, 107
government: antinuclear movement attitude toward, 104; Gofman's view of, 140; and licensing of power plants, 139, 171; and quantity predictions for nuclear waste, 109; radiation limits, set by, 119
government compensation: for black lung disease, 118; for Saint Helens disaster, 37
government subsidy: for nuclear research, 43; for solar energy, 43, 78, 86n
granite, radiation from, 17
graphite, 181
graphite moderator, 8, 175; in HTGR, 8, 181; in TRIGA research reactor, 175
Great Britain, *see* United Kingdom
greenhouse effect, 62
*Greening of America, The* (Reich), 99

half-life, 15, 38; of activation products, 41; of fission products, 108, 109; of krypton, 111; of plutonium, 34–35, 108
*Handbook of Chemistry and Physics*, 109
Hanford Nuclear Reservation: and Mancuso study, 120, 121; and waste disposal technology, 39, 117; and radioactive waste leaks, 12, 38; and weapons-waste disposal, 40; hard energy, xii, 69
Harvard/M.I.T. study, on cost effect of construction and licensing delays, 171
Hayes, Denis, on solar energy usage, 74
Health, Education and Welfare, Department of (HEW), 143–44
health consequences: and AMA comparative energy study, 134; and China's study on radiation, 19, 144; of coal usage, 32, 60, 61, 117, 118, 118n; low-level radiation, 19; and Nader's antinuclear argument, 117–18; of nuclear and coal-fired plants compared, 18; of nuclear energy, 17, 18, 19, 32, 134; of nuclear energy and natural gas compared, 134; of nuclear moratorium, 62–63; from nuclear waste and petro-chemical full use compared, 41; and pro-nuclear arguments, 59, 134; and Sternglass's opposition to nuclear energy, 122; of uranium mining, 5, 12–13, 51, 60, 61, 118, 118n; *see also* cancer; deaths; occupational risk
heat engine, cogenerator use of, 89
heating reactors, 183n
heat sink, earth as, 22
heat transfer, and liquid sodium, 9
heavy water, 8; *see also* CANDU
heavy-water research reactor, 55, 58
helium, as coolant in HTGR, 8, 181, 182
Hendrie, Joseph M., 30
high-level waste, 39
High-Temperature Gas-Cooled Reactor (HTGR), 8, 48, 180–82, 181n
Hinkley Point B reactor plant, (U.K.), 45
Hiroshima: and effect of A-bomb, 19
home heating; and cogenerator, 90; comparative cost efficiency of energy sources, 68, 80 (*see also* solar heating); and industrial waste heat, 64; and use of photovoltaic cells, 76
homeowners, and conservation measures, 77
homeowners insurance, and nuclear accident coverage, 36
Honicker, Jeannine, *see* Honicker Case
Honicker Case, 133–35; and allowable exposure dose, 136; appeals hearings of, 134n, 137; Gofman's testimony in, 133, 135, 136–37, 138; Sternglass and, 133; and unconstitutionality of nuclear power, 133; and wasted energy, claims, 137
HTGR, *see* High Temperature Gas-Cooled Reactor
Huff, Lawrence, *Dome*, 162–64
humanist, 103, 107, 107n
Humboldt Bay reactor study, 130
Hunsterston reactor (Scotland), 49
hydroelectric power, 64, 65, 71, 76, 76n, 147; and environmental impact, 104; hydroelectric dam failure and nuclear reactor accident compared, 22
hydrogen, 7n, 8, 90
hydrogen bubble, at TMI accident, 25, 28
hydrogen cyanide, compared to plutonium production, 34
hydrogen explosion, and TMI accident, 28, 141–42
hydrogen recombiners, 33

# Index

# Index

photovoltaic cell, 76, 80, 87–89, 88n; and Commoner Patent Streetlight, 81–83; residential use of, 76, 80

photovoltaic electricity: arguments against, 87–88; 89; conventional utilities, and effect of, 77, 80n, 91, 149; and hydrogen production, 90; technology for, 76

Pilgrim II nuclear plant, 48–49, 102

pipe rupture, 20, 35

pit-mined coal, efficiency of, 67

plutonium, 34; acid bath fuel rod disposal and, 10; comparative toxicity of, 34, 35, 53, 180; destruction of, in reactor core, 60; and diversion from reactor for weapon use, 56 (see also plutonium bomb; terrorism); as fuel in reactor, 5, 7, 38, 53, 108–9; half-life of, 34–35, 108; illegal acquisition of (see terrorism); India's explosive device and, 55, 58; and Iraqi production of bomb-grade, 56; isotopes of, 54 (see also plutonium-239; plutonium-240); in natural state, 5, 53n; as nuclear waste, 33; as poison, 13, 33, 34, 35, 52, 53; production of, and argument against breeder reactors, 5, 12, 33, 35; production of in nuclear reactors, 12, 53; reactor-grade as bomb material, 36, 54, 164 (see also plutonium bomb); safeguards against theft of, 52, 53, 54; and spent fuel rods, 38; treatment of in fiction, 162; waste of, through disuse, 178; and Windscale reactor production of, 18

plutonium-239, 15; in breeder reactor, 8; fissionable nature of, 5; half-life of, 34; illegal weapons proliferation, 57; and nuclear bomb, 5, 36, 52, 53, 54, 58; and U-238 transmutation, 5

plutonium-240, 5, 36, 54

plutonium bomb: an argument against nuclear power, 13; beryllium reflectors in, 183; and Pu-239, 5, 36, 52–54 passim, 58; and reactor-grade plutonium, 5, 36, 53, 54, 164; requirements for, 115

plutonium explosion, 36, 157

plutonium reprocessing plant, and Silkwood incident, 150

plutonium-uranium-thorium breeder reactor, and fuel for HTGR, 182

Poisoned Power (Gofman and Tamplin), 140–42

poisons, radioactive and stable compared, 34, 45

politics: Commoner's involvement in, 91, 93; and mass movements compared, 96; and nuclear power, xii–xiii, 100; and pro-nuclear factions in Europe, 98; see also left-wing politics; liberal politics; Libertarian party, right-wing politics

Politics of Energy (Commoner), 74, 86, 91

pollution, see air pollution; thermal pollution

polonium, 27, 60

Portsmouth Shipyard study, 151

potassium, 27

potassium-40, and body radiation, 15

Poverty of Power (Commoner), 74, 93

power density of nuclear reactor, 8, 181

press coverage: and Clinch River Breeder Reactor project, 154–55, 157; of Fermi I reactor accident, 154–55; of foreign nuclear energy programs, 154, 155; at Mt. Saint Helens, 27; of TMI accident, 26, 27, 28; see also news media

pressure vessel, 20, 22, 181

pressurized coolant, 22, 22n

pressurized-water reactor, 6, fig. 1–2 (p. 7); and boiling-water reactor compared, 7, 22n, 168; containment building for, 181; cooling system in, 22n, 24; at Three Mile Island, 24

Price-Anderson Act, 24–25, 36, 37, 142

profit motive, and morality, 173

Prometheus Crisis (Scortia and Robinson), 161–62

property damage: or hypothetical meltdown accident, 12; from meltdown and hurricane compared, 23; RSS report on accident probabilities, 23

proportionate mortality methodology, 121

protons, and atomic structure, 3–4, 5

psychic numbing, 115

Pu, see plutonium

public opinion, 112, 164; and attitude toward nuclear energy, 100–1, 104–7 passim, 142; and mass movements, 95; of utilities, 99–100

public policy, and democracy, 93, 97

pump failure, and nuclear accident, 20

rad, 16n; carcinogenic level of, 131

radiation, 4, 11, 13–20, 119; and BEIR study, 118–19; Caldicott on, 113; cancer, and relation to, 15–18 passim, 20, 123–24, 136n, 137; carcinogenic nature of, 118, 119; Chinese study of health hazards of, 19, 144; from coal-fired plants, 62, 139–40; in common energy sources, 59; common sources of exposure to, 11, 13, 16, 17, 29, 119; dangerous limits of, 15; in decommissioning, 12; genetic effect of, 19, 20, 113; Gofman on, 138; in granite, 17; at Indian Point reactor, 17; natural, 15, 17; from nuclear accidents, 11, 18, 20–21, 25; perception of, 102–3; safe levels of, 135; see also radioactive emissions; radioactivity

radiation, natural, 15

radiation dosage, see rad

radiation exposure: and airline travel, 17, 132; allowable, 136, 141; of average American, 16, 119; and cancer (see cancer); of HTGR and NRC regulations compared, 181–82; NRC measurement of, 29; of population around TMI accident, 29, 143–44; risk to fetus, 136

radiation monitoring, 33

radioactive contamination, 22

radioactive elements, half-life of, 15, 38, 67, 108

radioactive emission: allowable level of, 16, 119, 131; cancer producing level, 131; and California referendum requirement, 103; and color television, 16, 29, 119; at Grand Central Station and Indian Point compared, 17; and Kemeny Commission, 30; and NRC regulations, 16, 29; and nuclear accidents, 18, 20–21, 27, 29, 30, 158, 159; nuclear and coal-fired plants compared, 61, 139; at Saint Helens, 27; see also reactor emissions

radioactive fuel, supply of, 54

radioactive isotopes, 4, 38, 108; of hydrogen, 7n; of potassium, 15; see also specific elements

radioactive waste: from coal-fired plants, 62; Erlich on, 151–52; in China Syndrome, The, 170–71; see also nuclear waste

radioactivity: in boiling-water reactor steam, 7n; of decommissioned reactor, 41; fission products and, 4, 12; of glassified nuclear waste, 39; of moderator of light-water reactor, and HTGR compared, 181; of plutonium, 34; in waste from coal-fired plant, 61; see also radiation

radioiodine milk contamination, 29

radium, 34, 60

radon, 27, 51, 59, 118n

# Index